CW00650503

"I have known Cindy Jacobs for nearly two biblical voice who has helped to bring much sc of Christ. This book will be required reading for our entire local church leadership team and the thousands of churches we oversee worldwide. The house of God, in this day, has multiple generations that are fatherless and have not been parented—naturally or spiritually. This book is a manual for raising up and equipping spiritual mothers who will help the Body of Christ fulfill its destiny. Read, memorize and teach from this modern classic. With its contents, let's change our world!"

Bishop Harry Jackson, pastor, Hope Christian Church;
host, *The Hope Connection*

"Dr. Cindy Jacobs has demonstrated for many years the title of this book, *Women, Rise Up!* Cindy has risen to be an international minister who is called upon to minister to thousands of leaders and saints in numerous nations. Every Christian woman should read this book to discover her calling and how to fulfill it."

Bishop Bill Hamon, Christian International Ministries Network;
author, *God's Weapons of War*

"Watching Cindy Jacobs fulfill an international prophetic calling at the highest of levels for more than thirty years has been both a joy and an inspiration. We all study to become; some become the study. Cindy has modeled in life what she has now put on paper. Every woman—and man, as well—should read this book."

Dutch Sheets, founder, Dutch Sheets Ministries;
author, *Intercessory Prayer*

"*Women, Rise Up!* is a powerful book! It will encourage, console, inform and correct you, make you laugh, and compel you to go beyond your comfort level into the fullness of God's destiny for you. Cindy Jacobs covers everything from personal issues and challenges to the theological concerns of women stepping into biblical governmental positions. This is a great book, and I highly recommend it!"

Barbara Yoder, lead apostle, Shekinah Regional Apostolic Center

"I love reading books that inspire me to do great things for God and to live radically unto Him. *Women, Rise Up!* does just that! Cindy Jacobs, a great apostolic-prophetic pioneer of faith, taps into the enduring legacy, catalytic impact and unique influence of Spirit-led women fearlessly pursuing their calling in God. I encourage you to pick up this breakthrough book, full of wisdom and biblical insights. It does not matter if you are a woman or a man, be transformed and inspired from generations of resilient women paving the way for revival and reformation in every sphere of influence around the world."

Ché Ahn, president and founder, Harvest International Ministry;
international chancellor, Wagner University

"The new millennium has revealed a new order in the Body of Christ. Cindy Jacobs captures this new order in *Women, Rise Up!* Women have been recognized in the Church as prayer warriors, but not particularly for their ability to exercise God's authority on the earth. We are about to see faith-filled women arise and change the course of history. This book you are holding will help women determine their call, role and future as a key weapon in the hand of the Lord."

Dr. Chuck D. Pierce, president, Global Spheres Inc.;
president, Glory of Zion International Ministries

"Cindy Jacobs brings clarity and insight to the controversy surrounding a woman's place in ministry. Delicately, yet boldly, she presents a fresh, historical and biblical interpretation of God's Word on the issues facing today's woman of destiny."

Beth Alves, president, Increase International, Bulverde, Texas

"Every woman who is struggling with God's call on her life should read *Women, Rise Up!* Every man who questions a woman's call needs only to read it with an open heart and mind. A vital contribution to the literature of gender reconciliation, this book is biblically sound and long awaited."

Bishop Joseph L. Garlington Sr., senior pastor,
Covenant Church, Pittsburgh, Pennsylvania

"As the Holy Spirit labors over the Church to bring forth reconciliation among believers, our focus has been on racial or denominational issues that separate God's people. All the while, however, the greatest single issue of unbiblical discrimination has been the widespread posturing against women in ministry. Cindy Jacobs's voice deserves to be heard—and taken seriously. It just may be another gentle whisper of the Spirit saying, 'Open your hearts wider.'"

Jack Hayford, founding pastor and pastor emeritus, The Church On The Way; chancellor emeritus, The King's University

"In a day when there is considerable confusion over gender issues in the Church and in the home, Cindy Jacobs cuts through the fog like a spiritual laser beam. No other book I know on this subject matches the superb combination of biblical and pastoral integrity."

C. Peter Wagner (1930–2016), author, *Finding Your Spiritual Gifts*; former apostolic ambassador, Global Spheres; founding chancellor, Wagner Leadership Institute, now Wagner University

WOMEN, RISE UP!

Books by Cindy Jacobs

Deliver Us From Evil

Possessing the Gates of the Enemy

The Power of Persistent Prayer

The Supernatural Life

The Voice of God

Women, Rise Up!

WOMEN, RISE UP!

A Fierce Generation Taking Its Place in the World

CINDY JACOBS

a division of Baker Publishing Group
Minneapolis, Minnesota

© 1998, 2012, 2019 by Cindy Jacobs

Published by Chosen Books
11400 Hampshire Avenue South
Bloomington, Minnesota 55438
www.chosenbooks.com

Chosen Books is a division of
Baker Publishing Group, Grand Rapids, Michigan

Previously published by Regal Books as *Women of Destiny*

Printed in the United States of America

All rights reserved. No part of this publication may be reproduced, stored in a retrieval system, or transmitted in any form or by any means—for example, electronic, photocopy, recording—without the prior written permission of the publisher. The only exception is brief quotations in printed reviews.

ISBN 978-0-8007-9911-3

Library of Congress Cataloging-in-Publication Control Number: 2018040726

Unless otherwise indicated, Scripture quotations are from the New King James Version®. Copyright © 1982 by Thomas Nelson, Inc. Used by permission. All rights reserved.

Scripture quotations labeled AMPC are from the Amplified® Bible, copyright © 1954, 1958, 1962, 1964, 1965, 1987 by The Lockman Foundation. Used by permission. (www.Lockman.org)

Scripture quotations labeled NASB are from the New American Standard Bible®, copyright © 1960, 1962, 1963, 1968, 1971, 1972, 1973, 1975, 1977, 1995 by The Lockman Foundation. Used by permission. (www.Lockman.org)

Scripture quotations labeled NIV are from the Holy Bible, New International Version®. NIV®. Copyright © 1973, 1978, 1984, 2011 by Biblica, Inc.™ Used by permission of Zondervan. All rights reserved worldwide. www.zondervan.com

Scripture labeled NIV1984 taken from the HOLY BIBLE, NEW INTERNATIONAL VERSION®. Copyright © 1973, 1978, 1984 Biblica. Used by permission of Zondervan. All rights reserved.

Scripture quotations labeled RSV are from the Revised Standard Version of the Bible, copyright 1952 [2nd edition, 1971] by the Division of Christian Education of the National Council of the Churches of Christ in the United States of America. Used by permission. All rights reserved.

Scripture quotations labeled TLB are from The Living Bible, copyright © 1971. Used by permission of Tyndale House Publishers, Inc., Carol Stream, Illinois 60188. All rights reserved.

Scripture quotations labeled KJV are from the King James Version of the Bible.

Excerpt from *Intimate Friendship with God* by Joy Dawson, copyright © 1986. Used by permission of Chosen, a division of Baker Publishing Group.

19 20 21 22 23 24 25 7 6 5 4 3 2 1

In keeping with biblical principles of creation stewardship, Baker Publishing Group advocates the responsible use of our natural resources. As a member of the Green Press Initiative, our company uses recycled paper when possible. The text paper of this book is composed in part of post-consumer waste.

This book is lovingly dedicated to my mom,
Eleanor Lindsey,
March 27, 1926–February 22, 2016
a great woman of faith and prayer,
and my heroine

Contents

Foreword

We are living in the most exciting time in history to be a woman!

When I was sixteen years old, God spoke to me in an audible voice telling me I was called to preach His Word. I had never heard of a woman preacher, although some were beginning to emerge. So I asked the Lord to show me somebody doing now what I would be doing then, so I could have a picture of what that would look like. He replied, "Jane, there is no one doing now what you will be doing then because I will be doing a new thing!"

Today there are many strong, anointed, prophetic women arising in every sphere of society. I believe we are now living in the days of "the new thing."

Genesis 1:26–28 tells us that women are created in the image of God, just as men are, to be co-heirs of His Kingdom with the mandate to "be fruitful and multiply; fill the earth and subdue it; have dominion. . . ." Women are to be strong, capable partners in raising families, producing resources and ruling the earth. Sadly, since the fall of Adam and Eve, women have struggled in most cultures as an oppressed underclass, with little more vision or purpose than childbearing and mere survival. Rather than fulfilling their creation mandate to subdue the earth, women have been subdued and ruled over. Rather than producing resources, women have been some of the earth's most impoverished. Their strength and leadership have been stifled, holding women in the bonds of silence and limitation.

When Jesus came to save humankind, He also began to restore women to their place of full function. When Mary sat at His feet to hear Him teach—which was against Jewish custom—Jesus validated her as a disciple. Jesus first revealed Himself as Messiah to the Samaritan woman and then released her to go preach to her city. Women were last at the cross, first at the tomb and the first to proclaim His resurrection. Throughout the first century, women were an integral part of establishing the early Church. Women like Mary, Lydia, Priscilla, Junia, Chloe, Phoebe and others are among those Paul commended for laboring with him for the Gospel.

Yet because of religious mindsets in the Church and the spirit of prejudice in the world, women were pressed back behind barriers, awaiting a new dawn of reformation. Even in dark times in history, though, we find inspiring women leaders such as Vibia Perpetua, a martyr for Christ who kept a stunning journal while she awaited execution; Joan of Arc, who led armies to battle because of heavenly visions; Florence Nightingale, a social reformer who founded modern nursing; Clara Barton, who founded the American Red Cross; and Harriet Tubman, an abolitionist who rescued many from slavery. Catherine Booth, Sojourner Truth and Maria Woodworth-Etter were just three of many early women preachers and healing evangelists.

These women are examples to us today that we can and must embrace our original creation mandate to subdue and rule the earth, dealing with injustice, poverty and pain, bringing the freedom of the Kingdom of God everywhere we go. God is sounding a clarion call for women to find their purpose, passion and authority to lead, whether in the Church, the business world, government or another area in society. It is true that women have been victimized, marginalized and immobilized by their culture, by life experiences, by lack of proper identity in Christ and by the inability to imagine the success and influence for which they were created. But God is doing a new thing!

For this reason I am grateful to Cindy Jacobs for writing this masterpiece, *Women, Rise Up!* It is a timely resource for cutting through the chains of religious mindsets and Scripture misinterpretation to bring us into "the new thing." Both the biblical and modern examples of women fulfilling great endeavors for the Kingdom of God will inspire you to rise up and lay hold of your created purpose to bring righteousness and justice into your world. Women, rise up!

Dr. Jane Hamon, co-apostle of Vision Church @ Christian International; author of *The Deborah Company*, *Dreams and Visions* and *The Cyrus Decree*

Acknowledgments

As I have written this book, there are many people I want to thank. First, of course, is the Lord Jesus Christ. Thank You, God, for helping me through the writing on the controversial subject of women in leadership.

Next, I want to thank my husband, Mike, who loves me and has been there for me throughout the ups and downs of writing *Women, Rise Up!* I also want to thank my family and friends for giving up time that they would like to have had on a personal level so the women of the world could be blessed!

To all my good friends at Regal, thanks for believing in me and for wanting a book to be written that would release women into everything God has called them to be. Thank you, Kyle Duncan. You lifted me up time and time again through our phone conversations when I would hit a slump in trusting God that I could, indeed, finish the course. Bill Greig III, you have been great to allow me to write what has been in my heart. Kim Bangs, thank you for suggesting that women in the 21st century need to be challenged and encouraged in their calling and destinies.

The two guys who spent the most blood, sweat and tears in the writing are Dr. Gary Greig and Bayard Taylor. Thanks for putting up with my lists of questions and inquiries about what the Greek and Hebrew really say concerning the woman question. You are going to have a special star in your crowns for this project.

To all those who have prayed for me, I could not have written this book without the prayer shield you put up for me. I pray God will pour back abundant blessing upon your heads. Please don't stop praying. We have just begun!

Last, but not least, I want to thank Jim and Becky Hennesy, my pastors, who are brave to agree to be my spiritual covering. You're the best! Thanks for standing with Mike and me throughout the years of our friendship and for believing in the call of God upon women.

Cindy Jacobs,
Dallas, Texas,
March 26, 2018

Introduction

There can be no doubt that God has used and is going to use women in extraordinary ways in every generation. Why do I think this? We women love to fight injustice. From the beginning our Creator said that our seed would bruise the head of the serpent. I believe this is true (see Genesis 3:15). While this might be Messianic in its interpretation, it could also be said of our legacy, both spiritually and physically. There are great injustices around the world that need someone to "dance upon injustice" and rise up and fight.

As I both write my story and highlight the importance of women in leadership and society, I believe there are many issues about which we have been quiet—and need to be "silent no more."

From sexual exploitation through being trafficked to intimidation and unwanted advances in the marketplace, and in the secular world as well as the church world, we need to speak out. We cannot refuse to speak regardless of the consequences. This needs to be done, not only for ourselves but for the generations to come.

I have written extensively in this book about women who were unafraid. I pray their stories give you great courage to fight against ignorance and injustice. Women in many countries of the world are, at this moment, facing death, simply for believing in Jesus.

When I started ministering in nontraditional roles for women, such as preaching, I did not really know any role models with whom I could study and ask, "What is my role as a woman in the Church today?" In time, God brought some women into my life who helped me sift through my multitude of questions.

I have written *Women, Rise Up!* to show from a personal level absolutely that women have a right to fulfill any ministry in the Church—and in life. To controversial issues such as "Does a woman have a right to preach to men?" some today might respond, "Cindy, haven't we gotten past all of that now?" I wish. While there have been major strides in many areas, as of 2017 women made up only 9 percent of senior pastors in Protestant churches.[1]

One of the most important reasons for writing this book—for me, as a woman—was to find out whether or not I had a right to stand in the pulpit to preach. I did a deep study in this regard. I delved into the writings of those who do not believe women can hold roles of authority, as well as those who differ from my stance on the role of the husband in the home.

Taking this journey along with me were two scholars, Dr. Gary Greig and Bayard Taylor. I must admit there was quite a bit of "spiritual jostling" as we debated different Scriptures. It was all done with deep respect for one another, and the end result is what you read in this book.

God is exposing the exploitation of women around the world today. The subject of this book is a serious one. Every woman wants to fulfill her destiny in God. All of us want to reach our full potential. This book is for us to reach not only our *personal destinies* but also our *corporate destinies.* We need to work together to bring change. When we do that together, it strengthens us and gives us the courage that is found in sisterhood.

If you and I were able to sit down together, you might say to me, "Cindy, why should I read this book? I am not called to be a woman preacher. My ministry is in the marketplace," or "I am called to fight human trafficking," or "I'm called to join the fight to end abortion." In reply, I can only tell you that I have received calls from women in government who are fighting massive gender inequity, and glass ceilings exist, across the board, in almost every endeavor. All the things I have mentioned, and others besides, are ones to which you have a calling.

This book will strengthen you in your resolve to fight for justice, to change laws, to teach your children or to be a great student leader in your university. Sexual exploitation is no new problem, but we never need to be afraid to "blow the whistle" on those who would try to victimize us. We must find both our individual as well as our corporate voices.

The process of writing this book about the role of women in bringing biblical change has caused me to ponder the plight of women, in my own generation, throughout the world: Although the burning of brides is now illegal in India, torture and other atrocities continue to be perpetrated on women. Also, abortion clinics advertise with statements like, *"It is better to spend $38.00 now to terminate a female fetus than to spend $3,800 on her dowry later."*

Chinese women are forced into unwanted sterilizations, and gendercide is a stark reality in societies that value the male gender over the female. I pray that some of you will be champions for causes that stand up to these injustices. I have heard that baby girls have been typified as "maggots in the rice."

Impoverished women represent the majority of civilization's poorest people. We need more women who see systemic poverty as their enemy and will stand against this societal plague. Together we must be a voice to stop such atrocities.

While talking to women across the world, I have heard their pain. Even now, pictures of hurting female faces flood my mind: women with lovely almond-shaped eyes spilling over with tears, and some with beautiful ebony complexions—all yearning for an answer to life. Again and again they ask: *Cindy, what does God want from my life?*

As I have gazed into those eyes and listened to the brokenness in their voices, I see mirrored images of years past when I, too, struggled with that same issue as a young woman aching to find purpose and destiny. Certainly Christ is the answer, but the subject of women in leadership has caused great debate in most Christian circles. Earnest men in the pastorate, who want to release the women in their churches, are seeking a balanced and solid biblical basis to do so. Some who are dealing with gender-to-gender issues that are potential firebombs of destruction to marriages are feeling their way in the Spirit for a path of reconciliation.

According to the World Health Organization 2017 report, around 200 million girls and women have been genitally mutilated to date, mainly from thirty nations.[2] Women make up 70 percent of the world's poor and 75 percent of the sick and disabled in the world.[3] According to a study by the U.S. Centers for Disease Control worldwide, one in five women in America has been raped. These numbers vary depending on the study taken. Some estimate that as many as two million women in America have been raped.

It is for these women I have written this book. Their only hope is the Gospel of Jesus Christ, for where the Gospel is preached, its transforming power changes lives.

The subjects I have tackled in this book deserve to be studied by both men and women in the Body of Christ. Thank God for men such as Ché Ahn, and, of course, my own husband, Mike, who have stood up for women both in ministry and leadership. Lee Grady has been a pioneer voice in helping to see women renounce their fears and stand up as leaders in society.

It is my hope and prayer that a whole new generation of emerging women in leadership will read this book and find fresh courage to conquer huge problems that exist in the world today. You might find yourself weeping, laughing or saying, "I've found myself!" It is with that hope tucked snugly in my heart, and with much love to all women who fervently desire to be used of God, that I have written this book to say, *Women, Rise Up!*

Blessings,
Cindy Jacobs

ONE

The Journey

I am starting this book with my own story because I want us to be friends. As you read, I want you to know me and my own journey and how I got to be the Cindy Jacobs that people recognize today. While my own story and calling began with a calling to preach, yours might be in the marketplace, the classroom or home with your children. All of us, however, are called to rise up and make a difference.

The year was 1950. A struggling seminary couple knelt in earnest prayer, presenting a very special request to God. It seemed strange for them to ask such a thing in light of their present circumstances. "Lord," they prayed, "please give us a baby girl." They had lost one child through miscarriage but had a precious son. God answered their heartfelt petition in August 1951, and that is how my journey began.

I have always been deeply touched when I think about my parents' prayer. It has given me a sense of destiny and purpose through many turbulent times as a woman minister. Perhaps the Lord knew I would need the extra confidence that such a blessed beginning gives so that I would have the strength to finish the course God had set for me.

People sometimes say to me, "When you were a little girl, did you ever dream you would be traveling around the world speaking to thousands of people?" The answer is no. I had absolutely no inkling. I have, however, always had the sense of God's hand on my life for something very special, even as a tiny child. Maybe you have felt something similar.

Even people who have been in terrible rebellion but have a call of God on their lives will later recount how God saved them from disaster or a potentially life-threatening circumstance time and time again. If you are praying for lost loved ones or rebellious children, this should give you great comfort. God is faithful—always!

I have chosen to start this book with an intimate sharing of my life because most who will read it will be women, and a woman is born with a God-given need to know about people in a detailed fashion that is somewhat foreign to male thinking.

If you are a man reading *Women, Rise Up!*, please feel welcome in the following pages. You are extremely important in helping women find God's plan for their lives, and you may even be called of God to affirm and bless the work that God is doing through your wife and daughters, female friends or the feminine gender in your local congregation.

I Love You, Daddy

The man who influenced my life the most as a child was my daddy. I adored my daddy as I grew up. He was a Baptist church planter and had a passion for starting churches. During those days, we had no understanding of the role of the apostle in the Church, so Dad rather puzzled us. He would start a church in one place, and it would grow rapidly. Then he would go into a building program, and within a period of only a few years he would have a thriving congregation. Then, to our great consternation, he would get an itch or need to move on and do it all over again! We now know that he was called as an apostolic leader to raise up new works.

As you can imagine, I moved quite a bit. I guess it could have really messed me up except for one factor—there was a lot of love in my family. I did not doubt for one minute that I was loved. Dad, even though he had been a gang member in New York City, had been born in Georgia, and he still had a bit of a soft drawl at times. Often, I would reach for his big hand that wore a size twelve ring, look up into his face (he was almost six feet tall) and say, "I love you, Daddy."

And he would always reply with a grin, "I love you, too, darlin'."

Food was not always easy to come by in those days. I remember times when we would receive big cardboard boxes full of food. The church called it "a pounding," because some considered this kind of gift receiving food by the pound. It sure was fun to receive. We would get all kinds of exotic delicacies that people had been given for Christmas but had not sampled—pickled pigs' feet and things like that. I loved it!

A Matter of Relationship

Prayer was important in our home. Each night, until we all were eventually scattered asunder by jobs, school and the like, we would kneel by one of our beds to pray. I was always small for my age, so my nose never reached the top of the bed in a kneeling position. We would take turns praying, one at a time.

For some reason the youngest always started, which was fine with me, because I am the middle child and that put the pressure on my sister, Lucy. I am convinced my life as an intercessor began on that bedroom floor—down on my knees, listening to the deep rumble of my daddy's voice and the sweet, soft Texan accent of my San Antonio mom.

My parents had an effective way of teaching, which went straight to the heart. I especially remember one day when I was in college. The Jesus People movement was in full swing, so it was vogue to pray "Dear Jesus" instead of "Dear God" or "Our Father."

That evening after I prayed for the meal, my daddy looked up, his gray eyes filled with sadness as he queried, "Honey, how did Jesus teach His disciples to pray?"

I replied, "Our Father, who art in heaven."

"Then pray that way," he softly instructed me.

Another time, I decided I would call my daddy, "Father." I thought it sounded rather important. Dad was working on something in the backyard at the time. He stopped and simply said, "Sweetheart, your Father is in heaven—I'm your daddy." He was not being mean. I knew what he meant. The awareness of God in heaven was often brought to the forefront in our home.

If you read my book *The Voice of God*, you know that my daddy went to be with the Lord when he was 49 years old. I have thought, from time to time, *Now I have a Father* and *a daddy in heaven*.

Born to Bear Fruit

Because Dad loved to start churches, circumstances were usually in a pioneer stage. This was great training for me as I learned to canvass neighborhoods. (If you are not familiar with the term *canvass*, it simply means going from house to house either to visit or leave a flyer about the new church.)

Early in life, I begged Mom and Dad to let me take piano lessons, so I played hymns for the church from the time I was ten years old. And because Sunday school teachers were often scarce—because we usually had quite a few new converts—I would sometimes teach the little kids younger than I with big, colorful, poster-sized Sunday school pictures that told the story on the back.

Life as a Baptist pastor's daughter was not always easy. I remember moving to a little Texas town during the third grade where everyone was either Catholic, Czech or somehow related. My life in that community was often full of rejection—subtle and otherwise. Years passed before I realized there was not something terribly wrong with my personality and that my being overlooked and left out was simply a matter of another person's prejudice. Thank God for the secondhand bike my dad fixed up for me. I loved to whiz down the country roads exploring God's world and sensing the weight of His presence. God and I talked—a lot.

When I was nine, I went to church camp in Prescott, Arizona. The presence of the Holy Spirit was precious during the meetings, and I loved to hear the missionaries' stories. I relayed in *The Voice of God* how the Lord called me during a camp session. One thing I did not tell was my struggle over what I was to be. The night service was sweet as we sang the old hymns of faith, such as "Count Your Many Blessings,

Name Them One by One." I felt very close to God. I had surrendered my life to the Lord that afternoon in my quiet time, but now I knew I needed to "make it public," as we called it.

Finally, the moment came when the speaker gave the invitation. Wafting through the night air came the strains of the camp song I loved, "I have decided to follow Jesus; no turning back, no turning back." I knew I could not turn back. I had to go. Feeling nervous and a little embarrassed, I moved out from the wooden bench where I had been sitting. Quietly, I knelt at the front. The song went on, "Though none go with me, still I will follow." Tears coursed down my cheeks; my heart was bursting with love for the Lord. I sang over and over with the melody, "I will go, Lord—anywhere. Just tell me what You want me to do."

At the end of the invitation time, one of the workers handed me a commitment form to fill out. I sat down and studied the boxes: *pastor*, *evangelist* and *missionary*. I was not sure about missionary, but I never dreamed I could be a pastor or evangelist, so I signed up with the Lord to go to the mission field. Little did I know that decision would lead me to worldwide ministry.

It is interesting how choices we make even in our earliest years affect our lives. My interests as I grew up were in interior design and music. No one in my family played the piano, but as I mentioned earlier, I had an intense desire to learn. Unfortunately, there was no money, so my mom wrote to my grandmother, who sent us the money for my lessons. My first piano had been stored in an old firehouse, so the keys were warped and looked rather wavy. I did not care. One piano teacher told my mother that I was too little to reach the pedals and that my hands were too tiny to stretch wide enough to play, but that did not daunt my mom. She believed in me and found another teacher.

Years later the piano lessons placed me in good standing: I was granted a music scholarship to what was then Grand Canyon Baptist College. I honestly believed I had discovered my niche in life. This must be what God wanted of me.

I once heard the parable of a beautiful tree that grew beautiful flowers as it matured. The tree, seeing the flowers, came to the conclusion that it was a flower tree and that it would always be a flower tree. But as spring progressed, the flowers dropped off and little hard balls began to form where the flowers had once given the tree its sense of splendor. This was most confusing to the tree, which no longer knew what it was. Time passed, and the little hard balls eventually matured into luscious ripe apples. Eventually, the tree realized it was meant to bear fruit and not flowers.

The apple tree's story is much like life's passages for those whom God calls. Many times, a young leader will assume what his or her eventual destiny will be by the beginning flowers of his or her calling. That is exactly what happened to me with music. I loved to play Bach, Beethoven and so forth—so much, in fact, that I thought this would be my call.

Years later, I was offered a job teaching voice at a Bible school, and my desire to take the job was so strong that I had a hard time hearing God's will for me. Even though my schedule was full of speaking engagements that I would not be able to fulfill if I took the vocal teaching job, I still struggled for a yes from the Lord. Finally, in the wee hours of the morning, the Lord gently instructed me to finish the course by preaching the Gospel, not by teaching music. I heard Him say in a still, small voice, *Cindy, the call to music is the call of your soul [or emotions], but the call of your spirit is to preach the Gospel.*

God Will Make a Way

Emotions can color the decisions we make along the way, and they will eventually affect our destinies. We must be cautious when feelings begin to dictate our actions. Let me explain.

When I first started ministering in Argentina during 1990, I fell so in love with that nation that I wanted our whole family to move there. I even dialogued about the move with some Argentine leaders. One day, when I was riding in a taxi to a meeting in Buenos Aires, the voice of the Lord said in my heart, *Daughter, I will allow you to give your* heart *to this nation, but not your* life. *I have called you to the nations of the earth, and you must not move here—you would get so focused on this one place that you would not fulfill your calling.* I knew I had to obey His voice rather than the voice of my emotions.

I completed my bachelor's degree in music and went on to study a fifth year for my master's in teaching music. The fact that I studied music and desired to use my gift for the Lord will help you understand one of the challenges, or tests, that came before me as a young married woman in my church.

Mike and I lived in California and attended a little fellowship with only about fifty members. Mike worked all night for an airline and would sleep during the day, so I often attended church alone on Sunday mornings. One Sunday, the pastor approached the back of the church, where I was sitting, to talk to the man on the other side of me. He leaned across me and in a quiet voice asked, "Homer, would you stand and lead a song this morning? We don't have anyone who can do it."

Homer, obviously very uncomfortable with the thought, shot back, "Pastor, you know that I can hardly carry a tune!" The pastor walked away and led the song himself.

Now, Mike and I were personal friends of the pastor, and he was well aware that I was working on my master's degree in music. In fact, the week before, for my orchestral conducting class, I had observed my professor as he directed the Burbank Symphony. Part of my training was in conducting symphonies, but now, *because I was a woman*, I could not even stand in front of my church to lead a hymn! As a 23-year-old woman who wanted to use her gift for God, that was a heartbreaking moment.

What did I do? Well, I knew I had several options: One, I could go away bitter and never return to the church. Two, I could stir up trouble against the pastor. Three, I could make a godly choice and seek the Lord as to how I could use my musical training in this church that did not believe women had a place behind the pulpit. I chose to pray and forgive the pastor; then I started a youth choir.

What transpired was glorious! That little choir became the best sound around, and many of the youth made commitments for the Lord Jesus. I really grew through that experience.

Young leader, man or woman, please read this carefully: God will always make a way for you if you are obedient to Him. Nothing will stop you from using your God-given gifts. If a door closes, look for the window. Be creative. When life is full of frustrations and tests, never give up.

God will always make a way for you if you are obedient to Him.

Many people ask me, "Cindy, why has God used you all around the world for His Kingdom?" Well, it is not because I am more gifted than most, or a better speaker. I earnestly believe it is because when there were obstacles in the way of what God called me to do, I trusted Him to make a way where there was no way. Has it been easy? No. Has it been worth it? Yes!

Ladies, you may at times experience unique challenges in pursuing your destinies, but your attitude along the way will make or break you. If you choose bitterness or anger, or you get eaten up inside at how unjust the system is or how prejudiced some men are against women, then you will never survive in the ministry or be successful in your life, either. And remember, being prejudiced against men is just as ungodly as the other way around.

It takes a lot of courage to follow the call of God—many times more courage than you can personally muster. This is why you need to have an intimate walk with the Lord.

Obstacles are inevitable. There will be storms. And friend, sometimes God does not take the storm away—He just tucks you in the eye of the storm, where you will be protected from its raging.

My War, His Will

At other times, however, the storms we experience come from our own struggles to follow His will. God touched me when I was 31 years old and told me to pick up my cross and follow Him in taking the Gospel to the nations. Well, I had a terrible struggle accepting the call. In fact, during that time, I had a brilliant idea. I would offer my husband, Mike, in my place! You see, I never dreamed I would be the one preaching. For some time I had prayed and believed God that Mike would preach and I would be his loyal intercessor. That nice, neat package would not have offended anyone.

My wrestling with God began in earnest when I realized God was not negotiating. He wanted *me* to preach, not Mike. Now, this was about as foreign to my thinking as my signing up for the "astronaut program." Anyone who knows me would double over laughing at the thought of my doing anything that requires athletic ability. When we played volleyball in school, I ducked when the ball came my way.

The war was on! I gave the Lord plenty of reasons why I could not possibly preach. "God," I pleaded, "didn't You notice that I am the *wrong gender*? Besides, Lord," I further whined, "I don't like women ministers. They have those high, squeaky, unpleasant voices. So, God, don't ever ask me to preach, especially over radio!" (I have lost track of the number of times I have preached or been interviewed on the radio throughout the world since that prayer.)

The next horrible thought that zinged through my brain was, *Oh, God! What about my children?* I winced at that. You see, I lived in a little Texas town where some of the men did not have a very high regard for women ministers. I did not want anyone to hurt my kids. I am afraid my next statement was not very spiritual: "God, I'm not laying my children on the altar of any ministry." I was unwilling to see my children mocked, made fun of or isolated as I had been.

For nearly a two-year period, I paced the floor after everyone was asleep at night, fighting the call. Again and again the voice in my head screamed, *No, no, I won't do it!* Rebellion was running deep. *Why me, God? Please, God, no!*

Struggling Veterans Who Preceded Me

I began to read autobiographies of others who had struggled with their sense of destiny.

Aimee Semple McPherson

One day I came across a book about Aimee Semple McPherson, who founded the Foursquare denomination. The story related her struggle with the Creator. She had been a missionary wife whose husband died while they were newlyweds on the mission field in China. Aimee was widowed, with a small baby to care for. In desperation, she came back to America to raise her little daughter.

About that time, Harold McPherson, just six months older than Aimee, asked for her hand in marriage, declaring his love for her and her little girl. Aimee agreed to wed, with one stipulation: because all her heart and soul were really in the work of the Lord, "If at any time in my life He should call me back into active ministry, no matter where or when, I must obey God first of all." They married on February 28, 1912, under those conditions.[1]

For a while, Aimee attempted to stay at home and forget the call of God upon her life. She and Harold were living at her mother-in-law's lovely home in Rhode Island. She had also given birth to a baby boy during that time, and she took up collections for The Salvation Army in order to augment their income. Finally, however, as Aimee tells in her own words:

> All through these strenuous days and that of the comparative quiet of our Providence home, a Voice kept hammering at the doorway of my heart. It shouted, "Preach the Word! Do the work of an evangelist!"
>
> "Impossible, Lord!" I would protest. "Impossible!"
>
> "I have called thee a prophet unto the nations," echoed the Voice.
>
> "No, Lord, I cannot go!" I would reiterate. Then would come a paralyzing silence which ensues when a telephone is disconnected. Returning to the privacy of my own room, I weepingly sobbed, "Oh Jesus! Jesus! Jesus!"[2]

Aimee's health broke under the strain. She suffered a major operation and steadily grew worse. All the time, the Voice inside kept bidding her to keep her pledge to preach the Word. To continue in her words:

> Finally, my condition became critical, and I was taken into a separate room to die. A nurse sat by me in the early hours of the morning, watching my flickering pulse. Through the death silence, which was broken by my own painful breathing, came the Voice of the Lord in trumpet tones, "NOW WILL YOU GO?"
>
> Lying there face-to-face with the Grim Reaper, I realized that I was either going into the grave or out into the field with the gospel. I made my decision and gasped out the words, "Yes—Lord—I'll—go!"
>
> Instantly, new life and warmth surged through my being.[3]

It helped to know that I was not the only one who had ever kicked against the pricks to answer the call of God (see Acts 9:5; 26:14). Not only did I realize that, but the consequences for saying no suddenly loomed large before me. Maybe it would not be healthy to tell God no—I did not want to take that chance.

Sister Gwen Shaw

Other women have also wrestled with accepting the fact that God had a call on their lives. One of them was Sister Gwen Shaw, who was the head of the End-Time Handmaidens. The Handmaidens consist of a large network of intercessors who must fast 21 days before they can become an official part of the organization. In her book *Unconditional Surrender*, Sister Gwen tells the story of her call to China during a revival in her Canadian Bible school days:

> It was around 11:00 PM when I entered the building and found my way to the classroom downstairs, where students were praying. As soon as I knelt, I felt a great burden for intercessory prayer come upon me. I put my head down under the chair and the Holy Spirit began to travail inside of me. Hour after hour I wept and wept. Today as I look back, I know it was that God would give me another chance to do His will and fulfill His calling on my life.
>
> After this experience, I looked at my watch. It was now 3:00 AM. In the other room there was still a lot of praying going on, so I got up and went in there.

> As soon as I went in, I saw something I had never seen in my life before. One of the students was travailing for China. The Holy Spirit was weeping and calling through the student, "I'm calling you to China. I need you in China. Won't you go to China? China. China."
>
> I looked around at those in the room and I wondered, "Who could God be calling to China?" The fact that it might be me never dawned upon me. After all, God couldn't call me—I was married now, and anyway, I didn't like the Chinese people. I was even afraid of them.[4]

The call of the Spirit persisted until one teacher asked Gwen, "Why don't you pray about it?" She consented and tells the result in her own words:

> Immediately, I began to feel a strange new burden grab hold of me for a nation I had never thought about. "I must be imagining this," I thought. God surely wouldn't call me. What would Dave [her husband] say?[5]

Gwen's heart was so full of questions that at last she said, "Lord, if it is me You are calling, then You will have to put me on the floor. I'm staying in this chair."

> Suddenly the power of God hit me like a stroke of lightning and threw me on my back on the floor. I thought God was killing me! "Lord, I'll go! I'll go!" I cried in desperation.[6]

Upon arriving home, Dave was not at all happy about the decision his wife had made. He announced sarcastically that she might go to China but he was "going to Hawaii." Gwen's heart was broken, so she cried out to God. The Lord faithfully intervened. The same Holy Spirit who had dealt with Gwen later prophesied through a visiting prophet over Dave that he was called to North China.

This account should be encouraging to you if you feel a call of God even though your spouse does not.

As a matter of fact, I came close to calling off my wedding because Mike insisted that he did not have a call of God on his life. I broke up with the poor guy about ten times because of it. The last time we broke up, Mike moved from Phoenix to Los Angeles, where we had met at a Baptist church.

After Mike left, I was terribly sad. I did not eat, and I was totally miserable. Finally, Mike called and quoted Matthew 18:19–20: "Again I say to you that if two of you agree on earth concerning anything that they ask, it will be done for them by My Father in heaven. For where two or three are gathered together in My name, I am there in the midst of them."

"Honey," he said, "somehow I feel that if we will let God be in the midst of our marriage, everything else will turn out okay."

Later on, Mike did receive a call and we started Generals of Intercession together in 1985. We have had many challenges, but God has truly been with us all the way.

Beginnings

People often ask, "Cindy, what happened after you said yes to God and accepted His call?" The truth is that I had no idea what to expect after I surrendered my life to full-time ministry. There certainly did not appear to be much danger of anything too drastic happening to me because, after all, I lived in Weatherford, Texas—population twelve thousand. How could anyone find me there? In fact, some of us used to say jokingly, "Can any good thing come out of Weatherford?" We had not even started Generals of Intercession yet. What a good place to hide, right? Wrong! God can find you anywhere. (Read Psalm 139.)

When I agreed with God to preach the Gospel, I taught Children's Church and led worship. Sundays were busy because I had to arrive early to work with the praise team, lead the worship for our little church, slip out and teach forty to fifty children from ages five to twelve and then slip back in to finish the service at the piano. It may sound overwhelming, but I actually thrived on it. God was at work! The children were praying for each other and God was causing short legs to grow, mosquito bites to disappear and warts to fall off. We had a great time. Nearly one hundred children were born again within a year's time.

When God Calls, He Equips

God actually started things off in a big way when I visited my in-laws in Phoenix, Arizona. We went to lunch with Faye Darnell, the women's pastor of a large charismatic church with nearly five thousand members and between two hundred and three hundred women in the weekly women's meetings. I had a nice time, and we agreed to meet the following day for the Bible study.

Had I known what God had in store for me that day, I would have been scared out of my wits. The Lord, however, had faithfully prepared me by waking me at six o'clock, impressing upon me to fast for the day.

At the meeting, I was puzzled by the strong sense of God's presence upon me—until Faye asked me to minister prophetically to twelve women. I agreed, and as I prayed, the Spirit of God moved powerfully. Not only did the twelve women fall under the power of God, but others in the room were also touched. Faye urged me to continue. The strong sense of God's Spirit rolled in like a thick cloud filled with His glory. I ministered for three more hours.

God wants to minister through you and me in ***His*** *power and not* ***ours.***

When I returned to Weatherford, I received a call from Faye, asking me prayerfully to consider ministering at her church's next ladies' retreat. She told me about the well-known person who had ministered the previous year and then said, "Cindy, we could get some big-name speaker, but we are hungry for the anointing, and we want you to come." Frankly, I was astounded.

Mike and I prayed, and we sensed this appointment was of the Lord, so I said yes. Then the struggle began. What had I done? To say that I was fighting intimidation would have been the understatement of a lifetime. It is in moments like this that the devil sits on your shoulder and whispers in an intimidating voice, *Who do you think you are? You know you can't do that! What will you say that will have any meaning to those people?* Actually, it really was not very difficult for him practically to demolish me with those cutting words, because they exactly mirrored my own. Fortunately, when you and I feel totally inadequate, we are actually ready. God wants to minister through you and me in *His* power and not *ours*.

My one "plus" was that I earnestly wanted to obey God. I had more fear of the Lord in me than fear of man. (Believe me, I had tons of fear of man in those days!)

Next, I was overcome with a deep sense of emotional insecurity. I rehearsed a list of names of numerous other women who could do a much better job, and I tried to get God to change His mind. (Some of you are grinning because you have had a similar experience or else you are going through one.) Perhaps by now I should have given up on convincing God to change His mind, but at times I can be very stubborn and hardheaded.

Throughout these emotional roller coaster rides, I was also earnestly beseeching God for the subject matter I was to teach during the ladies' retreat. Faye had asked me to teach three times. *Three times!* I thought with sheer terror. *God, I haven't taught more than one time anywhere in my life!* Major panic set in as I sought the Lord for something to say during *all that time*. Thank God for praying friends who helped me through that big step.

Leaping into the Dark

When I was young, my daddy used to preach about faith. I remember hearing him explain that it was like a little girl looking down into a dark basement and her daddy saying to this small child, "Jump, honey. I'll catch you!" The little girl cannot see her daddy, but she can hear his voice. That leap into the dark and into her daddy's arms is faith. Friends, I was leaping into the dark and hoping God was going to catch me.

The day the retreat began I felt assured about the message God had given me, but I had no idea how long it would take to teach this series of talks on "Releasing Bitterness and Judgments." I will never forget the first session. Faye introduced me, and I walked to the front. Fortunately, we had one of those old wooden pulpits instead of the new Plexiglas kind. Those Plexiglas pulpits are merciless: They show all of you—even your shaking knees. You cannot even take your shoes off if your feet hurt without the whole world knowing!

My knees were shaking and I was fervently praying, *Oh, God, please don't let them know how scared I am! Oh, God, help me!* But then, all of a sudden, I sensed the same presence of the Holy Spirit as I had at the weekly Bible study. It enveloped me like a garment, and the words simply flowed out of my mouth. Boy, was I ever relieved! In the end, not only did I have enough material, but I had too much.

God did all kinds of things that weekend. We laughed and we cried. People were able to forgive the unforgivable. The miracle anointing flowed. I will never forget when I gave a word of knowledge (supernatural insight about a certain type of action that is taking place) that someone had a corn on her foot and that God was healing the problem. Now, this was kind of corny (pun intended), because we were at a retreat center in *Cornville*, Arizona.

A woman named Juana laughingly said, "It's me, it's me!"

"Well, take off your shoe and look," I urged. She did, and the corn fell right off her toe and onto the floor. Wow! It was great.

People were set free, especially from bitterness. One woman, who began manifesting a demon, fell on the floor. I started casting the evil spirits out of her. And when I called out "rejection," the spirit manifested. It caused her to pound the floor as it left with a whiny voice, saying, "I'm the last one; I'm the last one." What a glorious deliverance!

What did I learn? I hardly know where to begin. I learned that if I stepped out in obedience, God would show Himself strong on my behalf. I learned that He is greater than my fears and insecurities and those thoughts that rise up to intimidate me. I learned that if He is working through me, I never have to worry about what I lack, because He will speak through me—and He is not at all insecure or lacking in any good thing. Good lesson, huh? In chapter 11, "Anointed to

Serve," I will share more about this and other lessons I learned while ministering.

God's Open Doors Stay Open

There was a real shifting of gears in my life that weekend. Other people quickly heard about what happened and sent me invitations to speak. It has always been my philosophy to let the Lord make the way. I have never sent out publicity résumés or tapes to solicit engagements. The Lord has opened all the doors. In fact, He has opened so many doors that I have had to run to keep up with Him.

I do want to balance my experience by saying that I know some people generate their entire incomes from speaking engagements. In those early days, Mike worked for American Airlines, so we did not have to use love offerings for living expenses. But people who live entirely by faith may have to initiate finding contacts and be selective about where they can afford to speak. Either way, if it is not the Lord's will, the doors will usually shut rather than open (see Revelation 3:7).

I thought we had quite a big measure of faith before 1991, but now I realize my faith was in Mike's paycheck. Today, God is the one who guides and provides every detail of our lives.

This was the beginning of my being thrust into ministry, which began in 1981. So much more that has transpired will be woven throughout the pages of this book. The next chapter, "Secret Pain," gives crucial information as you discover God's plan and purpose for your life. No matter what God calls you to do, striving to be a whole person in Christ is essential to finishing the race well. Let's take the journey together. . . .

TWO

Secret Pain

You will never be prepared to reach your destiny unless you are healed from past pain. It will always be there to trip you up just as you are on the verge of rising up. I went through much healing in order to be who I am today. I know the difference between women who have been healed and those who have not. Please do not skip this chapter. It is important for your life.

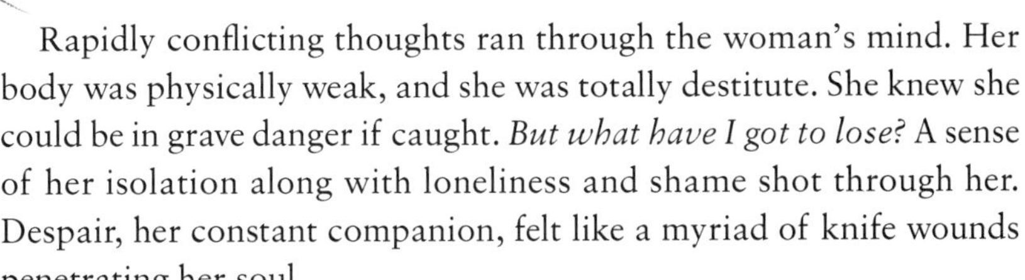

Rapidly conflicting thoughts ran through the woman's mind. Her body was physically weak, and she was totally destitute. She knew she could be in grave danger if caught. *But what have I got to lose?* A sense of her isolation along with loneliness and shame shot through her. Despair, her constant companion, felt like a myriad of knife wounds penetrating her soul.

Slowly, she dropped to her knees and began crawling through the crowd. Every once in a while, she would stand up to get her bearings and see how far she had come in executing what seemed like a fail-safe plan. The crowd was large, and many people were jostling and pushing each other just for a look at this incredible rabbi. Surely He would not notice just one more person tugging on the hem of His garment.

She inched her way toward Him and at last reached out. *Just one touch and I know I will be healed of this issue of blood*, she told herself.

At last she was almost close enough to touch the border of the fringe trailing from His side. For one split second, she faltered. *What if I am discovered and stoned because I have made the rabbi unclean? How could I possibly get away in this throng? Too late now*, she decided, and made the plunge.

What can be happening to me? Her thoughts were in turmoil as warmth emanated from her womb. The terrible pain subsided and a peace such as she had never known flooded her mind.

She came to herself quickly and looked around in a panic to see how she might hide and make her escape. Then she heard a voice calling out in the crowd. It filled her with wonder and fear at the same time.

"Who touched Me? I felt power leave My body."

And then she knew. It was the rabbi, the one they called Jesus. He was calling her.

Her first thought was to get away! But then she remembered the sound of His voice and was aware, in a keener way, of the strength and wholeness now coursing through her once diseased body. Gingerly, she stepped out of the crowd, fell down at His feet and said, "Rabbi, it was I. I am the one who touched the hem of Your garment."

She shyly lifted her face upward. *Those eyes*, she marveled. *Who could be afraid of anyone who has eyes such as His?* They were tender and loving, yet strong and full of power.

Somehow she knew she could trust Him. There was a sense of being fully protected from all those who would seek to harm her because she had come out into the crowd when she was unclean. With a trembling voice she told her story.

"Master, I've gone to the best physicians in the land for the last twelve years. I used to have quite a bit of money and many friends. Now I have spent it all, and no one has helped me but You. You were my last hope. I'm not quite sure exactly what has happened to me, but I know I am well. Oh, thank You, Master, thank You!" she exclaimed.

Lovingly, the Master looked down into her tear-filled brown eyes and pronounced, "Daughter, it was your faith that made you well. From this day you are whole and free of your disease."

The crowd melted back as she cautiously climbed to her feet. She *was* well! The weakness was gone, and joy burst from her soul. With one last look at Jesus, she practically floated away into her new life (see Matthew 9:20–22; Mark 5:25–34; Luke 8:43–48).

Private Pain in Public Pews

Have you ever asked yourself, *Why did Jesus call her out of the crowd?* It is unthinkable that a loving God would desire to humiliate the already broken woman. Did He have to ask, "Who touched Me?" Didn't He already know?

Perhaps He called her out of the crowd because her disease had not only affected her on the *outside*, but it had also greatly damaged her on the *inside*. The woman had suffered for twelve years and was weary of life. She had, in all probability, been separated from those she loved—at least from any kind of human touch—and most likely suffered deep physical and emotional poverty. I believe the Lord called her out of the crowd to bring healing to her inner person and lift the shame and disgrace off her. Jesus, the rabbi, pronounced her "clean."

Many people who enter our churches today come with secret pain they do not want to talk about. Maybe you are one of them. It deeply saddens me to know that people sometimes slip into church to find comfort only to leave again without being made whole.[1]

Why do people hide their pain? One of the many reasons might be that they have a big problem trusting other brothers and sisters in the Lord. There is also the issue of feelings of shame and rejection.

Let's take a look at the culture of the Church. In many cases, we come together and say to each other, "How are you today?"

"Fine, thank you," is the usual reply.

No matter how terrible we may be feeling, the polite response is, "God has been good to me." Well, I am not negating that God has been good to us, but many of us are not honest. We are *not* fine. In fact, we might have just told a big lie! There are situations in our lives causing us deep distress, and we need help.

Often our "How are you?" questions are perfunctory, and we seldom listen for a response. Eye contact is rare, and heart-to-heart sharing is rarer still. We need to listen not only to what people say with their words but also to what they say with their faces. We need to notice whether their eyes are happy or sad, and check out their expressions. Jesus, who was in a crowd and pressed on every side, took notice of someone who simply touched His garment for a moment. He is our example. I want to be like Him in everything I do and say. Unfortunately, I fall far short.

In Touch with the Out of Touch

Some people are in touch with others, but they are out of touch with themselves. They stuff their pain. They deny it and project it away by blaming others. But God did not create us to carry our hurts indefinitely. Pain that is not dealt with can destroy your destiny; it is like an infection that when left untreated can destroy your body. If you are to become all that God intends for you to be, you must allow the Holy Spirit to ferret out all the hurt places within you and heal your broken heart.

Pain that is not dealt with can destroy your destiny.

Healing begins with truth. You must be willing to look at what my mother calls "our beasts in the basement." The basement may be the floor of reality; instead of kicking all your junk downstairs, you need to have a spring cleaning. Of course, it is much easier to hide from the truth. Counselors call this *denial.*

I once saw a funny but true *Peanuts* cartoon. Lucy was trying to tell Snoopy (who was dancing around and around in glee) just how terrible the world is.

"Snoopy," rebuked Lucy, "with all the terrible things happening in the world today, how can you be so happy? You must be in denial."

Snoopy replied with a big grin on his face, "I'm the king of denial."

For some, denial is survival, but that is not God's highest and best. There is a lot of pain and cause for offense in daily life. The Bible says in Matthew 18:7, "Woe to the world because of offenses! For offenses must come." Whether we like it or not, we will all be challenged by offenses and the pain they cause.

In the early days of my ministry, every little word of criticism wounded my heart to the core. Rejection is one thing that women ministers usually receive quite a bit of (as does anyone in Christian leadership, for that matter).

A friend called me one day and asked what I was doing.

"I'm in bed," I told her, "and I've stapled the covers over my head, and I'm not coming out."

Everyone has days like that. Maybe you are having one today.

One of the most memorable prophecies I have received was this: "Daughter, I'm going to give you the hide of a rhinoceros and the heart of a dove." I have to admit that I am still very much in process on both counts. Initially, I was reluctant to write this book. I had to count the cost, because I know that not everyone will embrace the message it brings to women. I hope I have more fully developed my rhinoceros hide.

Secret Sins Cause Leaky Lives

Many people have so much secret pain stored up inside that it often spills out, hurting those around them. One day, I asked a counselor friend why a person we know acts the way she does. Her response was, "Cindy, that person is so full of anger that she's like a big sponge that is totally saturated, and it just leaks out all over people who get close."

What is important is that *you* are not the one who is leaky. One of my favorite prayers is, "Lord, keep me from secret and hidden sins" (see Psalm 19:12).

A pastor friend was terribly hurt by a breach in his relationship with a great and respected leader who had mentored him. He had given up all hope of reconciliation, but as we talked, he realized that a stronghold of offense had built up in his mind because he had been rejected. We made a covenant to pray and ask God to restore not only that broken relationship, but also other relationships in his life. One by one, we saw

God answer our prayers. Finally, the one breach that had caused him the most pain was mended in a supernatural way.

Does this pastor's story cause you to think of those with whom you have had a breach? It might be your mother, your child or a friend. It has caused a deep pain in your life. Believe God to heal the situation. Never give up on believing, because *nothing* is impossible with God.

If I am speaking to you, would you be willing to stop reading right now and make a list of those with whom you need to reconcile? You might even want to pray the following prayer:

> *Lord, I guess that I have believed there is something You cannot do. I have given up on trying to reconcile this situation, so I am going to believe there is nothing impossible or too difficult for You. Please heal this breach with ________ and restore our relationship.*

I thought about waiting until the end of the chapter for that, but I do not want you to suffer one moment longer. I pray that you feel a lot better right now.

How Can a God of Love Have So Many Rotten Kids?

Years ago, I began to come to grips with my own secret pain. Most of it resulted from being a pastor's daughter. In fact, by the time I was eighteen, I could not stand some church people. I had watched them behave ungratefully toward my parents, and sometimes they were downright mean. One day, I concluded that I loved God but I could not stand His children!

I remember standing by my mother when a woman approached her and started criticizing my dad. I was a sixteen-year-old fireball, who did not take this too kindly. My mom kept me a little behind her, probably so I would not tell the woman off. Actually, I was thinking, *Mom, if you will move a little more to the right, I'll let her taste my fist!*

My mom patiently listened to everything Mrs. Big Mouth said, and then with a look of peace on her face, she murmured, "I am so sorry that you feel that way, because *we love you so much*." All the strength went out of my anger as I listened in wonder to my mother show the love of Christ to this totally unlovable person.

By coming from the opposite spirit, the situation was reversed. Mom was a victor rather than a victim. Her victory came through her own choice and maturity in Christ.

We can make similar decisions in our lives. Scripture tells us to bless those who curse us and do good to those who hate us (see Matthew 5:44). If we do this, we will receive a blessing from above: "Blessed are you when [people] revile and persecute you, and say all kinds of evil against you falsely" (Matthew 5:11). Notice the Scripture does not say *if* but *when*.

Once, when I was sad because of false accusations spoken against me, my husband wisely said, "Cindy, Jesus was perfect, and they falsely accused Him." This brings us to an important principle:

> You will never be so perfect that you will escape being misunderstood.

At times when I hear what my accusers are saying about me, I chuckle and say, "I can't understand why they'd say those things about me, because I'm such a nice person!" (Well, mostly I am.) Honestly, many misunderstandings are cleared up when you meet the person you are having a problem with and sit down and dialogue with him or her.

Forgiveness: The Antidote for False Accusations

Let's pause for a few moments to deal with the subject of false accusations—an area of secret pain that is often pulled into the public arena. Accusations often get mixed up with gossip and multiply alarmingly. One time, for example, I had a little mole removed, and people phoned my office to verify if I had cancer! Why are we so apt to believe the worst about each other?

Could it be that we have been listening to the accuser of the brethren? The devil works day and night trying to kill our faith, rob our joy and destroy our reputations. We would be wise not to listen to him. Pastors are accused of manipulation and control because they try to correct sinful situations in their churches. Many women who are strong leaders are accused of being jezebels (i.e., controlling and manipulative women who act like Jezebel in 1 Kings 16–2 Kings 9. Would it make you feel any better to know that I have been accused of being one myself?). Accusations are not gender specific. At one time or another, all believers will have to learn how to deal with accusation.

So what should you do when you are accused? First, you will have to deal with the sting of it in your emotions. (The magnitude of the pain will depend on how much rhinoceros hide you have developed.) My friend Peter Wagner, who was a forerunner in the area of church growth, prayer and spiritual warfare, got shot at often. When he heard of a new criticism written against him, Peter would just grin and say, "Did they spell my name right?" I really admired that in him. I do not always fare so well. Sometimes my first reaction is to want to beat 'em up (a real joke for someone who is five feet two and three-fourths inches tall) or demand an immediate apology.

But forgiveness is what Jesus modeled, and so must we. After we work through the anger or hurt stage (or a mix of both) and we forgive, we need to pray for wisdom.

Although our first inclination might be to confront, that might not always be the best plan. John Maxwell is a foremost expert on leadership. He said this at a "Breaking the 200 Barrier" seminar at Fuller Seminary: "You can either add water or gasoline to a fire."

If you are not careful, you can make the situation much worse. (This is hard to believe at the moment it happens.) If the Lord tells you to confront the situation, follow the biblical pattern set forth in Matthew 18:15–17:

1. Tell the person his or her fault. Make sure it is between you and the offender alone. If the person hears you, you have gained your brother or sister (see verse 15).
2. If he or she will not hear you, take one or two more to confront (see verse 16).
3. If he or she refuses, tell it to the Church (see verse 17).

The gravity of some situations is so intense that if you are married, it is better to go as a couple—as in a case when the accusation has been made before a congregation. You may also want to ask someone in spiritual leadership to go with you.

Remember, Jesus acted like a lamb led to the slaughter before His accusers. Even though I have been written against and slandered on the radio, very few times have I answered my accusers.

One day, my teenage daughter queried, "Mom, who is (so-and-so), and why doesn't he like you?"

This was a perfect opportunity to model Christ's forgiveness before my daughter. It hurt me more that my daughter had heard the accusation and had suffered than the fact that I had been spoken against over the airwaves.

I might add that none of these people came to me to dialogue before they publicly bashed my name—a clear violation of the Matthew 18 passage. But I was still able to show my daughter how things should have been handled and explain that suffering an accusation can be a growing experience. Through suffering we learn more compassion and tenderness toward others. How we handle the situation can either work a weight of glory (see 2 Corinthians 4:17) or destroy us. I have a favorite saying about times such as this:

> Satan has meant to break me through this, but I choose to allow it to make me more broken before the Lord.

One of the powerful women leaders of my time is Christine Caine. In her book *Unashamed* (Zondervan, 2016), she tells the story of being the victim of racial abuse from her fellow classmates in Australia because of her Greek heritage. In addition, she was sexually abused.

Even though this could have destroyed her life and self-esteem completely, both the love of God and the love of a good man (her husband, Nick) broke the shackles of shame off her life.

She used the compassion she gained to start an organization called A21 that fights against human trafficking and the pain of its tentacles of abuse.

Purify My Heart, Lord

If you want to be a pure and broken vessel for the Master's use, your intimate prayer sessions with the Lord should include a time of asking God to uncover secret sins, anger, hurts and offenses. Allow the prayer of David in Psalm 51 to be your example. (At times I deceive myself that something did not really hurt, but later I make some kind of caustic statement about it and discover I have not fully dealt with it to the depth that is needed.) Warning: Do not pray this way unless you really mean it, because He will do it . . . sometimes in the most public places!

One time, for instance, I was speaking at a large church for the Sunday night service. I had spoken for its women's retreat just prior to the service and God had revealed a deep wound in my heart concerning the city where that church was located. You see, my dad had pioneered a church there, and it had been hard—very, very hard. Remember the story about Mrs. Big Mouth? This was the same city. I had, amazingly, shoved my deepest pain into a big mental closet. I guess if Snoopy was the king of denial, I was the queen.

Immediately after I was introduced, the Lord spoke to me in my heart: *Cindy, you can't get up and preach to these people. Your heart is not right. You hate this city and the denomination your father was a part of here.*

Now *hate* is a strong word, but it was true. I was angry about the mistreatment my dad and our family had suffered. Of course, a good Christian girl would not consciously harbor hatred and anger, so I was not in touch with those feelings at all.

Why was I so angry? The Lord gently whispered into my spirit, *Cindy, you believe they are responsible for your dad's death.* Wow! That insight hit me like a ton of bricks. It was true, though.

A little family history is needed to understand the depth of my emotions. For some time, while pastoring and planting churches, my dad had longed to become a missionary and wanted to be supported by the missions board. The board had helped us with $25 a week, years before, and now he was applying for regular support.

When Dad approached those who were in charge of missions at the denominational headquarters, he was offered a proposal: "Albert, how about cleaning the buildings for us while we process your application? We need a janitor, and you need to provide for your family."

My dad was a very humble man. Although he was a highly educated seminary graduate, he felt it was not beneath him to become a janitor. So night after night he would clean the headquarters building. Sometimes I would go with him and help. Never did I hear him complain that the job was too menial.

After a substantial period of time, Dad approached the missions board to find out what had happened to his missionary application. Although numerous churches had given him commendable references, his request had been denied because one church had submitted a negative reply.

To put this in perspective, that church had run off every pastor they had ever had prior to my father. In fact, the previous pastor had left in the middle of the night, leaving only a letter of resignation on the pulpit. Even though it was a tough place, Dad had stuck it out. The church grew and even added a parsonage. And now the church he had strived so hard to build and preserve had struck its final blow, ending my daddy's pastoral career.

From that day forward, my dad was not the same man. He never pastored again. Even though God used him mightily with handicapped high school students, he never quite recovered from that disappointment. Finally, he died at age 49—one month short of his fiftieth birthday. He was too young to die. I believed his death was the result of a broken heart.

When I finally got in touch with those feelings, a volcano of emotion began to erupt within me. Shaking, I explained to the congregation what was happening. I told them the story and asked the elders of the church to come forward to pray for me. Thank God for covenantal friends who can be trusted with sensitive issues of the heart. As I knelt, they came quickly and laid hands on me.

A confession flowed out of my mouth. God's Word tells us, "Confess your sins to each other and pray for each other so that you may be healed" (James 5:16 NIV). I needed to be healed because I was full of private pain. The reason that Scripture instructs us to confess sin is that confession is part of the healing process. I said some ugly things, such as, "I have hated that denomination, God, and I have hated its denominational leaders. They couldn't have killed my dad in a more painful way than if they had used a gun to shoot him in the head."

I could not believe what I was hearing myself say. The confession went on: "And, God, I hate this city for what it did to my family. It was such a hard place to start a church. We suffered so deeply, God. The church either wouldn't or couldn't pay us enough to even provide the basic necessities of life, and we were hurt."

I had flashbacks of going to the store with my mom and asking her to buy some cookies. Mom cried because she had only ten dollars to buy a week's worth of groceries—she could not afford to buy cookies. I grieved as I recalled images of Mom and Dad wearing old clothes that should have been discarded years before. (Pastors and their families often suffer deeply as they sacrifice to start churches.)

After I had vented for a while, I felt like a too tightly wound clock whose spring had let go. During those moments, I could also see how my brother and sister were hurt by what happened. Thank God He restores. Today (as of this writing) my brother is teaching English in China, and my sister has her degree in counseling. God is a redeeming God.

At last, a glorious sense of peace and joy filled my heart as my friends prayed for me to be healed. I was just beginning in ministry at that time, but I believe that as a result of my willingness to be open and honest, God honored what happened that day. God has opened doors all across the world for me since then. My dad may not have become a missionary on this earth, but I have! And I am believing God for a double portion of anointing to shake the nations of the earth.

You might be a pastor or the child of a minister, and you relate to this story. You might also have received wounds from people who do not understand how you could go into a professional life as a woman. Many times as I have shared, leaders' children have come and fallen into my arms, weeping. A pastor in Mexico told me how he has gone with holes in his shoes because there is not enough money to fix the soles.

Whether or not you are in full-time ministry, someone might have hurt you so deeply that you have never been the same. You are why I have written this chapter. I do not want you to hurt; most of all, your heavenly Father does not want you to keep carrying secret pain in your heart. My friend Ed Silvoso says that people get shipwrecked in certain areas and times of their lives and are never the same. It stunts their spiritual growth. The apostle Paul expressed it this way: "[Have] faith and a good conscience, which some having rejected, [and who] concerning the faith have suffered shipwreck" (1 Timothy 1:19).

Rebuilding from the Wreckage

I have seen shipwrecks happen to people other than myself. I have seen those with the gift of giving get hurt when large sums of money they gave to a ministry were misused and those in charge were proven unworthy of their trust. They became wounded and crippled in the area of their greatest strength. Thus, their strength became their stronghold. I have seen pastors so hurt that they left the ministry and never used their pastoral gifts again. They are now soured toward the ministry, and unless they are healed, their pastoral destinies will erode in the sea of bitterness where they were shipwrecked. Perhaps I am talking to you right now. If so, here are some suggestions to help you receive healing:

1. Pray, asking the Holy Spirit to reveal any areas where you are carrying secret pain.
2. Make a list of the people and situations in which you have been hurt, abused or offended.
3. Ask God to give you a person(s) who can pray with you as you confess your faults. (Of course, you can pray privately and forgive,

and ask God's forgiveness, but James 5:16 speaks directly about confessing our faults one to another.)

4. The more vulnerable and truthful you are willing to be about the situation and your pain level, the deeper the healing you will receive. (Helpful tip: Bring a big box of tissues, because you will probably need it.)

Years ago, I was diagnosed with a grapefruit-sized tumor behind my ovary. After the doctor read the sonogram, he advised me to have the tumor surgically removed. I asked him if we could wait ten days so my husband and I could pray for my healing. He was a bit skeptical but said it would not hurt to wait for that amount of time.

I began to seek the Lord earnestly for healing. Then one day, I received a call from an intercessor in California who gave me a word: "Find the root and pull it out; then you will be healed."

I began to ponder this. At first I had no revelation about what had hurt me enough to cause this large mass to grow within my body.

Suddenly, in a flash of inspiration, I knew what it was! I had been deeply hurt by a male pastor who did not believe that women should be in the ministry. The rejection had affected me in my femaleness. (I have found this to be the case sometimes for lumps in the breast. In fact, medical science is now making similar discoveries. Women who have lived with a critical father or husband often have problems with fibroid tumors or with other female-related illnesses.)

I began to search the Scriptures regarding healing. When I read James 3:16—"For where envy and self-seeking exist, confusion and every evil thing are there"—I knew I had found the key to my healing. We had already prayed and anointed with oil, but this one thing I had not done: I had not confessed to anyone else my hurt, anger and unforgiveness toward this pastor.

Mike and I invited a couple with whom we felt close to come to our house. I knelt down and confessed my pain in detail. As I confessed that I had not truly been able to forgive this pastor, even though I had tried, I started to weep until tears were wetting the carpet in front of me. Then, when I finished, they anointed me with oil and asked God to heal me.

I still had the pain in my body after the prayer (the tumor was pressing against my spine), but something was different inside of me. I knew I was healed. When I went back to the doctor, he was totally stunned and amazed. The tumor was absolutely gone! Not only that, but I had the blessing of witnessing to my Hindu doctor as a result of the miracle.

There are serious consequences when we do not forgive others and receive a release from the pain and bitterness of the situation. I like the illustration that Ed Silvoso, who is a forerunner on prayer evangelism, often gives about forgiveness:

> Suppose a visiting evangelist comes to your church and borrows your car. The man is a former drug addict who seemingly is being used of God in a wonderful way. Later, you find out the man has driven to the airport, sold your car and gone to South America.
>
> You would probably be furious, feeling betrayed by the evangelist. "He used me!" you would probably fume. "He was a minister of the Gospel!"
>
> Who must take the initiative to forgive? The thief? No, the one in the right! There is a deep vulnerability toward bitterness that he has to overcome. Does the thief have to overcome bitterness? No. He is in South America, oblivious to the pain you are feeling!

This reminds me of the story told in Matthew 18:31–35:

> "So when his fellow servants saw what had been done, they were very grieved, and came and told their master all that had been done. Then his master, after he had called him, said to him, 'You wicked servant! I forgave you all that debt because you begged me. Should you not also have had compassion on your fellow servant, just as I had pity on you?' And his master was angry, and delivered him to the torturers until he should pay all that was due to him. So My heavenly Father also will do to you if each of you, from his heart, does not forgive his brother [or sister] his [or her] trespasses."

Quin Sherrer and Ruthanne Garlock (two of my prayer partners for years) have some good insight on the need to forgive:

> Forgiveness through Christ is the cornerstone of our reconciliation and relationship with God. Knowing this, Satan attacks our capacity to give and receive forgiveness. He provokes us to indulge our grievances and hold on to our bitterness by telling us over and over, "The person who did this to you doesn't deserve to be forgiven!" Only Christ's sacrifice has the power to free us from sin and its bondage. Yet Jesus fixed a condition for that freedom in His parable of the unmerciful servant. In this story the king represents God and the servants represent us, His children.[2]
>
> We put forgiveness in its proper perspective when we realize that any injustice we have suffered from another person is small compared to our own sin against God.[3]

Some secret pain can only be forgiven through the grace of Calvary. One of the most powerful stories I have ever heard about forgiveness comes from the life of Corrie ten Boom. If you are not familiar with her story, Miss ten Boom and her family harbored Jews, in their home in Amsterdam, during World War II, for which they paid a high price. Almost all of her family died in concentration camps, including her precious sister, Betsie. The following story is her personal account of a time when, years later, Corrie came face-to-face with a jailer from the concentration camp where her sister had died:

> It was a church service in Munich where I saw him, the former SS man who had stood guard at the shower room in the processing center at Ravensbruck. He was the first of our actual jailers that I had seen since that time. And suddenly it was all there—the room full of mocking men, the heaps of clothing, Betsie's pain-blanched face.
>
> He came up to me as the church was emptying, beaming and bowing. "How grateful I am for your message, *Fraulein,*" he said. "To think that, as you say, He has washed my sins away!"
>
> His hand was thrust out to shake mine. And I, who had preached so often to the people in Bloemendaal the need to forgive, kept my hand at my side.

> Even as the angry, vengeful thoughts boiled through me, I saw the sin of them. Jesus had died for this man; was I going to ask for more? "Lord Jesus," I prayed, "forgive me and help me to forgive him."
>
> I tried to smile. I struggled to raise my hand. I could not. I felt nothing, not the slightest spark of warmth or charity. And so, again I breathed a silent prayer, "Jesus, I cannot forgive him. Give me Your forgiveness."
>
> As I took his hand, the most incredible thing happened. From my shoulder along my arm and through my hand a current seemed to pass from me to him, while into my heart sprang a love for this stranger that almost overwhelmed me.
>
> And so I discovered that it is not on our forgiveness any more than on our goodness that the world's healing hinges, but on His. When He tells us to love our enemies, He gives, along with the command, the love itself.[4]

Perhaps it is your own family that has hurt you. Many people have to forgive their parents, or even their own children.

I recall when I held unforgiveness against my still small babies. Mary (or Kyrin, as she prefers to be called today) hardly ever slept through the night, and I was bone weary most of the time. Then, later, when Daniel was born, the doctors said he would probably never walk because he did not have muscle tone in his left leg. I spent hours soaking off his little cast while he cried and cried. Even though I knew in my rational mind that it was not Mary and Daniel's fault, and that it was, in fact, the situation that frustrated me, little things the children did started to grate on my nerves until I was a wreck.

The Lord showed me that I needed to forgive my children. At first it seemed crazy that I should forgive a little baby and a small child for things that were not their fault, but I did what He asked me to do. One by one, I asked God to bring to my mind situations from their infancy to toddlerhood where I had resented what they did. One by one, I forgave. When I finished, I somehow felt clean inside—released from past frustrations—and I was able to be a much more loving, patient mom.

One of the hardest things to do is to love a rebellious or, perhaps, strong-willed child or teenager. My daughter has always been a young, emerging leader and thus tested my leadership to the max! I remember when we went to a Bible study at a very large church one time when Mary was only three. I turned my eyes away from her for only a few short moments when all of a sudden I heard a strident voice, coming from the direction of the church's bookstore, screeching, "Whose child is this?"

To my absolute horror my sweet child had spun a rack of little mini-books around so fast that they had gone flying all across the store. I was absolutely humiliated! I was tempted to look the other way and say, "Child? What child? Did I come in here with a three-year-old, blond-haired child looking just like that one?"

Sherrer and Garlock tell the story of how Audrey forgave the pain caused her by Vic, her prodigal son, in their book *How to Forgive Your Children*:

> A few days before 18-year-old Victor was to graduate from high school, he learned he'd failed his Advanced English course and would not be allowed to walk down the aisle with his classmates for commencement. Three days later, Audrey found a note on the windshield of her small yellow station wagon, which read: *Mother, Dad . . . I have to get away. Don't worry, Vic.*
>
> Audrey was shocked. "Vic had never given me any problem," she told me. "I had such high expectations that he would serve the Lord with all his heart in whatever career he chose. I had another child who was retarded, a husband who was terribly mixed up and not serving God, and now I had a lost son. I had to call on the Lord for help."
>
> Audrey searched frantically for Victor, and finally located one of his close friends. "If you hear from Vic, please have him call home," she begged.
>
> That night the telephone rang. A weak voice on the other end of the line breathed a terse message: "Mom, I'm all right!" Vic cut the connection, leaving her no clue as to his whereabouts.
>
> "I had one choice, and I knew it," Audrey shared as she recalled the experience. "If I were to survive emotionally, I had to forgive Vic for the disappointment I felt because he was not graduating and for his leaving home without so much as a good-bye. I also had to lay down my pride, my hurt and, finally, my anger. If I didn't, I'd be tormented over what

> he had done to me and worrying about where he was. So, I made the choice: I forgave Vic, releasing all my pent-up feelings as I committed him once again into God's care."[5]

Although Audrey changed her outlook, the prodigal did not immediately come home. In fact, it was three long months before he would come home. God led her to a friend of Vic's because she felt in her heart that he might be in the area. When she finally saw Vic again, he was thin, living in a bad section of town and wearing threadbare clothes.

Her first words were simply, "Hello, Vic."

He replied, "Hello, Mom. I missed you"—music indeed to a mom's ears.

Sometimes restoration is a process and not the microwave kind of fix we would like it to be. If you are in the midst of the process, I recommend Marcia Mitchell's excellent book *Surviving the Prodigal Years* (Emerald Books, 1999).

As you forgive and receive healing from the subsequent hurt, it may also help you to study some of the books written by Quin Sherrer and Ruthanne Garlock. They are excellent and go into depth in the area of forgiving in many different areas. (See the recommended reading section at the back of this book.)

The topic of this chapter is extremely crucial because a woman will never reach her highest potential, either in the home or the church, without being a whole person in every way.

You are going to love reading the next chapter. Part of our restoration as individuals comes through the friendships God brings into our lives on an everyday basis.

THREE

Dear God, I Need a Friend

The power and strength that come from having a good friend and prayer partner cannot be underestimated. One of my great joys is intergenerational friendship with young women leaders. Maybe you do not have a good personal friend, but I am praying right now that God will bring you not only one, but many!

My husband used to play basketball on Sunday afternoons at the little park near our home in Weatherford. He teased that he would hang around under the basket until the younger guys would throw the ball to him. (The truth is, Mike is actually a good athlete, but he enjoys luring an innocent partner who is quite rusty and out of shape onto the basketball court—rather like, "Come right in," says the spider to the fly!)

Mike had played with mostly the same group of guys for nearly six weeks, and I had even gone down once to be his best cheerleader. So one day when my sweaty, stinky-but-happy husband arrived home from an action-packed day on the basketball court, I queried, "Honey, what are the guys' names that you play ball with?"

A totally blank expression came across his face. "Names . . . well," he stammered, "well, I don't know any of their names."

Now, to my feminine mindset this was a shock! He did not know anything about these people he had played ball with *for six weeks*? Unthinkable! It simply did not compute.

Surely, I must have misunderstood that he knew *nothing* about them. So I probed deeper. "Well, then, are they married? Do they have children?" In searching his face, I saw to my dismay the same blank look. The realization that he knew absolutely no details of their lives finally dawned on me.

The Gender Gap

Have you ever watched men play basketball? They are really physical. After a good shot, they pat each other on the rear end and otherwise express glee in ways a woman would *never* think of. (Okay, some women who are on a college team might do this, but they would probably know a lot about each other first.) I was incredulous when I first noticed this. I would have to know someone really, really well to act physically like that, and then I still probably would not do it.

On the other hand, have you ever watched women get together for the first time? Their goal is to bond with each other, and they do so by gathering information. When two women have become friends, they know practically everything about each other—everything except maybe their social security numbers! I will go into more detail about the differences between men and women in chapter 7, "Gender to Gender," but for now, it is sufficient to say that the way in which most men cultivate friendship compared to the way most women cultivate friendship is quite different.

The Friend You Can Depend Upon

Does the title of this chapter, "Dear God, I Need a Friend," resonate in your heart? It does for most of us. And that is why I am going to talk to you about letting God be your very best friend. God, through His Son, Jesus, wants to be first priority in our lives. He is a friend who will never fail you. In fact, He is a "friend who sticks closer than a brother" (Proverbs 18:24).

The attributes of God are far beyond what even your best friend could attain. Let's consider a few of them together.

1. He is always available. (His line is never busy.)
2. He is never a gossip or willing to treat us unjustly.
3. He is unconditional in the way He loves.
4. He is generous in every way.
5. He is the most attentive listener.
6. He is the best counselor, always giving unbiased advice.
7. He is never selfish or self-seeking.

Pretty outstanding attributes, huh? In looking over the list, I feel I have a long way to go at being a good friend.

The Bible tells us that Moses was a friend of God and that "the LORD spoke to Moses face to face, as a man speaks to his friend" (Exodus 33:11). Imagine having that kind of closeness with Him!

Perhaps Moses could talk face-to-face with God because he did not have anything to be ashamed of. Moses must have walked before God with what the Scriptures refer to as "the fear of the Lord" upon his life.

So what is the fear of the Lord, and how does one develop it? I say *develop* because it certainly is not instinctive to our carnal nature. Joy Dawson, an international Bible teacher, author and intercessor, is one of the people who influenced my life most in learning about the fear of the Lord.

The Wise Friend Hates Evil

Joy Dawson taught me that one product of walking in the fear of the Lord is *wisdom*. I think I could safely say that we all want to be wise so we can help our families and friends; the Bible tells us "the fear of the LORD is the beginning of wisdom" (Proverbs 9:10). We begin to develop wisdom when we realize how casual our attitudes have been toward sin and how much our culture has polluted our thinking about right and wrong. You cannot be a friend of God if you have lost your understanding of what pleases and displeases Him in His holiness; sin is what separates us from God.

Joy Dawson gives four distinct levels of attitude toward sin in her book *Intimate Friendship with God*:

> *Level One:* The person who does not sin because the consequences are too great. This person lusts after someone else in his or her heart but does not commit the sin of adultery or fornication with his or her body because of the consequences being too great. Or he may hate someone else and wish that person were dead but does not murder him because of the consequences. Obviously, there is no hatred of evil and, therefore, no fear of the Lord.
>
> *Level Two:* The person who lives by the Golden Rule. He wants peace at any price and cannot understand anyone who is so radical that he would try to change the status quo of his life or anyone else's. This person can be full of the sins of selfishness and self-righteousness without being aware of it.
>
> He may go to church regularly every Sunday and give his tithes, pay his bills, grow six cabbages and give one over the fence to his neighbor. He often does good deeds. If you came up to him and said, "Do you fear the Lord?" he would be most indignant that you would even ask such a question of him. "Of course," he would reply. In fact, the "of course" could mean, "How could you have been so unobservant? How insensitive to the obvious!"
>
> If you asked him, "How long has it been since you spent more than an hour in prevailing prayer for the lost souls of men? What is the depth of your commitment to the Lord Jesus Christ for the lost souls of men to be reached by your witnessing to them on a personal basis? What is your prayer life in relation to the millions of Muslims, Hindus, Shintoists, animists, Buddhists, Communists, atheists, humanists, and nothingists who have no knowledge of God's plan of salvation or assurance of eternal life? What concern have you for the unreached millions of the world?" In all honesty he would have to answer, "Very little, or none at all."
>
> There is no fear of the Lord manifest in these sins of selfishness, prayerlessness, self-centeredness, complacency, and self-righteousness. There is no acknowledgment, let alone any hatred, of these sins in the person who lives on this level.

> *Level Three:* The sincere Christian who earnestly desires to please the Lord Jesus Christ. He does not want to sin and is deeply concerned when besetting sins are in his life. He wishes he could find an answer as to why he is always having to confess over and over again the same sins. Perhaps he commits the sins of criticism and of judging others; the sins of pride, always drawing attention to himself in conversation; the sins of unbelief in being unable to trust God, as manifested in fear, doubt, and disobedience. Or maybe it is the sins of lust, covetousness, jealousy or resentment—to God or man. He is deeply concerned and longs for freedom.
>
> *Level Four:* The person who has the fear of God upon him. He hates sin; therefore, he seldom sins. If he does, there is a quick awareness of sin, immediate repentance and a willingness to humble himself before others if directed by the Holy Spirit to do so. [1]

Joy Dawson goes on to say that "we have sinned because we have chosen to sin, because we love sin. 'Through the fear of the Lord, a man avoids evil' (Proverbs 16:6)."

As Joy's son and my friend John Dawson would say, "That will clean your plow." I have *the fear of the Lord* on me just typing the four levels!

Humility: The Quick Fix for Human Messes

I often think of how little puppies are sometimes trained with a very short leash. If they run out too far ahead, their owners pull back on the leash and they will find themselves splayed out on all fours. This is how the Lord is with me at times. Once I plant the fear of the Lord as my boundaries, if I simply think of running in the wrong direction, my heavenly Father, in His mercy, pulls back on that leash and I find myself falling on my face in an extremely humbling position.

I am thankful to know that God loves me enough to keep me from straying outside His love (see Hebrews 12:10). I want to clean up my messes quickly and run to fellowship with Him. I want Cindy Jacobs to be a person He can trust to do with integrity and compassion whatever He needs to be done. I know that it will take all of my life to be the kind of friend that Moses was with God, but then, God is no respecter of persons, so I believe it is attainable.

I have learned that one way God manifests Himself to us is through the friends He sends our way. Although our primary need is friendship with God, we can also ask Him for a friend "with skin on," so to speak. The unconditional love of a covenantal friendship is healing and a great source of strength and comfort (see Ecclesiastes 4:12). A real friend is one who sees you at your worst moments and still thinks you are special.

Ruth: A Model for Friendship

Both men and women need friends, but their friendship needs are very different. For now I will primarily focus on the kind of friends that women need. (Men, you might want to stick around and not tune out at this point, because the following insight will be helpful in your relationships with those mysterious beings called "women.")

One of the most beautiful stories of friendship in the Bible comes from the book of Ruth. This book flourishes with lessons we can apply to our daily lives. As you read about Ruth, notice the qualities she brought to her friendships and ask yourself which of these qualities you need to cultivate.

Let's begin by contrasting this book's main characters—two women brought together during distressing times in a covenantal relationship: Ruth, a young Gentile daughter-in-law, and Naomi, a bitter, disillusioned, older Jewish mother-in-law. The diversities of these two widows can conjure up all kinds of mental pictures for us. Ruth was probably quite beautiful and most likely could have had her pick of handsome young men. She did not need Naomi.

Plus, Ruth would have known about the notoriously strict religious laws of the Jewish people because she had married into a Jewish family. So why would she choose to go with Naomi to Bethlehem?

Undoubtedly, she knew that if she traveled with Naomi, she would be forfeiting the protection of her own people and choosing instead the hard, cold ground and hostile surroundings in order to make the journey. This was a serious choice weighted with possibly dire consequences. And yet Ruth made that choice.

Ruth Was Covenantal

The dialogue between these two women is often sung at weddings, representing the love between husband and wife, but it was actually a healthy, covenantal love between two women:

> Entreat me not to leave you,
> Or to turn back from following after you;
> For wherever you go, I will go;
> And wherever you lodge, I will lodge;
> Your people shall be my people,
> And your God, my God.
> Where you die, I will die,
> And there will I be buried.
>
> Ruth 1:16–17

Not only had Naomi won Ruth's personal affection, but her life had also caused her daughter-in-law to have a conversion experience for which she abandoned her pagan gods for the one, true and living God. What an impact a friendship can make!

As we read through the book of Ruth, we notice that Naomi had another daughter-in-law, Orpah. But her two daughters-in-law were quite different in the ways they demonstrated love and friendship. *The Woman's Study Bible* gives interesting comparisons of the two, including Ruth's "Love that bore testing" and "Resolute exercise of the will" versus Orpah's "Love that failed in adversity" and "Easy change of emotions."[2] Let's look at Ruth's character in more depth.

Ruth Was Patient

Bitter people, such as Naomi, are usually difficult to be around. And Naomi might have been short with Ruth from time to time as she processed the grief of her husband's death. But Ruth's love was so healing that even Naomi was softened by it.

I am convinced that the love of God can penetrate any soul, no matter how hurt or angry. I would encourage you not to abandon your friends when they are going through bitter times such as the loss of a child, husband or parent. That is the time when they need you the most. And that is also the time when they are least able to reciprocate your love. But the Scriptures tell us to love even when we do not receive it in return (see Matthew 5:44, 46).

Ruth Was Diligent

Personally, I admire Ruth as much as any woman in the Bible because of her excellent character qualities. She did not have a lazy bone in her body. Rather than going out to glean the fields, she could have said to Naomi, "Look, old woman, get up and go help me find some food. I have lost as much as you have. Not only that, but I'm also in this crummy foreign land, and I don't understand the customs!"

Ruth Was Long-Suffering

Instead, however, Ruth was tender toward Naomi—who must have been in deep shock and steeped in shame and embarrassment for having to return to Bethlehem empty-handed. Most likely, her old neighbors who had tried to dissuade her and her husband from leaving were wagging their tongues and saying to each other, "Didn't we tell them not to go to that God-forsaken place? Well, she got what she deserved!" Ruth was sensitive to the pain and shame of her mother-in-law. She had met the living God and her actions showed it.

Because Ruth was now God's child, He directed her right to the field of one who would become her husband and kinsman redeemer (i.e., a type of Christ; the kinsman redeemer was a relative who could "redeem" the inheritance of a dead relative. Isn't this a romantic story?). The Bible says Ruth *happened* upon the field of Boaz (see Ruth 2:3).

Ruth Was Grateful

Ruth worked tirelessly all day, and when she met Boaz, she fell at his feet in gratitude. (Probably, she lifted those beautiful brown eyes up at him through her long dark lashes, and he just melted!) What man could resist such a humble, grateful woman?

Ruth Was Committed

When Ruth ate the lunch Boaz provided, she saved some for Naomi, mindful that she was hungry at home. She could have reasoned that she, after all, was the one doing the hard physical labor.

By chapter 3 in the book of Ruth, we read that Naomi was being healed of her despair and wanted to see that Ruth had security. She advised Ruth to appeal to Boaz as her kinsman redeemer. This strategy was based upon knowledge of levirate marriage (see Deuteronomy 25:5–10). By this practice a widow became the wife of her husband's brother or another close relative in order to produce a child who would inherit her first husband's estate and preserve his name. Ruth's loyalty to the tradition of her husband's people and her desire to care for Naomi by marrying someone within the family were a tribute to her commitment to the family of her deceased husband.[3] Of course, we know that Boaz was a symbolic picture of Jesus, who is our Kinsman Redeemer—the Lord who redeems us from our sins and provides rest and relationship for all who lay their lives at His feet in submission to His lordship.

Ruth Was Teachable

Ruth did exactly as Naomi told her, which shows she had a teachable spirit and a willingness to listen and learn from her elders. When Naomi tried to instruct Ruth about how to approach Boaz, Ruth could have said, "Now listen, Naomi, I recognize that you know a lot about Israel, but I know much more about men than you do. You're from the wrong generation and obviously out of touch with how to get a man to notice you."

Ruth Was Obedient

There are great blessings to be gained from obedience—not blind obedience, but loving, godly obedience. The Bible says that obedience is better than sacrifice (see 1 Samuel 15:22).

I love to read *The Woman's Study Bible* because of the richness found in the margin notes regarding interrelations among women. At one point it discusses the mutual commitment between Ruth and Naomi—such as how the bitterness in Naomi's heart opened the way for creativity in Ruth, and how Naomi's counsel bore fruit as Ruth accepted and honored it.[4]

One of the great themes of the book of Ruth is that of restoration. Dr. Fuchsia Pickett says, "The book of Ruth ranks among the greatest books of the Bible for teaching true spiritual restoration, foreshadowed in the redemptive love of Boaz for Ruth."[5]

—

Godly Friendships Bless Both People

Naomi instructed Ruth to go to the threshing floor and lie down at Boaz's feet and say to him, "I am Ruth thine handmaid: spread therefore thy skirt over thine handmaid; for thou art a near kinsman" (Ruth 3:9 KJV).

In ancient Eastern culture, "to spread a skirt," or covering, over someone was a symbolic act offering that person protection. More than that, it involved entering into covenant with a person for the sake of redemption. Even today in many Eastern countries, to say that a man puts his skirt over a woman means that he married her.[6] (What a bold woman Ruth was! She was in all practicality proposing marriage to Boaz.)

In asking for Boaz to cover her, Ruth was declaring, "I need a redeemer. I am a widow, disgraced, with no inheritance. You can take my shame, my poverty, the bleakness of my future and give me an inheritance. You can totally redeem me, if you will."[7]

This beautiful friendship brought redemption and restoration to *both* women. Ruth got a new husband and had a young son. She became the mistress of the house where she had gleaned. Naomi received an inheritance, and her son's lineage was passed on. Not only were both women totally restored, but the generations also show that both King David and the Messiah, Jesus Christ, who redeemed the sins of the world, came from their heritage.

This story touches me deeply because my friends are among the greatest treasures God has given me. I have friends I can rely on to come to my aid for help on many different levels, as I would do for them. This is a covenantal love.

Some friendships, like that of Ruth and Naomi, go beyond simply being a satisfying relationship for a brief period of time—they are God-ordained. Joy Dawson has taught that God appoints the seasons of our friendships. New friends may have been brought into our lives just for the moment, or the meeting could be a God-ordained, lifelong connection that will change the course of our destinies.

New friends may have been brought into our lives just for the moment, or the meeting could be a God-ordained, lifelong connection that will change the course of our destinies.

The following are a few examples of friendships in the Bible:

- Esther and Mordecai: cousin and cousin
- David and Jonathan: shepherd boy and prince
- Mary and Elizabeth: mother of Jesus and mother of John

These kinds of covenantal friendships are supernatural in their purpose. Have you ever met someone with whom you felt an immediate bond in friendship? This is an indicator that God will be doing something significant through the meeting. Of course, this goes way beyond the feminine gender. Mike and I are extremely close to a number of other ministers and their families who have had a tremendous impact on our lives: Chuck and Pam Pierce, Peter and Doris Wagner, Ed and

Ruth Silvoso, Dutch and Ceci Sheets, Lou and Therese Engle, Pastors Jim and Becky Hennesy and others.

I do not hesitate to say that we are family to one another in many ways. We have laughed, prayed, cried and mourned together. Many of us have been on the front lines of the battlefield and been shot at so many times that we have had to pray each other out of intensive care. We know that we can call each other any time of the day or night, but we do not abuse the privilege.

Cultivating Closeness

One of my close female friends of many years is Beth Alves of Increase International. We have had numerous Holy Spirit adventures together. Several years ago, for example, I went through a deep valley of despair. Finally, in my intense discouragement, I decided to quit the ministry. I will never forget calling Beth on the phone and leaving a sobbing message. I was crying so hard that my voice was indistinguishable. Beth shared with me later that her husband, Floyd, heard my message and said, "Beth, who in the world is that woman?"

Even though my voice was almost unrecognizable, Beth knew. Beth is my friend, and it was not the first time she had heard me cry.

"Floyd, that's Cindy, and something is terribly wrong!" she exclaimed. Beth called and called until she reached me. When I explained the situation and my decision, she said, "Cindy, don't do anything rash. You go rest and let me carry your prayer burden for the next three days." Beth not only prayed, but she also *fasted*. Within three days, I was able to press on in the ministry.

Maybe you are thinking right now, *I sure wish I had a friend like that*. Well, friendships like Beth's and mine are forged in the trenches of life. We have walked through so much together that we have built a foundation of trust. I have stayed up nights praying for her and her children, and vice versa. Friendships such as ours require a substantial investment of time and energy. They do not just happen—they are cultivated over time.

I have a great friend and prayer partner named Cheryl Sacks. She is a minister and author, like me. We have been friends for more than thirty years. It is great to have a friend who is a peer whom I can call and have a prayer time with. Even though I live in Texas and she lives in Arizona, she never seems far away. The great thing is that Mike and I are just as close with her husband, so we often pray together as couples and even vacation together.

My own sister was one of the wisest women I ever knew, and it was always such a comfort to be able to talk to her on the phone. Lucy passed away in 2012 of melanoma cancer. I miss her to this day.

Many people are waiting for someone to knock on their doors with a cake and the announcement, "Hi, I'm your new best friend, and I've come to lift you out of your doldrums!" Even though this is not out of the realm of possibility, friendships usually do not happen that way. The Scriptures tell us that "a man [or woman] who has friends must himself [or herself] be friendly" (Proverbs 18:24).

Sowing Seeds, Reaping a Harvest

Because we moved so often when I was a young girl, I remember feeling unbearably lonely. Then one day in the fifth grade, I made a decision that if I was going to have friends, it was up to me to start the relationships. I did not know that I was actually tapping into a scriptural principle. It just worked! When I met someone I hit it off with, I would invite that person to my house after school. I also began thinking of kind things to do for people, and before long, they were responding. I was not interested in joining the most popular crowd—I just sought out people with similar interests who liked to read and discuss books or ride bikes with me.

When my family moved, I corresponded with friends from that area as long as they wrote back so that I would not be entirely disconnected from relationship. I introduced my new friends to my old friends through their letters, and the cycle of friendship expanded.

I also learned to develop friendships with people of all ages. I talked to neighbors when they were outside—especially those who were senior citizens. I had many hours of great fun while I raked the leaves in their yards, walked their dogs or sat and ate cookies with them. One of my grandmother's neighbors, whose name was Mrs. Lippy—I always called her "Mrs. Mississippi"—left me a one-hundred-year-old plate when she died. What a treasure!

Now I am learning from the next generation and feel a great call to them. Many have told me about their fears and challenges, and although we relate on a different level—some call me "Mom"—they enrich my life. I once came home from a trip to find eight of them in the house while my own child had run an errand. "Hi, Mom," they chorused. Bewildered, I searched each face to see if I recognized any of them. I did not. But they let me know that my kids had told them they would love me and that they could call me "Mom."

Over the past years, I convened a roundtable of emerging women leaders. They are extraordinary women who are working to stop human trafficking and abortion, and they have a 24-hour house of prayer in Hollywood, California. Each woman is an extraordinary speaker in her own right. I am very proud of them and their exploits for God.

Letting God Be Lord of Our Friendships

Friendships have periods of ebb and flow, and these transitions should not be threatening. If only young girls could realize this when they feel their lives are over because "Dottie" has a new best friend. There are times when I am extremely close to a particular person, but then the Lord seems to start taking us in different directions for a season of our lives. It does not mean we no longer have deep affection for one another; it simply means that we are going different ways. One or two years later, we might just take up at the same place again. Of one thing you can be certain: If God is giving you a friend who is part of your future destiny in Him, He will see to it that you find each other again.

Friends like Laurie Cole and Margarita Jones have helped me in ways that have made my life as a traveling minister much easier. Another friend, JoAnna Cinanni, rescued me before I went on a prayer journey to Vietnam. Right before we left, I became very, very sick. The day before I was supposed to leave, I was so sick that I could not even get out of bed to pack. JoAnna came to my house, looked in my closet and packed everything for my trip. It was an adventure simply to discover what was in my suitcase on that trip! Thank God for the gift of friendship. Cheryl Sacks has been my prayer partner for years. Julie Zylstra has been my vacation buddy and intercessor, too.

What keeps people from developing close friendships? Sometimes it is fear. They may have been deeply, deeply hurt through what might be called "friendly fire."

Maybe you have been "wounded in the house of [your] friends" (Zechariah 13:6). This is a very deep pain; however, you will be the loser if you do not allow your heart to open and receive the healing of the Lord that comes through friendships. It is a risk worth taking.

Some married women expect their husbands to give them the kind of friendship they need to receive from women. This expectation can actually put a strain on the marriage. While I do consider my husband my best friend, I know he does not like to hash, rehash and go over the details of situations to the degree I need to. When a woman gets hurt, she needs to talk about it—sometimes more than once. This can actually lessen the pain for her, but it can also drive a man crazy, as they usually discuss an issue once, conquer it and put it to rest, in most cases.

Friendship Qualities That Enrich Our Lives

Women in countries other than the United States sometimes express friendship in different ways than we North Americans do. In Argentina, I would think nothing of holding hands and walking down the street with my good friend Marfa Cabrera. In America, however, I would be reluctant to do so. I think Americans often rob themselves of the sweetness of pure relationships in which they can hug or even kiss on the cheek without feeling strange. I used to love to hold my mother's hand. Often when we were at church and someone prayed, she would reach out and take my hand. What a precious, precious gift that was!

Have I convinced you to enrich your life with deeper friendships? I hope so. Here are some tips for growing and finding new friends:

1. Pray, and be honest before the Lord. Tell Him, "God, I need a friend." You might even be specific, just as I was about my need for a friend, Beth Alves, who could help me at home during that personal crisis.
2. Be open to looking at past friendships and allow the Lord to heal you of any bitterness, pain or abandonment that would cause you to build walls and not receive the good gifts God wants to send your way.
3. Look around you for people in your neighborhood or church who are alone. Many singles need community in their lives and might enjoy spending holidays and other special times with you.
4. Pray for your neighborhood or perhaps your co-workers, asking how you can express Christ to them through friendship.

One of the greatest women of prayer I have known was Mary Lance Sisk. Mary Lance taught about neighborhood praying. She told me the story of how a young mother moved into a developing subdivision where only a few houses had been built. This mom would bundle her little ones up and put them in a stroller to walk and pray over every lot on her street. She would ask the Lord for the salvation of each person He wanted to move onto those lots. Years later, Mary Lance reported to me that almost every person on her whole block was a Christian.

I pray God will give you a strategy for your neighborhood. Maybe you will have a ministry of baking bread for new people who move in, or organize block parties where you open your home. You can make a difference in the world through loving, interactive friendships. Do not wait for another person to initiate a friendship; you be the one to reach out. There are many lonely people in the world who would make great friends if you were willing to invest a little time in them.

With this theme of allowing God to use you to make a difference in the world you live in, I invite you to turn to the next chapter, "Women of Destiny."

FOUR

Women of Destiny

Have you ever asked yourself, *Why was I born?* Do you struggle with a sense of purpose and belonging? Each person has been uniquely formed and is destined by God to accomplish specific tasks and goals. And yet, I have talked with many women who have said they wish they had been born a man! They tell me, "Life would be so much easier," or, "Men have it so good, and women have it so much tougher."

The point is that if you are born a female, God wanted you to be one. You were given life by God to be a woman of destiny and to impact the lives around you. But in order to do that, you must discover God's purpose for your life and fulfill it to the very best of your ability. Sadly, I have ministered to women from around the world who feel that being born a woman was a curse and not a blessing because of their cultures.

Perhaps you could make an impact like Susanna Wesley, whose children John and Charles grew to be mighty reformers for God's Kingdom. Remember, the Lord has called you for "such a time as this," just as He called Queen Esther (see Esther 4:14).

It is true that some women will have bigger mountains to climb and greater challenges to overcome than others. Some will have been raised in abusive homes, in the drug culture or in other difficult places. Others will have had the advantage of more money or greater educational opportunities. Fortunately, it is not what you have but Whom you know that makes the difference.

Little Becomes Much in God's Hands

History is full of examples of women who believed God would turn their dire circumstances around and, therefore, saw amazing miracles. Consider the woman from 2 Kings 4:1–7. Talk about a bleak situation! Her husband had died, and the creditors were threatening to make slaves of her two sons if she did not pay the debt her husband left behind. (You may be in a similar circumstance, although you are more likely to be in danger of eviction than the enslavement of your children.) This woman needed a miracle. What did she do? She went to the prophet of God, who asked, "What do you have in your house?"

This probably seemed like a strange question to the widow, but she graciously replied, "Nothing at all, except a jar of olive oil."

Often, we think we are in a barren place, without hope, but I assure you, there is something in the house—either a talent, an ability or a tangible item, such as a jar of oil, that God can multiply to bless you. He will not leave you comfortless.

This widow was in a seemingly deep-end situation, but God had a plan for her. The prophet told her to borrow as many empty pots and pans from her neighbors as she could find. Then he instructed her to lock herself in the house and pour oil into the vessels from the one full container she already had. When she obeyed the prophet, she stepped into the realm of the miraculous.

Imagine the scene . . . her boys running back and forth borrowing pots, eyes wide with amazement as the oil kept pouring and pouring. Finally, perhaps a little out of breath, the boys said, "Mom, that is the last pot." Surely she must have looked around at the full vessels of oil and marveled!

She must have gathered up her skirts and gone running to find Elisha. I am certain that he would have been grinning when he instructed her to go pay her debt and then live off the money she made from selling the rest of the oil.

God Knows Your Address

Several years ago, I was ministering in Argentina at a large church. The meeting was packed, and the balconies were overflowing with people. Right in the middle of the meeting, I stopped, and the Lord spoke quietly into my heart, *Cindy, someone here is planning to commit suicide. Tell the person not to do it.*

Feeling the urgency of the situation, I interrupted the message and gave the word from the Lord. When I finished the sermon, the pastor gave an appeal for the suicidal person to come forward. Slowly, a woman about thirty years old, dressed in a white blouse and dark skirt, made her way to the front. Softly, in a rather muffled voice, the young woman whispered that she was being evicted from her house and had planned to shoot her three children and herself when she arrived home from church.

At that point, she drew a gun out of her purse and put it in the pastor's hand. "Pastor," she said, "when I heard God speak to me through Cindy, I knew He would make a way, and my children and I would not be out on the street."

No doubt, the woman had prayed, and God had intervened. I sure was glad I had been faithful to the Holy Spirit's nudging and stopped in the middle of the message to tell her God had a better way!

Anchored in the Purposes of God

You may feel stuck in and controlled by the circumstances around you when, in reality, God has a plan to lift you out of the midst of your problems or despair. The apostle Paul wrote, "And we know that all things work together for good to those who love God, to those who are the called according to His purpose" (Romans 8:28).

If you study this verse carefully, you see that things work together for good to those who have the anchor of "purpose." All things may not be working together for good, because we are aimless and do not know our purpose. We could interchange the word *purpose* with *destiny*.

Down through the ages, God has used women in powerful ways to influence their families, churches and nations. Many women have told me, "I know that God has called me to be a mother." Other women, such as my Mexican friend, former congresswoman Rosi Orosco, feel their place is to fight human trafficking. The issue is not what you are doing, but whether you are doing what God has ordained for your life at this time. Romans 8 promises that nothing will be able to separate us from the love of God, but sometimes we are unsuccessful and miserable because we are not in our place of purpose, or destiny.

Women of Courage and Valor

History reveals that no matter what their beginnings, women have been able to rise to the forefront when God was involved. Catherine Booth, for example, was a sickly woman who often stayed in bed for days at a time, yet she never let her poor health stop her from doing the Lord's work. She sacrificed to "reclaim" women from lives of prostitution, and she persevered until 1890, when she finally died of cancer at age 61. By the time God called her home, Catherine Booth had impacted the whole world through The Salvation Army.

Another woman who greatly changed the face of our nation was Frances Willard. When I went on a prayer tour of the Capitol building in Washington, D.C., the marble statue of her standing beside a pulpit engraved with the words *For God and Country* impressed me. I was inspired to scurry to the history books, where I learned that this great woman of God lived from 1839 to 1898 and was one of the best-known female temperance leaders of the nineteenth century. She was active in founding and directing the Woman's Christian Temperance Union (WCTU), the largest nineteenth-century women's organization.

Frances Willard's life and ministry illustrate how closely the temperance movement was aligned to religious activities. In spite of intense opposition, temperance work offered the only viable public ministry for many women of the nineteenth century. Frequently, the religious activity associated with the WCTU involved evangelistic outreach to men.

The WCTU department of evangelistic work sponsored Bible readings and Gospel work in prisons and police stations, as well as among railroad employees, soldiers, sailors and lumbermen.

Willard's work was not limited to the United States. Indeed, the WCTU was probably the first large-scale women's organization to spread worldwide. By the 1880s, the White Ribbon Missionaries were organizing chapters in Asia, Africa, South America and elsewhere throughout the world.

Closely connected with her work for temperance was her support of women's suffrage, for she believed that laws supporting prohibition would be enacted only if women had the ballot. As with her temperance work, Frances Willard claimed the direct leading of God:

> While alone on my knees one Sabbath, in the capital of the Crusade state, as I lifted my heart to God, crying, "What wouldst Thou have me to do?," there was borne in upon my mind, as I believe from loftier regions, this declaration, "*You are to speak for women's ballot as a weapon for protection for her home.*"[1]

Frances worked with Dwight L. Moody during his Boston campaign, and Moody even invited her to preach at a Sunday afternoon meeting. Although she eventually felt it was not God's will for her life, she later said, "I deem it one of the choicest seals of my calling that Dwight L. Moody should have invited me to cast in my little lot with his great one as an evangelist."[2]

Today, women's organizations such as Justice Speaks, started by Sharon Ngai in Hollywood, California, and Unlikely Heroes, founded by Erica Greve, are platforms for women to fight against the abuse directed toward men, women and children. They are rising up to stand against injustice.

Career Woman Is Not a New Term

Some women of destiny are called to business, such as the woman referenced in Proverbs 31:16, who bought a field and planted a vineyard. In this biblical family, it seems that both the mother and father did some work outside the home. Women today (especially Christian women) often feel guilty for having careers, and yet this Proverbs 31 woman was clearly praised for her contribution.

I believe God is raising up an army of women in ministry as well as women who own businesses. Through the years, our ministry, now called Generals International, has been working with business leaders to help them develop prayer strategies for their companies. This, in part, led me to the study of an Asian woman named Lydia, one of the most fascinating and least talked about women in the Bible. Her story is told in Acts 16:13–15.

The events that led to Lydia's conversion are significant. Paul had received a vision from the Lord of a man who said, "Come over to Macedonia and help us" (Acts 16:9). Prior to this vision, Paul had intended to go instead to Asia. Although the Lord restrained him from going there, the Lord had a plan to begin to touch Asia through this one woman.

Lydia was named after a province in Asia Minor, in which the city she came from, Thyatira, was located. Lydian women were famous for the manufacture of beautiful purple cloth made from the purple dye of the murex, a mollusk.[3] But I have often wondered how Lydia came to live in the city of Philippi in Macedonia, because the two cities appear to be more than three hundred miles apart. Did she come by a caravan, riding on the back of a camel? How did she, a single woman, manage to overcome the obstacles that might have come her way? Evidently, God had a plan for her life that included being in the city of Philippi, on a riverbank, seeking to know more about Him—at the same moment Paul came into town.

The very fact that she was worshiping by a river is important historically. The place was probably a *proseucha*, a place of prayer and worship when there was no synagogue. It was usually a spacious, uncovered amphitheater.[4] A regular synagogue could be established only when a core group of ten adult men was present. For some reason, only women were in attendance when Paul arrived on the scene.

Lydia was hungry for truth. Notice God's strategy. Paul did not go into Asia, but his first convert in Europe was Asian! The Lord knows when the heart is ready to receive the truth. Not only was Lydia born again, but also her whole household received Christ and was baptized with her.

I believe Lydia had a gift of giving that influenced the church in Philippi, which was started in her home. Do you remember Paul's letter to the church at Philippi?

> As you well know, when I first brought the Gospel to you and then went on my way, leaving Macedonia, only you Philippians became my partners in giving and receiving. No other church did this. Even when I was over in Thessalonica you sent help twice. . . . At the moment I have all I need—more than I need! I am generously supplied with the gifts you sent me when Epaphroditus came. They are a sweet-smelling sacrifice that pleases God well. And it is he who will supply all your needs from his riches in glory.
>
> Philippians 4:15–16,18–19 TLB

It might even be possible that Lydia, in some way, helped to start the church in Thyatira referred to in the book of Revelation. The letter to the leader there says: "I am aware of all your good deeds—your kindness to the poor, your gifts and service to them (Revelation 2:19 TLB).

It is also interesting to note that the church in Thyatira had allowed the false prophetess Jezebel to bring heresy into the church. This is certainly a sobering note. We women must be very careful to stay godly and not manipulate or try to control.

When God Called, She and Her Hatchet Went

One of the most colorful leaders in American history was a woman named Carrie A. Nation. Her fame was based largely on her "smashing" of saloons with a hatchet. This activity was a result of what she described as a "divine call," saying, "One day . . . I opened the Bible with a prayer for light, and saw these words: Arise, shine for thy light is come and the glory of the Lord is risen upon thee."[5]

At the time, Carrie worked with the WCTU in Medicine Lodge, Kansas. Her smashing was often accompanied by the preaching of an evangelistic message. What did it mean to "smash" a saloon? In her own words:

> I threw as hard and as fast as I could, smashing mirrors and bottles and glasses, and it was astonishing how quickly this was done. These men seemed terrified, threw up their hands and backed up in the corner. My strength was that of a giant. I felt invincible. God was certainly standing by me.[6]

Remember, this occurred around the beginning of the twentieth century, in the days of the Wild West at a time when saloons were a place of sexual exploitation and alcoholism. I would not recommend that you take this exact approach today! But what if God called you to pray earnestly every day for the pornography stores to close in your town or city? Would you be willing to answer that call?

According to Darrow Miller, the porn studios in America produce eleven thousand movies a year. It is a ten-to-fourteen-billion-dollar-a-year industry. Approximately 28,258 internet users view pornography every second, choosing from more than 4.2 million possible pornographic websites. Just writing these statistics—and it is greatly probable, in reality, that they are much higher—makes my heart cry, "Is there not a cause?" I pray that many, as you read these statistics, will rise up and become an active force to fight against such a horrible problem as porn.[7]

Many women are being called by God to stand up for righteousness in their countries. If you were to see some of them, they might not appear that impressive at first glance. Many are silver-haired praying grandmothers. Others are teenagers taking a stand for abstinence in their schools. I like what Aglow International says: "Ordinary women—extraordinary God!"

United We Stand, Divided We Fall

In 1985, I entered a time of prayer and fasting for the United States of America. On the third day of the fast, I asked the Lord, "How has Satan made such inroads into the United States? He isn't omnipotent or omniscient!"

The Lord answered, *He has a strategy, and My people do not. Call together the "generals" [prayer leaders], and when each comes with a piece of the strategy, I'll reveal Myself in their midst.*

My first book, *Possessing the Gates of the Enemy* (Chosen, 1991), tells the specific instructions I received. What I want to emphasize here is that the Lord told me that we would be like John the Baptist, preparing the way for a move of unity. He said, *If the intercessors come together in the 1980s, the pastors will come together in the 1990s.* Of course, that is just what happened!

With help from many friends such as Sally Horton, B. J. Willhite and others, we "generals" had a great first meeting. I will never forget looking around the room of great prayer leaders that night, thinking, *Lord, this is going to take a big miracle!* You see, some people had tried to discourage us from even attempting to get men and women from such diverse backgrounds together for prayer. They thought it would never work.

It was a challenge. As I scanned those in attendance, I reflected on what I knew about the organizations and churches they represented. One thought that everything was the result of demons; another thought Christians could not be oppressed by demons at all. Another believed we were perfected through suffering; the next one did not think we should ever suffer anything as Christians. Interesting . . . very interesting.

God met us in a powerful way, and the next morning I was still basking in the goodness of God. We all felt that we needed to get together again for prayer and strategizing. Right in the middle of the afterglow of success, however, the phone rang. Have you ever noticed how the devil follows you around on the heels of a great blessing?

A distant relative of one of Job's friends was on the phone: "Cindy, my pastor said that if God was going to bring together the prayer leaders, He certainly would not use a woman."

I could not believe what I was hearing! Truthfully, I was deeply shaken by the phone call. That night, I did not mention the call to Mike because he was really tired when he came home from work. I thought to myself, *You can handle this. Don't make a big problem out of it.*

The next day, while I was minding my own business, the phone rang again. It was a woman. (I have generally found women to be much meaner to me about being in the ministry than men.)

The voice on the phone said, "Cindy, my pastor said that [Oh, no! I could hear it coming, and I knew it was not good!] *even if* God wanted to use a woman to gather the generals, He wouldn't use a woman your age."

At the time, I was 33 years old. (The year for both the crucifixion and the resurrection. At that moment, we were in the crucifixion part.) Immediately, in my mind's eye, I had a picture of myself with a big bun on the back of my head, hair shot through with gray, rolled down hose and varicose veins.

I felt like shattered glass inside. One of my biggest fears was that I would fall into presumption and move out of the will of God in my life. *What have I done?* I wildly thought. *How could I have been so stupid and ignorant?*

Any time God calls you to something new, it seems that old slew foot sits on your shoulder and asks, "Who do you think you are?" When I wrote *Possessing the Gates of the Enemy*, the devil tried to tell me again and again that nobody would read that book. As of this writing, it has been translated into thirty-plus languages. After I wrote it, different people said to me, "Well, I knew everything in that book, and I could have written it." My response to them was, "But you didn't!" There are many outstanding revelations God gives people, but they are not willing to be disciplined enough to sit down and do the work of writing.

I remember when Peter Wagner was compelling me to write what became *Possessing the Gates of the Enemy*, and I woefully complained to him, "But I am too busy to write a book." He gave me that unique Peter Wagner look that he got when he became a bit disgruntled, and shot back emphatically, "You aren't busier than I am! People do what they want to do!"

When I wrote my second book, *The Voice of God* (Regal, 2004), a "friend" said sagely, "Well, Cindy, you know some people only have one good book in them." Panic struck! I had signed a contract without being enlightened about that particular bit of info.

I called my mentor and spiritual dad, Peter Wagner, once again, and poured out my heart to him. "Do you think I only have one good book in me?" I asked fearfully. "Have I overextended myself?"

Thank the Lord that Peter was home to walk me through that valley of doubt. Peter explained that many people experience those same feelings when they write their second book. To say that I was relieved was a big understatement. When we finished talking, the peace of God had settled deep into my heart. *The Voice of God* has been used to start Schools of the Prophets across the face of the earth. I am so glad that I took Peter's good advice and went ahead and wrote the book.

The Taunting Goliath Takes a Tumble

By the time I received the second phone call after the first generals meeting, I was struggling intensely. I remember thinking, *Oh, God, I've been in terrible presumption! How could I do such a thing?* Mentally, I started making a list of both men and women older than I who could finish the vision.

When Mike arrived home that night, I was in a deeply spiritual state, but it was not the right spirit! I was depressed, discouraged and sitting on our bed crying my eyes out. (Believe me, I was not a pretty sight. Mascara was running down my face, my eyes were swollen and my nose was running.)

Mike took one look at me and said, "What is the matter with you?" Then he grabbed a fist full of tissues, put them in my hand and instructed me to blow my nose.

"Oh, Mike," I sobbed with that high squeaky voice women get when they have been crying, "I've made a horrible mistake. I thought that God spoke to me to gather the Generals of Intercession to pray for the nation." I then proceeded to tell him about the two phone calls.

Poor Mike. He has put up with a lot from me throughout the years. There is going to be a special star in his crown just for being married to me. When I had cleaned myself up a bit, he said, "I'm going to pray and get the word of the Lord for this situation, and I'll let you know what God says to me in a couple of days."

Good as his word, several days later Mike shared what he had received. "Honey, this is what the Lord spoke to me. When little David went to the camp of the Israelites, all the men were in battle array. Goliath came day after day and taunted them and mocked the God of Israel. Only David rose up to face the giant with the words, 'Who are you, you uncircumcised Philistine—to dare defy the armies of the Most High God!'"

He went on to say, "Cindy, you weren't God's first choice. He tried to call a man. You weren't God's second choice. He tried to use someone older than you. [This was getting more encouraging all the time.] You were God's third choice, but He knew that if He asked you, you would do it because of your obedience. He knew that you would do anything He asked you to do."

From that time on, Mike and I were partners in a new way, co-founding, as I mentioned earlier, Generals of Intercession in 1985, and even though Mike worked with American Airlines until 1991, we conducted many meetings to gather leaders together to intercede and bring healing to their nations. We now have a fifty-state prayer network and the United States Reformation Prayer Network (usrpn.org), and we team together in our endeavors.

The Lord also sent some encouraging prophecies my way from people I hardly knew. One of them admonished me not to give the vision God had given me to another. The spiritual warfare in the early days was so strong (what am I saying—there still is a lot of warfare) that every time we had a meeting, Mike and I would decide on the way there that it was the last one we would ever do. Then some prophet would show up at the place and start prophesying, "And the Lord says, I want you to take this vision around the world." Have you ever felt really unspiritual, as if you wanted to kick the prophet? We did not want to go around the world. Just getting to that one little meeting was so difficult we wanted to quit.

I am glad that we persevered, because we now have a worldwide media ministry with our TV program *God Knows*, and it is broadcast in a number of different languages.

Building Faith Muscles

I have to say that faith does grow with the vision. While our faith almost failed a number of times, we can believe for much more now than we could in the early days. I remember when we opened an office outside of our home, in 1991. We wondered how we would ever make the two-hundred-dollar-a-month payment. Now we believe for hundreds of thousands of dollars for projects on a regular basis. As of this writing, the newsletter we started in 1992 goes out worldwide through generals.org. We also learned that faith is "always in the red." When you are comfortable believing Him for one thing, God shakes you out of your comfort zone and says, "Now do this."

In this hour, God is calling women, not as militant feminists who insist upon their rights and demand a place of service, but as those who will find their place in His Kingdom.

In this hour, God is calling women, not as militant feminists who insist upon their rights and demand a place of service, but as those who will find their place in His Kingdom.

What is the difference between a godly woman's movement and a militant, feminist one? First of all, we are not angry and demanding. We are for, not against men. We are always looking for God to open doors, and we are courageous to go through them, even in the face of opposition, but we do not kick them down.

If God does not open the door for you, then it is not one that you should go through (see Revelation 3:7). Beverly LaHaye describes God's call of women in her book *The Desires of a Woman's Heart*:

> Each woman's call is unique. For some obedience to God means being "thrown to the lions," so to speak, or cast into a hostile climate in which Christians and the Bible are scorned as out of date and puritanical. For others, obedience to God may lead to a more quiet, private existence. The important thing, however, is to be obedient to God and "Stand firm. Let nothing move you. Always give yourselves fully to the work of the Lord, because you know that your labor in the Lord is not in vain" (1 Cor. 15:58).[8]

LaHaye goes on to say:

> Hundreds of thousands of women today are involved in organizations such as Concerned Women for America, Christian Action Council, Eagle Forum, American Life League, Enough Is Enough and Mothers Against Drunk Driving, to name just a few. These women know who they are. They are confident of their worth; they see the decline in American society, and they are actively involved in trying to stop it.
>
> The committed women of Concerned Women for America [the organization LaHaye founded], for instance, are working in churches and neighborhoods to build a network of prayer and action. They are actively working at the local, state and national levels to derail legislation and education that will harm their families. They are concerned about protecting the rights of families rather than their own personal rights. They are not primarily concerned about self-fulfillment, and they are not chasing some nebulous ideal of happiness. They are seeking to fill a concrete need: preserving the nuclear family and society from destruction.[9]

Remember the story in chapter 1 about the apple tree that thought it was a flower tree? This story is symbolic of the many passages or stages that both men and women go through in life. Throughout the years, we all experience changes in focus, occupation or even roles. Few of us know what we will eventually do; however, the prophetic word will sometimes give us an inkling.

Believe His Prophets and Prosper (2 Chronicles 20:20)

When Dick Mills prophesied in 1984 that I would have a worldwide ministry, I could hardly comprehend what he was talking about. At the time, I was speaking at local women's meetings, with many invitations, and had only ministered in Canada outside of the United States. I had to grow into the prophecy Dick Mills gave, which did not say in detail, "Next year I'm going to speak to you about a prayer army you'll eventually call Generals International; then you will speak to national congresses and meet with presidents all around the world."

But I am glad not to have known. I was not ready yet. Frankly, it would have scared me to know. To give you a frame of reference for how far I have come in speaking before large audiences, I need to explain about the days when we would have Wednesday night "seasons of prayer" at my church. I was only in my twenties, and I fought a measure of shyness. Each Wednesday, the congregation would pray aloud in what amounted to sentence-type prayers. Week after week, I would say to myself, *The next time we have that time of intercession, I'm going to pray aloud.* Somehow, when the time came, my tongue felt glued to the roof of my mouth. I just could not get the words out.

If someone had told me then that I would speak to twenty thousand people at a time, I would have gone into a catatonic state! Thank God, He gives me only what I can bear at the moment.

Later, after I had children, I was often frustrated that I did not have more time to pray and intercede. The Lord would often assure me, *Cindy, the day is coming when your children will be in school and you'll be able to spend hours in prayer.* I learned to have small prayer breaks while I was washing dishes or rocking a baby. I would usually pray late at night or get up early to have my devotions.

Maybe you are a frustrated young mom or maybe you are spending countless hours starting a business of your own or taking care of needy relatives, and you are feeling terribly guilty because you want to do more for the Kingdom of God. Let me assure you that if you are feeling called of God and you are willing to remain obedient, a day will come when you will be able to do all that is in your heart.

Trusting Through the Seasons of Life

Life is a series of seasons, and we all experience winters, springs, summers and falls. As you read about these four seasons, ask God to show you where you are and what He wants to teach you during this season of your life.

Winter "Wonder Why It Is Not Happening" Land

If you are in a winter season, you may feel rather dead or unproductive. It could be that God wants you to take a rest and allow the ground of your life to replenish itself. This is one of the hardest seasons for "type A" people (such as myself).

After I finally stopped struggling and accepted the call of God on my life, He then asked me to give it back to Him and take a hidden role of intercession. I felt like a spiritual Ping-Pong ball. Now that I had said yes, I had all this fire and wanted to go take on the world for Jesus Christ. Instead, He said, *Cindy, be still and know that I am God. I don't waste the anointing. Be assured that I know where you live and will use you in the proper time.*

Some days I would cry out to Him, "God, I'm afraid that You are going to come back again before I get to preach even one time." Oh, it was so hard to wait! When you are in this state, you feel as though God moved and lost your address. The heavens are as brass, and you can even struggle with feelings of abandonment. But these preparatory times are necessary because they develop character and cause your roots to go deep, deep down into the soil of the Word.

Once the plan of God unfolds, it is as if you are on fast-forward. That is when you will need all the Word you have deposited in yourself to survive the blessings of the other seasons.

Spring Is Bursting Out All Over

Life seems to be the most exciting during spring. This season is usually accompanied by a sense of great anticipation—you often feel as though you are about to burst inside with new life. You get this sense that something wonderful is about to happen, but you do not quite know what it is. That is how I felt in 1989, when Mike and I went to a prayer summit in Washington, D.C., sponsored by the late Ray Bringham.

One night during the summit, I tried to sleep but was not able to for all the excitement I felt. (I guess the only experience I can relate it to is how I felt on Christmas Eve as a little girl. We opened our presents on Christmas morning, and I could hardly wait to pounce on my parents and drag their tired bodies out of bed.) The next morning, we drove over to an executive council meeting for the National Prayer Embassy with Peter Wagner, his wife, Doris, and Leonard LeSourd, vice president of Chosen Books, whom we had just met. Peter and Doris watched as we modeled prayer between England and the United States in something we now call "identificational repentance." They were fascinated and plied us with questions about how to heal nations.

I had started writing a book about prayer and had prayed some rather radical prayers such as, "God, if You want me to write a book, You'll have to help me. I need a mentor, and I don't have a clue how to find a publisher." Right in the middle of our conversation, Len leaned over and asked me, "Have you ever written a book?" Then he handed me his card.

Peter chimed in, "Cindy, I'm meeting with Jane Campbell, editorial director of Chosen Books, at 4:30 today because they want a book about prayer. They don't need my book; they need your book. Meet us in the cafeteria at 4:30 and I'll introduce you."

Since then, my life has been a whirlwind. Peter Wagner became my mentor, and he gave me guidance on my first book. In fact (to my absolute horror), he threw the first three chapters I had written into the trash! The point is that spring is a time for birthing new things into our lives.

At times during the spring of your life, you may be on the verge of a new thing and feel like a pregnant woman in her ninth month: You are sort of grouchy and touchy; you know that God is about to do something, and you can feel it move inside you, but you have no idea what it looks like. Every day you live with the hope that God will reveal it to you so you can get on with your life.

Summer's Fruit Is Sweet, but Some Days Are Hot!

Summer is mostly a fruitful time. Although it may be rather hot in the amount of spiritual warfare you experience, this season is generally quite productive. This is also the hour when you sense God's refreshing and blessing. It is during this time that you experience the richness of seasoned friendships.

Autumn Leaves Me Feeling Frazzled

Autumn is harvest time, when the seeds you have planted have ripened in the summer sun and are ready to be picked. The vastness of your responsibilities during this season, whether personal or in the Body of Christ at large, can feel overwhelming. Be cautious of great presumptions. If you move too quickly on the plans of God for the harvest, you can move prematurely and cause great destruction to the harvest. And if you fail to watch for signs of storms in relationships, you can actually see most of your life's work destroyed. This is a critical time to gather others around you who can speak into your life.

I do this on a number of different levels, both ministerially and as a woman. I have friends, who have a special love for our family, with whom I can share heart to heart when I am struggling. Others know more about what I am going through as a minister.

This was not always the case. In the early days of ministry, I knew no other women in leadership. Even later on, those I knew either had no children or were much older than I, so they had different time factors to consider. Since I have usually been the youngest of my peer group, I have felt a little "out of sync," so to speak, with the rest of my group. I have had unique responsibilities and always felt as though I was doing some kind of juggling act: trying to be supermom, the best wife in the world and yet spend enough time with God. Yes, autumn can be busy.

In addition to harvest, autumn is also a time of dying to self. Just as nature reflects transitions in its seasons, likewise God usually calls for the greatest changes in your life during autumn. Often He will reposition you for greater effectiveness. Sometimes He will have you leave one ministry to work in another or ask you to quit your job to stay home more. It seems to me that God is currently repositioning a large part of the Body of Christ to prepare His Church for the end-time thrust of the Gospel. Many people are physically moving to new cities, and this kind of change requires great flexibility and patience. But the result will be greater effectiveness for His people and greater glory for His Kingdom.

Breaking the Mold to Recast the System

Women of destiny have great challenges before them. At times, God does not choose the most likely or even the most talented for high places. There are some women who have been in the winter season—in a seemingly hidden time—whom God is getting ready to release as a great blessing to the Body of Christ.

Young Esther was a woman such as that. The Bible tells us that she was an orphan. In addition, she had suffered the trauma of exile, not to mention the fact that she was the wrong race. She had at least three strikes against her. Obviously, Esther was too dysfunctional for God to use for anything important. Right? Wrong. He created her as a woman with great physical beauty, and her adoptive father, Mordecai, must have worked hard at developing her inner beauty. I wonder if she dreamed of being a queen when she was a little girl? Maybe, but probably not.

Esther was a woman who broke the mold for what a good Jewish girl should be. It must have required great courage and flexibility on her part to answer the king's summons. And yet, God is calling women today who are willing to respond to anything He asks with a simple, "Here am I, Lord, send me."

This response may mean breaking the mold for society's stereotypes. The feminists cry, "You'll never be fulfilled unless you have an occupation outside the home." Other voices say, "You are a bad person if you feel God has anything for you other than keeping house."

Kari Torjesen Malcolm discusses some of the issues that prevent women from reaching the place and calling God has for them in her book *Women at the Crossroads*. I like her perspective when she says:

> We forget so easily that Jesus promised that if we seek first His kingdom and His righteousness, all the rest shall be added to us (Matt. 6:33). If our love relationship with Him takes first priority, then all other relationships will find their rightful place in our hearts and schedules. The woman who focuses on Christ will therefore become a better wife and mother than the one who stays home all day out of a sense of duty, as a reaction or as a cop-out. To a woman who loves the Lord, the Word of God will burn as a fire in her bones, so that she must speak up for her Lord, whether the crowd be small or large, or whether the people be her own kin or those from a different culture.[10]

Breaking the Strongholds That Strangle Destiny

In looking back over my life, I can identify at least five major strongholds that I had to deal with in order to be released into my destiny. I think many women will relate to a number of these on differing levels.[11]

1. Stronghold of the Mind

I like the way Ed Silvoso describes a *stronghold of the mind*: "a mindset impregnated with hopelessness that causes the believer to accept as unchangeable, situations that we know are contrary to the will of God."[12]

In other words, some of the ways we think and feel about ourselves and our situations are contrary to God's will. Basically, there are ways we think and feel about ourselves that can actually stop us from reaching our destinies in God. These can be things such as childhood traumas, insecurities or inferiorities.

One of the major endeavors I believe all women should participate in is prayer. The enemy wants to make you feel that your situation is hopeless, your husband will never be born again, your child will always stay in rebellion and so on. These strongholds must be cast down as vain imaginations so that we can run the race with diligence in intercession.

2. Stronghold of Fear

One of the biggest strongholds we women struggle with is fear. Fear comes in many packages and hides behind lies. We sometimes self-righteously dress up our fears as, "It's simply not *me* to stand in public and pray."

We often fear others' opinions. Remember, at the end of our days, the Lord will ask each of us what we did with our talents. I hope none of you has a backyard full of talents you have buried, such as gifts of music, writing, organization, serving and more. Fear will not be an acceptable excuse when we stand before the King of the universe, because He has given us all the ability to be overcomers through the blood of the Lamb. If we are feeling overtaken with fear, it has not come from God! He gives us power, love and a sound mind (see 2 Timothy 1:7).

Some of you need to dust off your talents and dreams and give them to the Lord. The difference between women who find their places in God's Kingdom and those who never find it may simply be a willingness to be used by God. Everyone can do something. You can join a group that intercedes for your local schools or makes meals for shut-ins or some other form of service that will get you out of yourself.

3. Stronghold of Intimidation

Intimidation often binds women. It occurs when we look at our shortfalls rather than at the greatness of God. Whether we are called to sing or testify, the enemy might say something such as, "People will think that you are full of pride if you do that." He often points out the weaknesses in our personal lives and family situations, or tries to compare our abilities with those of others, in order to produce an oppressive feeling that will restrain us from reaching our full potential in God.

4. Generational Stronghold

Some strongholds start long before we are born. We inherit them. You might say, "Wait a minute, Cindy, that's not fair!" Exodus 20:5 tells us that God visits the iniquities of the fathers upon the children to the third and fourth generations. While we have been redeemed from these iniquities, we need to appropriate our freedom through the name of Jesus Christ. I give a lengthy teaching on this subject in my book *The Voice of God*. These strongholds can produce curses such as sickness, poverty, insanity and so forth.

5. Stronghold of Tradition

Having grown up in the South, in the United States, I found that tradition was another of my big strongholds. Good Southern Christian women simply did not travel around the world and preach the Gospel! As you can tell from reading this book, I struggled intensely with accepting the call of God upon my life as a minister of the Gospel. It took me two full years before I even admitted to anyone that I was a minister—even after I was licensed. I just could not seem to get that "m" word out of my mouth. I guess I was afraid of people's reactions. Now, I am proud (in a righteous way) of sharing what I do in God's Kingdom. I tell people, "I have a great boss and the retirement plan is out of this world."

I have often wondered if Queen Vashti, in the book of Esther, refused to come when summoned by the king because it was not traditional for her to do so. When our King summons us, we must be sure that we are not being held back by tradition.

Lord, Send Me into My Call

You may have a genuine desire to become a woman of destiny and fulfill the high calling of Christ Jesus for your life. Be assured that the Lord is raising up a vast army of women all around the world. Never be bound by the opinion of man (or woman). Simply follow God's leading. If God calls you to stay home full-time even after the kids are grown, then do it! Maybe you are single, and God is calling you to the mission field; step out! (We will have a lot to say about this in the next few chapters.)

Please pray the following prayer with me right now:

Lord, I want to be a woman of destiny. I give You all of my life, my family and other people's opinions of me. Here am I, Lord. Send me into my call. Help me to break down any strongholds that stop me from completely serving You. I will go anywhere You ask me to go and do anything You ask me to do as long as I know it is Your will for my life. In Jesus' name I pray. Amen.

One way to strengthen your resolve to be a woman of destiny is by studying other heroines of the faith. You might consider the next chapter as a great "Hall of Faith" for those who have pioneered and paved the way for future generations. Maybe you will find someone of whom you can say, "Lord, I want to be like her. She's my heroine. If she did it and finished the course, I can, too!"

FIVE

Heroines of the Faith

Isn't it amazing how God chooses the foolish things to confound the wise? Some of the greatest works for the Lord have been done by women who by their physical form, background and other circumstances seemed the least likely to be used for God's Kingdom purposes.

Those who opposed them underestimated the strength and determination of these women. They were fearless—even when commitment to Kingdom work meant the sacrifice of their very lives. In this chapter, we meet three of them.

Lottie Moon

During the Reconstruction Era in the United States after the Civil War, a lovely young woman, standing just four feet three, received a call from God to spend her life in faraway North China. This young lady came from a wealthy, aristocratic family during a time when women were considered beautiful ornaments. Her home, Viewmont, in Albemarle County, Virginia, was not far from the homes of three American presidents. If you have seen the movie *Gone with the Wind*, you get a perspective of the culture during this time period. Young women of her day turned flirting into an art form, which they used to twist the hearts of unsuspecting young men around their little fingers.

But this was not the case with Lottie Moon.

Lottie received from her family not only a strong religious heritage (her father was descended from a prominent Quaker theologian and her mother was a staunch Southern Baptist), but also a focus on education. She was one of the first Southern American women at that time to earn a master's degree.[1]

When her younger sister, Edmonia, left for China in 1872, Lottie's heart turned toward the mission field as well. She received her own call to China in the spring of 1873 when she was 33 years old. Lottie was in love with a young professor, but when he embraced Darwinism, she broke the engagement and never married. At times she would be racked with deep pangs of loneliness on the mission field.[2]

Lottie set up housekeeping with her sister and quickly adopted Chinese dress and ways. Eventually she looked quite Chinese. She wore a plain Chinese gown and embroidered satin shoes, slept on a brick bed and cooked her food in Chinese kettles. She traveled from village to village in a mule litter and commonly slept in vermin-infested inns.[3]

Lottie stirred the ire of many by suggesting that women in China had the right to demand equality with men. She received further criticism from other missionaries, such as the wife of a Congregationalist missionary who suggested that Lottie Moon was mentally unbalanced for her "lawless prancing all over the mission lot."[4]

Still, Southern Baptists answered her call to give money to help relieve suffering in China. To date, following their first offering of $3,000 in 1888, nearly a billion dollars have been donated to world missions in Lottie's name.

Lottie suffered many hardships, and she grieved the martyrdom of many Chinese Christians during the Boxer Uprising. Life became harder and harder financially until revolution broke out in 1911. But the more her Chinese friends suffered from war, sickness and poverty, the more Lottie Moon gave to feed the poor. Finally, in her seventies, she simply stopped eating.

In December 1912, Lottie bowed to the pressure to return to the United States. She was frail and dying of starvation when she boarded the ship. Four days later, this faithful warrior of the cross slipped into glory.

Ten years earlier, Lottie Moon had said, "I would that I had a thousand lives that I might give them to the women of China." Her tombstone in Virginia reads: "Faithful unto death."

As I finish writing this story, tears are coursing down my cheeks. Inside me there is an answering cry that says, "Oh, God, I want to be a heroine of the faith like Lottie Moon! I want to be faithful unto death." In fact, I have stood on the spot in Cartersville, Georgia, where Lottie gave her life for China, and I vowed to give my life for the nations. It is not that I would desire to be a martyr, but if the time came when a choice was given me between denying Christ or living—well, I settled that question a long time ago. In fact, I did so when I was only twelve years old at church camp.

I will never forget the night when my counselor chose me to be in a skit where this question of martyrdom was being portrayed. The skit was acted out in the outdoor amphitheater on the campgrounds at night. Spotlights illuminated different situations in nations all around the world where Christians were given the choice of dying or denying Christ.

My part was set in a Communist country where we were ordered to kneel with guns pointed at our heads and given this ultimatum: "Denounce Christ or die on the spot!" While getting ready for the skit that night, those words played repeatedly in my head, *Denounce or die . . . denounce or die!* What would I do if the situation were real? Would I choose Christ, or be a coward and make the decision to denounce Him?

Later that night the play seemed to come to life before me, and when I knelt on the hard, rocky ground, I suddenly had no doubt what my answer would be. I would never, never, never deny Him! From that night forward, I became a "living martyr." In a way, I died that night when I made my choice.

Vibia Perpetua

History is full of women who gave their lives for the cause of Christ. One of the earliest was Vibia Perpetua (c. AD 181–203). Perpetua, a Christian noblewoman, lived in Carthage, North Africa.[5] This story especially fascinates me because North Africa, as of this writing, is currently a stronghold for Muslim fundamentalists. (We are earnestly praying and believing for this situation to change!)

Roman Christians brought the Gospel to this part of the world during the reign of Emperor Septimius Severus. Because Severus feared the rise of Christianity—a strong Christian community resided in North Africa—he issued an edict prohibiting any teaching or making of converts. New believers came to Christ realizing that they had little chance of surviving for very long.

It is inspiring to study the writings of these early Christians, knowing that martyrdom was just a part of life. In fact, it was considered a privilege to be a martyr. Early writings tell of Paul's conversion after the martyred death of Stephen. Most of us would not consider martyrdom synonymous with evangelism, but the early Church thought very much in that manner.

Perpetua was keenly aware of this at the time of her own baptism. She said as she came out of the water, "The Holy Spirit has inspired me to pray for nothing but patience under bodily pains."[6]

Perpetua was soon arrested. Can you imagine yourself in the place of this young woman in her early twenties? How would you react if you were arrested? Her father pleaded with her to recant her faith. To add to the intensity of the situation, she was nursing her baby!

We have Perpetua's own words from the journals she maintained right up to the time of her death. As I read her words of watching her child suffer, my heart was gripped as I thought of my own two children. She gave the child to her sister to raise, and, when the infant was brought to her for the last time, she confessed, "God so ordered it that it was no longer required to suck, nor did my milk inconvenience me."[7]

As I have studied the life of Perpetua, the following passage of Scripture has come to me again and again:

> "Do not think that I came to bring peace on earth. I did not come to bring peace but a sword. For I have come to 'set a man against his father, a daughter against her mother, and a daughter-in-law against

> her mother-in-law.' . . . He who loves *father or mother* more than Me is not worthy of Me. And he who loves *son or daughter* more than Me is not worthy of Me. And he who does not take his cross and follow after Me is not worthy of Me. He who finds his life will lose it, and he who loses his life for My sake will find it."
>
> Matthew 10:34–35, 37–39 (emphasis added)

Perpetua marched with a joyful expression from the prison to the arena, where she would be slain by the sword. "Perpetua . . . took the gladiator's trembling hand and guided it to her throat. Perhaps it was that so great a woman, feared as she was by the unclean spirit, could not have been slain had she herself not willed it."[8]

Truly, the world was not worthy of you, young Perpetua! Oh, God, I pray that I will follow You with such ardent love as my sister from Carthage.

Joan of Arc

One heroine of the faith who was guided by God through visions and was used to change the fate of a nation was Joan of Arc. She is often called the Deborah of France.

Joan of Arc, a shepherdess from a small French village, lived from 1412 to 1431. She had a short life indeed—only nineteen years. Apparently, her visions began when she was about twelve years old, and they continued until she started her mission in France at age sixteen. Although some of the visions and voices she heard seemed to be from strange sources, such as martyred saints, I believe the Holy Spirit was speaking to her. Perhaps, in her ignorance, she did not have a complete understanding of the voice of God, but the fruit of what she heard was good.

She called the Lord *Messire* ("my Master"), and what she heard from Him was sweet and direct:

> Whenever I am sad because what I say is a command of Messire is not readily believed, I go apart and to Messire I make known my complaint,

> saying that those to whom I speak are not willing to believe me. And when I have finished my prayer, straightway I hear a voice saying unto me, "Daughter of God, go, I will be thy helper." And this voice fills me with so great a joy, that in this condition I will forever stay.[9]

(A parenthetical note: If you are a teenager reading this book, God is going to use your generation in a powerful way! The Lord wants to find Deborahs in your generation to serve Him to change their nations—maybe not in exactly the same way, but in the way He would choose for your life.)

To understand a little of the political situation during Joan of Arc's time, France and England were in dispute over the crown of France. The armies of England's Henry VI occupied much of the northern part of the kingdom, and strength was added to his cause through allies living in France, the Burgundians. Circumstances looked dire for the French heir to the throne, the Dauphin Charles.[10]

Joan's village was situated directly between the land of the Burgundians and those of the Dauphin. When Joan was only sixteen, she started receiving more and more supernatural instruction and spoke up in response to her country's cry of distress. An older relative traveled with her to go see the captain of the French garrison, who sent her back to her parents.

Joan was a mystic accustomed to waiting for spiritual guidance, so she simply went home and waited. This time she received more specific instructions, which she relayed to the captain. Impressed with her calmness and piety, he allowed her to go to the Dauphin. But before she went, Joan proceeded boldly to cut her hair to a pageboy length and exchanged her red dress for the uniform of a soldier. She was highly criticized for this, and yet because she believed she had received divine guidance to do so, the criticism did not faze her. Dressed as a man, she was able easily to ride a horse and travel with the soldiers to meet with the Dauphin.

After being questioned initially by ecclesiastical authorities, she was questioned further for three weeks by eminent theologians, watchful for any heresy. Finally, the eighteen-year-old was allowed to proceed with the divine guidance she had received earlier from the Lord to lead an army into battle at Orléans. She must have been an incredible sight, because the Dauphin put her in a glistening coat of armor to lead the troops. For a weapon, Joan chose a sword that had five crosses, given to her by a church, and she carried a banner sprinkled with holy water to represent her company.

I would love to have been a witness to this young Deborah of God as she told her company to repent, renounce their sins and take the sacrament together. God's favor to fulfill her mission was remarkably evident as Joan admonished the hard-drinking, foul-mouthed soldiers, warning them that God would not give them victory unless they became moral people. Astonished by her words, many soldiers made dramatic changes in their lives. A noticeable change came over the men and they rose to the standard put before them. At the front of her company marched priests chanting psalms and hymns. (Reminds me of Jehoshaphat [see 2 Chronicles 20:21]!)

The troops of the Lord took Orléans that day, and Joan went on to lead four more victorious battles. She then instructed the Dauphin to proceed with his coronation, and saw that he was anointed with oil. At last she knelt before her king, King Charles VII.

Later, after the crowning, Joan, at age nineteen, was captured by Burgundians, handed over to the English and tried as a witch and a heretic before a pro-English tribunal. She stood steadfast in her obedience to God as she responded to the charges. At one point, her accusers threatened her with torture in order to force her submission to the court. She answered that even should she be torn limb from limb, she would not reply differently. In any case, she told them, she would simply maintain afterward that they had extorted by violence any statements at variance with her beliefs. They decided that torture would be useless.[11]

History tells us that her final judgment was based on twelve points. Among them were a denial of her gift of prophecy and the wearing of masculine clothes.

On May 30, 1431, Joan was tied to a stake and burned alive. Not once did she beg to be released, for she was not afraid of martyrdom. She had finished the course and fought the good fight. Her last words were simply the sweetest ones human lips can utter . . . *Jesus, Jesus.*

It was reported that the English, upon returning to camp, could only mutter, "We are lost! We have burned a saint!"[12]

King Charles VII, who had failed to come to her aid, later reversed the verdict against her. She was declared the patroness of France in 1922. Joan, like Jeremiah, did not consider her youth to be an obstacle in the path of her destiny in God. She died having fulfilled the purposes of God for her life in her generation (see Acts 13:36).

Does this story speak to your heart? Perhaps God is calling you to be a Deborah in your generation. There are women in the United States Congress right now who are there because they feel a distinct call of God to help change America. Other women in nations all around the world are receiving similar calls. Even if you are not called to be a Deborah, I would encourage you to study the women of the Bible and find the one(s) you most relate to. God is raising up Esthers and Naomis (godly grandmothers) to bring healing to their generations through their lives.

Avenging the Blood of the Martyrs

Recently, the Lord gave me a word that He is getting ready to avenge the blood of the martyrs. This will occur through many receiving Christ in places where the blood of Christians is crying out to God from the ground (see Genesis 4:10).

The first time I gave this word publicly was at an Aglow conference. A woman from Rwanda, where hundreds of thousands have been killed, spoke the morning after the prophecy was given. When she stood to share, she started by saying, "I am so encouraged because I know God has heard my prayers." She went on to say that God had miraculously spared her life during the massacres. "However," she said quietly, "others of my Christian friends did not make it." She continued, "As I looked at their dead bodies, I looked up to heaven and cried, 'God, avenge the blood of the martyrs.'"

I know that it will be so. God is getting ready to avenge the blood of the martyrs throughout the world. Many thousands of people will turn to Christ in a great revival in Rwanda, as they will in Italy and Spain and other places where so much shedding of Christians' blood has occurred.

Why is this chapter about heroines of the faith so important? One reason is that throughout the years, many books have been written about heroes, but very little emphasis has been placed on the exploits of great women. I believe mothers should read stories to their daughters about the women of God who have gone before them to prepare the way. In doing so, young women can learn from both the weaknesses and the strengths of these heroines to be more equipped for the unique questions a life of service to God will bring. For instance:

- Should I marry if I have a call of God on my life?
- What about having children?
- What kind of husband should I marry?
- How did other women settle these issues?

I have certainly made mistakes along the way that I believe could have been avoided if I had received a book such as this one to help guide me.

In the next chapter we will continue looking at many other brave women whose stories inspire us. God wants women all over the world to rise up against the atrocities of our generations. We need to stand firm with fierce determination in the face of mountains of adversity, in spite of rising rivers of persecution and hatred. Remember, as Mike says, we are not better than Jesus. He was perfect and yet He was persecuted. Selah!

SIX

Moms and Other Great Women of Faith

I hope that this chapter will not only encourage you but comfort you—particularly if you have been accused of being "crazy" because of the call of Christ on your life. I have often (more in the early days of ministry) felt totally misunderstood and sometimes wondered if I *were* off the wall in my ministry of intercession.

In fact, let me interject something of my own personal life here. One day, I had received even more than the usual criticism about being a woman minister, and I was weary of it. (You see, not only am I a woman minister, but I am also one who teaches about healing nations and how to do spiritual warfare and the like.) Truthfully, I was murmuring to God about my situation.

"God," I said, "it's not bad enough that I am a woman minister, but one who teaches on spiritual warfare! If I have to be a woman minister, couldn't I teach about color typing or something less controversial? Lord," I went on, "I'm tired of being controversial."

Even though I deserved to be zapped with fire from heaven right on the spot, God had mercy on me and replied gently, *Cindy, the controversial things of today are the commonplace of tomorrow. Controversial people do great things for Me. Just do My work.* He went on to remind me of the barrage of criticism John Wesley received for using bar tunes for hymns. For his time, that was simply outrageous!

As I have pored over piles of books about great women who have overcome rejection, hardship, ill health and poverty in order to "just do His work," one determining factor has leapt out at me again and again: the influence of godly mothers on their sons and daughters. We begin there because, even if you do not have biological children, or nieces or nephews, you can have many spiritual children.

Moms of Merit

Many of the greatest leaders, reformers, theologians and thinkers were deeply touched by the lives of their moms who, like Eunice, the mother of Timothy (see 2 Timothy 1:5), and Mary, the mother of Jesus, believed in their sons.

Motherhood has somehow been considered a secondary calling to many women today. I believe, however, that nothing could be further from the truth! If the Lord had not called me to preach and travel, I would gladly have stayed home with my children until they were grown. In fact, after I finished my fifth year of college, I quit teaching to stay home with my daughter, because I did not want a woman other than me to raise her.

Chrysostom's Mom

Godly moms have touched even the pagan world. Anthusa and her husband, a high-ranking military officer who left her a widow at age twenty, lived in Antioch, where Paul had begun his three missionary journeys. Their son, John, was born AD 347. Her piety and devotion to God caused her son's tutor to exclaim, "What wonderful women are found among Christians!"[1] Libanius, a famous pagan orator and one of John's professors, stated his longing for the young man to take over his position of leadership in the school, "had not the Christians stolen him from us."[2]

Being renowned as an eloquent and zealous preacher, John was given the Greek surname "Golden-Mouthed" or "Chrysostom."[3] He was also a prolific author and is honored as a saint.

Like many women today, Anthusa was concerned about the corruptions in her city. During Chrysostom's formative years, Anthusa taught him to love the Bible and studied it together with him. This gave him a deep love for Scripture, which could later be seen in the many homilies he wrote. As a result of his mother's godly influence, John Chrysostom, who became archbishop of Constantinople and who died in AD 407, was one of the greatest expository preachers the Church has ever known.

Augustine's Mom

The prayers of Monica (AD 331–387) helped to bring the young Augustine out of rebellion and to the Lord. Augustine pursued a life of unabashed depravity. At sixteen, he took a mistress and had a son by her. Then he entered into the sect of Manicheans, a heretical group. All the while his mother bathed her prayers in weeping. Augustine writes in his autobiography, *Confessions*, of how God "drew his soul out of the profound darkness, because of his mother who wept on his behalf more than most mothers weep when their children die."[4]

> For she wished, and I remember in private with great anxiety warned me, "not to commit fornication; but especially never to defile another man's wife." These seemed to me womanish advices, which I should blush to obey. But they were Thine, and . . . I knew it not; and ran headlong with such blindness, that amongst my equals I was ashamed of a less shamelessness, when I heard them boast . . . and I took pleasure, not only in the pleasure of the deed, but in the praise.[5]

Monica's war for the soul of her son was not won overnight. In fact, he went deeper into sin. He was a prodigal in every sense of the word.

Augustine finally moved from Carthage to Rome and then Milan. His mother, a widow, followed after him, even though it was extremely dangerous for a woman to travel alone in those days. She, like Paul, even had a vision in the midst of a storm that all would be safe and gave this prophetic word to the sailors aboard the ship.

In Milan, Monica went to see her son and encouraged him to give up his mistress of fifteen years. She was delighted when he sent his mistress back to Africa, only to witness him taking another one in her place!

Finally, as a prodigal at the end of himself, Augustine, alone in a garden, entered into an intense struggle between his flesh and his spirit where he cried out to God:

> So was I speaking and weeping in the most bitter contrition of my heart, when, lo! I heard from a neighbouring house a voice, as of boy or girl, I know not, chanting, and oft repeating, "Take up and read; Take up and read." Instantly, my countenance altered. . . . Checking the torrent of my tears, I arose; interpreting it to be no other than a command from God to open the book, and read the first chapter I should find. . . . I seized [the epistles], opened, and in silence read that section on which my eyes first fell: Not in rioting and drunkenness, not in chambering and wantonness, not in strife and envying; but put ye on the Lord Jesus Christ, and make not provision for the flesh, in concupiscence [Romans 13:13–14]. No further would I read; nor needed I: for instantly at the end of this sentence, by a light as it were of serenity infused into my heart, all the darkness of doubt vanished away.[6]

Augustine rushed to tell the good news to his mother. A short time later, he and his mother decided to return to Africa with friends. They stopped at Ostia, which is at the mouth of the Tiber River, to rest. How sweet it was for Monica to spend long hours talking about the Lord with her son!

Unfortunately, her joy this side of heaven was short-lived; while she was still in Ostia, Monica became very ill and died a swift death (within nine days) at the age of 56. She had spent many years of her life crying out to God for the prodigal to come home and had been there to welcome him with open arms.

Augustine went on, with the help of the Bishop of Hippo, to champion Christianity when the Roman Empire disintegrated. It often seems that the greater the call of God, the more Satan fights for a person's soul.

Is there a prodigal in your life? If so, I pray that this story will encourage you not to give up praying and fighting for his or her soul. Many times the battle is much longer and fiercer than you think you have the strength for, but if you do not grow weary in well doing, you will win. Your prodigal will turn. Do not look at what your natural eyes see, but intercede with eyes of love that see the destiny God has planted within your son or daughter's heart.

John and Charles Wesley's Mom

Other reformers were greatly impacted by the lives of their mothers—men such as John and Charles Wesley, whose mother, Susanna, I briefly mentioned earlier.

Susanna was a beautiful woman with silky dark hair and deep blue eyes. The last of 25 children, Susanna was the daughter of a well-to-do cleric and grew up in London in the late seventeenth century. During this time when few women were educated, Susanna's father taught her Hebrew, Greek and Latin. She could write as well as any man, and her keen mind allowed her to discuss theology as articulately as any seminary student.

Susanna and Samuel Wesley had a tempestuous marriage at best. He was a poet and dreamer who kept them in debt. They had nineteen children together, and nine of them died. Their home was burned to the ground twice, and Samuel abandoned Susanna for long periods of time.

In the midst of all her sorrow, Susanna homeschooled all ten of her children, teaching them to read Hebrew and Greek and memorize Scripture. She also found time each evening to invest alone with one of the children, taking each in turn. A rigorous taskmaster, she set high standards for the home, not allowing the children to use coarse language or fail in their studies. Susanna called this her "method" of arranging the day. This term must have had an impact on her children, because two of her sons later called the new move of God "Methodism."

She suffered one of her moments of greatest terror when her five-year-old son, Jackie, was caught in the upper story of the rectory, which was awash with flame. Some young farmhands stood on each other's shoulders and plucked him out of a window. Jackie went on to become known as the great reformer John Wesley.

Her husband, Samuel, for all his faults, was a firm believer that God wanted to send revival to England, and he prayed for it diligently. Susanna loved Samuel all the days of his life, in spite of his many failings.

Incredible as it may sound for a woman with so much knowledge of God, Susanna did not really know Him as her personal Lord and Savior until the very end of her earthly life. She had heard about the inner witness and read how Christ warmed others' hearts, but she did not really understand until one day when taking Communion she came to the realization that Christ died for her personally. What a life-transforming thought! She was changed eternally.

Susanna died in July 1742, with her children gathered around her. As she looked from face to face, she said, "Please, my children, as soon as I'm released, sing a psalm of praise to God."[7]

Never underestimate the power of a praying mother. Susanna's sons changed the face of Christianity and brought tens of thousands to Christ. Today she lives on through the Methodist churches established around the world.

Making It Personal

It has occurred to me that you, like Susanna Wesley, might have gone to church most of your life but have never had a personal experience with Jesus Christ. Maybe someone gave you this book, and although you love God, you do not really know Him.

Why not take a minute with me right now to pray, asking Jesus Christ to come into your life? You will then have accepted Him and the price

He paid for you on the cross. He loves you and gave His life for you. Will you give your life to Him?

Pray this prayer with me:

Dear God, today I ask Jesus to come into my heart and be my personal Lord and Savior. Please forgive my sins and wash me from all the wrong things I have done. Be the Lord of my life. Thank You, Jesus, for coming into my heart. In Jesus' name, Amen.

Perhaps you already know your Savior, but you need to rededicate your life to the Lord. Perhaps you have a cold heart toward God, or you have been living a selfish life and are far from Him. Please pray this prayer of rededication with me:

Dear God, I realize today that I have been far away from You in my heart. Although I once prayed to receive Jesus Christ as Savior, He really hasn't been the Lord of my life. Lord Jesus, I now enthrone You as King over my heart. Take my life and use it. Make me a woman of destiny. In Jesus' name, Amen.

Holy Handmaidens

I prayed that last prayer with you in my own heart. My heart burns to do more with my life for the Lord Jesus than I am doing now. Part of my struggle in writing this chapter is the many women of faith I have to leave out. I have been humbled to read of the great sacrifices so many have made. But I must highlight here two more women whose courage inspires us, and then we will turn to other modern-day heroines who show us how to rise up and take our places in the world alongside them.

Amy Carmichael

Amy Carmichael (1867–1951), a Western missionary born in Northern Ireland, was probably the most famous woman missionary of her time. She also wrote 35 books on missions and established the Dohnavur Fellowship in India in 1901 to rescue girls from temple prostitution.[8] In 1916, Amy founded the Sisterhood of the Common Life to help steer young women, who were called to be single, into single-minded ministry.

I particularly encourage those of you who are single to study her life. She, like Lottie Moon, grappled with the thought of not marrying. Women missionaries of her time were often expected to live single lives as career missionaries at a huge cost. And even though they had no physical children of their own, God gave them many, many spiritual children who considered the women missionaries their mothers.

Amy later relayed her struggle, during her early missionary service in Japan, before going to India, in the following manner:

> On this day many years ago I went away alone to a cave in the mountain called Arima. I had feelings of fear about the future. That was why I went there—to be alone with God. The devil kept on whispering, "It is all right now, but what about afterwards? You are going to be very lonely." And he painted pictures of loneliness—I can see them still. And I turned to my God in a kind of desperation and said, "Lord, what can I do? How can I go on to the end?" And He said, "None of them that trust in Me shall be desolate." That word has been with me ever since.[9]

Amanda Smith

Any chapter dealing with heroines of the faith would be incomplete without honoring the role of African American women in Kingdom work. Among the most noted and courageous of these women was the Methodist revivalist Amanda Smith, who lived from 1837 to 1915. Amanda was born a slave in Maryland, yet she rose to become a Methodist Holiness evangelist, undertook mission work in Africa and founded an orphanage for African American children.[10]

As I studied her remarkable life, I felt great admiration for her as a pioneer who has gone before me to set an example of perseverance for my generation. I have suffered persecution at times and even hostility, but nothing compared to what Amanda must have encountered.

Elliot Wright put it like this:

> She was an unusual sight in post–Civil War America—a black woman evangelist, an ex-slave, traversing north and south, preaching to all races and then spending fourteen years evangelizing in England, India, and Africa. She, too, was part of the Holiness movement.[11]

Amanda Smith's story is also a tribute to the godly example of her mother and grandmother. Where would we be without the mothers of the Church?

Amanda received opposition from the Black African Methodist Episcopal Church (the AME) as well as from white churchgoers. When the AME held its first general conference south of the Mason-Dixon line, Amanda decided in her heart that she was going to go. Her appearance caused quite a stir, even though she says in her own words:

> The thought of ordination had never once entered my mind, for I had received my ordination from Him who said, "Ye have not chosen Me, but I have chosen you, and ordained you, that you might go and bring forth fruit."[12]

Oh, dear Amanda, your sisters down through the ages and those of today respond to your statement with a joyful, "Amen, sister, amen!" If it is not God who is calling us, then why would we ever want to say yes to being handmaidens of the Lord?

Challenged by the Call

As I have studied the women of God down through the centuries, there is one glaring unifying theme: Most of them, like myself, were extremely reluctant to become women in ministry, or to accept any kind of leadership role in the Church. It was not easy then, and, although much has improved since Amanda Smith's time, it still is not easy today. (We will discuss this more in later chapters.)

Because so many more women of faith deserve to be recognized in this book, it is with a certain amount of anguish that I close it with a few contemporary heroines whose well-known stories touch our hearts. I encourage you to read some of the excellent books that have been written by and about courageous women (see the recommended reading section) and find yourself in the pages. Read about Gladys Aylward, for instance, an English maid called by God to China under impossible odds. Her story never ceases to inspire me to have faith in God despite the biggest mountains of adversity. Truly there are many of whom the world was not worthy.

I also suggest that you read these stories to your sons and daughters. We need examples of mothers of the faith as well as fathers. Pastors need to preach about these heroines from the pulpit and inspire the generations to follow their examples.

The last several women mentioned in this chapter have had great impact on my life. Each of these women has given me something very special and unique in love and nurturing for which I will be eternally grateful.

For me personally, Margaret Moberly and the leaders of Women Ministers International helped mentor me. Great women such as Marilyn Hickey, Jane Hansen Hoyt and others have touched my life by their friendship. I will be weaving more of their influence on my life in further chapters.

Lisa Bevere

Lisa grew up as a "heathen." Her family was utterly dysfunctional; her parents divorced twice, and her grandmother was married four times. When Lisa was five years old, she was diagnosed with retinoblastoma—a type of cancer that resulted in her having one eye removed; because they caught it so late, she was given six months to live.

Knowing of the Lisa of today, it might surprise you to learn that she was a "nightmare of a child." (Using her own words!) She attended summer school at Purdue University and the University of Arizona, where she majored in partying (no degree) because she was a wild child.

God has His ways with people like her, and He arranged for her to meet a young, cute guy named John. Lisa told John that she feared her mother had joined a cult because she had become a charismatic. He shared the love of God with her and Lisa was born again. John then told her that salvation meant wholeness. That sparked her interest, because Lisa was lactose intolerant. John prayed with her and she was healed.

At the age of 21 not only did Lisa receive the Lord, but God brought her her life's partner, both in marriage and in ministry. John and Lisa married when he was 23 and she was 22. Right away they decided that they would serve God together as a team. They both served in their local church, then John served as a youth pastor for two and a half years.

The ministry was growing, but they felt as though they were dying inside. They resigned and launched out on their own with five hundred dollars to their name and two kids.

When Lisa was pregnant with her third son, God began to push her outside her comfort zone. He told her that He was calling women. She protested, "But I don't like women!"

The Lord countered her excuses by replying, *I like women!* He challenged her to be that woman she had always looked for. In fact, she came to understand that God created woman as the answer for the first problem: "It isn't good for man to be alone."

This was not easy for Lisa. She had no mentors and no idea how she was supposed to start. Finally the Lord spoke to her to write it backward—this meant writing the story of what she had wished had been. He was not looking for mentors; He was looking for mothers. Mothers want more for the next generation. They want to see them go further and rise higher.

In 1996 she wrote her first book, *Out of Control and Loving It* (re-released by Charisma House, 2006). It deals with issues of fear and control. At that time they had four boys.

Since that time Lisa has gone on to write many more books and studies. She is a *New York Times* bestselling author, and the organization she and John co-founded, Messenger International, has given away more than 17 million resources in 106 languages worldwide. Even though she is known across the globe, she is still humble, sweet, passionate and, having raised four amazing sons, is now a grandmother.

Beni Johnson

One of the finest women leaders that I know is Beni Johnson. Beni and Bill Johnson have seen many, many miracles through their church, Bethel, in Redding, California. In fact, the healing centers that they have developed have become a pilgrimage place for people around the world to come and receive outstanding spiritual encounters, along with being healed.

Beni was raised in the church and became a believer when she was quite young. When she was eighteen, she moved from Redding to Santa Rosa, California, to go to a discipleship school called Genesis.

Even though she knew the Lord, Beni found herself falling into depression. She cried out to God in her anguish to deliver her from the depression, and she was instantly set free. She never had that problem again.

Later, as she found out that her calling was to be an intercessor, she realized that she had become what I now know to be a "wounded burden bearer,"[13] an intercessor who helps carry the burdens of others who are unable to give their pains and griefs to the Lord and allow Him to carry them. In addition, she had a strong gift of discernment that, at first, she did not know how to work with! In the early years this resulted in her becoming depressed as she tried to fix everyone's problems as well as felt the emotions of others' depressions and anxieties.

Bill and Beni got married when he was 21 and she was 18. After going back to Redding, Bill served as the singles' director for his dad's church.

After that they took a church in Weaverville, California, and she became busy raising her children. (They are quite successful leaders today. You might also have heard of their son Brian and his wife, Jenn, of Bethel Music. Their son Eric now is the pastor of Bethel Church, like his father and grandfather before him.)

One service while she was in the balcony, taking care of the children, a visiting prophet called her down to the front. As she walked forward, she told the Lord, *I want any gifts You have, but please don't call me to intercession*. At that time she pictured intercessors as old, constipated-looking women, which she did not want to be!

The prophet, however, was listening to the Lord and not Beni, and he prophesied over her that she was called to be an intercessor. The world is glad that she answered that call, because she wrote *The Happy Intercessor* (Destiny Image, 2009), and showed us that prayer warriors are among the most joyous people on the planet today!

Freda Lindsay

One of the giants in God's Kingdom, and one who struggled with the call, was Freda Lindsay. Freda was born in Canada on a large wheat farm near Burstall, Saskatchewan, and was one of twelve children. Her German-origin parents grew up in White Russia and met and married in the United States, but later heard of great opportunities in Canada. It seems that God had a plan for little Freda to be Canadian! (Do I hear an "Amen!" from the country to the north of the United States?)

Although Freda fervently wanted to attend high school, her father was from the old school that believed women did not need to be educated. Fortunately, the same tenacity that was to stand her in good stead later in her life was apparent when she convinced her mother that she would find a job if her mother would talk to her father about her education. It is not surprising at all that Freda found that job and was able to move to town to attend school.

Later, Freda visited her sister, who told her of a revival meeting in progress in Portland, Oregon, held by a young evangelist named Gordon Lindsay. She tells of her struggle to accept the Lord in her book *My Diary Secrets*:

> After the dismissal prayer, I . . . made my way to the altar at the front of the church. There the devil told me I would live a dull and drab life

> if I were to become a Christian . . . that I would never have any friends, and on and on he went. Nevertheless, with the Holy Spirit tugging at my soul, I surrendered my life to the Lord that night and was gloriously converted.[14]

At the altar that night, Freda heard the same Holy Spirit tell her that Gordon would one day be her husband. Five years later they were married.

Years later, I was driving through Stanley Park in Vancouver, British Columbia, with Mrs. Lindsay and some other ministers when she pointed to a lovely site and said with a sweet tenderness in her voice, "That is where Gordon proposed to me." I listened with a sense of awe and felt privileged to be a part of such a time of sweet remembrance.

Freda and Gordon's life together was about as far from boring as a couple could ever imagine. Volumes could be written about their work during the "Voice of Healing" days when they were working with great men and women of God such as William Branham. *The Voice of Healing* (a magazine dedicated to the revival and miracles that came out of the movement) was started on April 1, 1948. The Lord led them to buy an old nightclub in Dallas, Texas, and gave Gordon the vision to build a Bible school, Christ for the Nations Institute (CFNI). My sister and brother-in-law are both graduates, so my own family greatly benefited, as did my friend Dutch Sheets, and many other friends in ministry.

March of 1973 was, as usual, a busy one for the Lindsays—by then they had three children: two boys and a girl. Toward the end of that month, when they went to the lake, Gordon requested that 1 Corinthians 15 be read for the family devotions. The chapter deals with the resurrection of the dead, which is personally interesting to me because when we went to pick up my dad's effects after his death, the only passage marked in his Bible was this same one.

On April 1, 1973, Gordon Lindsay slipped out to glory while sitting on the platform at CFNI. Freda and Gordon had been married 35 years.

Freda began to receive prophetic words from respected leaders revealing that Gordon's mantle had fallen upon her shoulders, and one day after the funeral, the board of CFNI voted for her to succeed her husband.

The weight of the massive responsibility of that huge work for the Lord came down upon her shoulders, seemingly crushing her small frame. Inside Freda Lindsay, however, lived a big God whom she had served unreservedly since she had knelt at that altar in Portland, Oregon.

Following the funeral, Freda reported:

> After friends and family had returned to their own homes, I was left alone with Carole [her daughter]. I started to get out of bed the next morning and found I had no strength even to stand. I lay back down and called Carole into my room. I told her the task was too great—the responsibility of our missionary work that was reaching into over 100 nations was too much . . . the finishing of the Institute building . . . the 300 native churches we were at that time helping to build . . . the Bible school in Zerka, Jordan, that we had just started to build . . . they were more than I could carry.
>
> Carole said to me, "Mother, let's just pray. And let's just take it one day at a time. The Lord will give you strength for just today." So I crawled out of bed and prostrated myself on the floor. For some time I lay there sobbing out my inadequacy at the immensity of the task when suddenly the Holy Ghost took over.
>
> Then I bathed myself, dressed and went to work. And the Lord has each day provided strength sufficient for all the needs that have arisen.[15]

Freda Lindsay was reunited with her husband, Gordon, when she passed away on March 27, 2010, at the age of 95. She had only stopped going to the office at age 94. Christ for the Nations Institute has built 11,000 native churches in Third World countries, has 44 affiliated Bible schools, and 26,000 students have come through the doors of the Institute. Some naysayers claimed after Gordon's death that the doors of CFNI would close within six months. Guess they sort of missed it—do you think? All because of one little girl from a family of twelve siblings who gave all of her heart, soul and mind to loving and serving her beloved Savior.

Christine Caine

One of the most courageous women leaders in the world today is Christine Caine. I mentioned earlier her influential organization called A21 that is fighting human trafficking across the world. It has fourteen offices in twelve countries. Among other recognitions, she received the Mother Teresa Award, given by Gandhi's great-grandson, for her work. Her story is one of beauty to ashes.

Christine was raised in a Greek family in Australia. It may surprise you to know that there was really horrible racism against the Greek-speaking people in those days. When she started school, for instance, her mother packed her a nice sandwich with pungent Greek cheese. The other kids at her lunch table jeered and remarked, "What is that stink?" She was humiliated, threw her sandwich away and went hungry. This became a regular occurrence for her.

At age 33, after her father died, she found out to her shock that she had been adopted. While she had wondered why she never could bond fully with her mother, she was stunned to find out that neighbors, as well as others, knew she had been adopted.

She went to talk to her older brother, George, who deepened her despair by saying he had just received a letter, as she had, revealing that he had been adopted also! He called the government office and was told all about it. Evidently the laws had changed after all the years since their adoptions, and "closed adoptions" were now open.

Christine went to talk to her mother, who wept, saying, "I never thought you would find out! Your dad did not want you to know. Christine, do you want to know the whole truth?"

Thoughts swirled around in her head after that. She asked, "Am I still Greek?" She found out that yes, she was Greek. When she finally obtained her birth certificate, she saw that it read: "Unnamed; Number 2508 of 1966."

Unnamed. Her birth mother had not even given her a name. She was just number 2508. Christine felt other emotions, too; the biggest one was shame.

Then the Lord took her on a healing journey. Through her pain, God gave her amazing healing by personalizing Isaiah 49:1 for her: *From the matrix of your mother, I have named you.*

Later, she understood that God had named her in the womb. Whose voice would she believe? That of the ink on her natural birth certificate or that written from the Father heart of God?

She founded the ministry called Propel in 2015 and began filling arenas, bringing healing to tens of thousands. Her powerful book, *Unashamed* (Zondervan, 2016), tells her story of healing and reveals how one little Greek adopted girl can change the world. Now it can be truly said that she sees the petals rather than the thorns on the rosebush.

Whatever you have gone through, God wants to heal you and make you whole and use your life as a testimony of overcoming.

Vonette Bright

Some of God's women leaders received the call to minister through the vision the Lord gave their husbands. Bill and Vonette founded the ministry called Campus Crusade for Christ (now called Cru).

I asked Vonette Bright one day at a Focus on the Family meeting for "AD2000 and Beyond" if God called her independently of her husband. She stopped and thought a moment, then said, "Bill received the vision to help reach the world for Christ and to begin on the college campus. We assumed that God's call for Bill was also my call. Afraid of what that meant, I asked God for a heart to respond. Bill calls me co-founder."

Of course, this great woman was not only an author, but she was also used of God along with others to call together the great prayer congress in 1984, which some people feel was the beginning, in some respects, of the prayer movement encircling the globe today. Vonette went to be with the Lord on December 23, 2015.

Corinthia Boone

Dr. Corinthia Boone is one of the greatest modern-day leaders that I know. She has been a good friend to Mike and me for many years, and we greatly admire her.

Corinthia was born in Prince George County, Maryland, to an African American family. Her mother's side was Baptist and her daddy's was Pentecostal. Corinthia had an experience when she was eight years old that was to mark her life forever.

One day, while sitting in the back of the church, Corinthia was suddenly engulfed in the presence of God. To tell it in her own words, "God had answered my desire to know Him." A change was evident in her life, and she would often be called to the altar to lead in prayer. As usual, the Holy Spirit led her in a way that affirmed her primary ministry: prayer.

The impact of this touch from God was deep and lasting. When Corinthia speaks of this, her voice sings with the joy of the Lord. She told me, "After that experience the trees sang and nothing looked the same to me." A couple of years later, Corinthia began to attend a Holiness church where she began testifying, prophesying, singing in the choir and speaking.

The first time I heard her story, I thought, *No wonder the Lord said, "Let the children come unto Me."*

Children are often underestimated with regard to their abilities.

The Lord led this mighty pioneer of God to earn her bachelor of science in education from Bowie State University. Later she earned her master's in administration supervision, a Bible school certificate from Baltimore Bible College followed, and then, at last, a hard-earned doctorate from Union University in philosophy, with an emphasis on counseling.

Corinthia worked for years with Bishop John Meares at Evangel Temple in Washington, D.C. She helped set up the Sunday school department and worked in many other areas of the church. She also served as an ordained elder.

In 1985, Corinthia was appointed unanimously to be chairperson of the Greater Washington National Day of Prayer. She has founded

Together in Ministry International (TIM), a fellowship of pastors finding new relationships, friendships and inspiration in a multicultural setting—an oasis of refreshing through worshipful prayer. Her ministry, the International Christian Host Coalition, is a multiethnic group of leaders who are committed to community transformation. This ministry (ICHC) is the umbrella ministry for TIM and the Greater Washington National Day of Prayer.

"The testings . . . have plowed long furrows upon my back, but without those furrows there would be no place for the seed. Without the opening of the seed, it could not fall into the ground and be fruitful."

I asked Corinthia if she would share some wisdom with those who read this chapter. She began by quoting Psalm 129:3 (KJV): "The plowers plowed upon my back: they made long their furrows." She went on to explain, "I have learned more from testings than anything else in my life. The testings I have gone through have plowed long furrows upon my back, but without those furrows there would be no place for the seed. Without the opening of the seed, it could not fall into the ground and be fruitful. Yes, I have had many testings, but I've always determined that they will only cause me to bear more fruit."

Corinthia, my friend, or should I say Corinthia Boone, B.S., M.S., Ph.D., I commend you for your courage. You are a true pioneer and heroine of the faith with many lessons for people of all ethnicities. I salute you for not becoming bitter from the storms of life. Thank you for your example.

Doris Wagner

Doris Wagner was born on a dairy farm in St. Johnsville in upstate New York. Her father was a German immigrant who had settled just outside this one-stoplight town, population fifteen hundred. (This story proves that we should never despise the day of small beginnings, because one day little Doris would grow up and lead to the Lord a young man getting his degree in dairy farming, whose grandfather had been the country doctor in St. Johnsville.) I wonder if Doris ever dreamed as a teenager of whom she would one day marry. Any daydreaming she might have done would probably never have touched upon the fact that she would eventually help start an organization that would influence the whole world in prayer.

One day, Doris went to a farm in another town and saw a young man milking a cow. The year was 1949. This young man was interested in the bright-eyed Doris, but the two of them were worlds apart in their thinking. He was a gambler and a drunkard, and she was a committed Christian who had just given her life to Jesus a week before.

Although Doris shared with him the Gospel message, the young man was reluctant to become a Christian, knowing that, if he did, he would have to give up his lifestyle in the fraternity house at Rutgers University. This young man had such a brilliant mind that he could factor the odds at draw poker and was a perpetual winner. In fact, his gambling was providing his spending money at college.

Finally, love and the Lord won in the battle for his soul, and he asked Doris to marry him. She, however, looked him straight in the eye and said, "I can't. I'm a born-again Christian, and I promised the Lord I would only marry a Christian."

He replied, "Well, what does it take to be a Christian? Will you show me how?"

"In a moment," she said. "But I must tell you something else first. I have also given my life to God to be a missionary."

"Missionary?" he said. "What's that?" When she explained, he said, "I think I'll be a missionary, too!" So he gave his life to the Lord and became an ex-gambler and ex-drunkard. That was in January 1950.

Now, I know some of you may highly suspect his motives, but the years have proven that he sought more than just a pretty face with dimples. Dr. C. Peter Wagner went with his wife, Doris, to Bolivia, where they were field missionaries for sixteen years. They returned to America to spend the next 25 years at Fuller Seminary, where Doris served as Peter's personal secretary before they launched Global Harvest Ministries.

Global Harvest Ministries was founded to coordinate the "United Prayer Track" of the "AD2000 and Beyond" movement. In 1996, Doris and Peter moved the ministry from Pasadena, California, to Colorado Springs in order to become founding partners of the World Prayer Center. Peter Wagner went to be with the Lord on October 21, 2016.

Doris Wagner now works with Chuck Pierce and Global Spheres, Inc., which is headquartered in Corinth, Texas. She has an ongoing ministry of deliverance and speaking. Many around the world affectionately know her as "Mom."

Doris was my buddy in the early days when I first went to Argentina and stayed busy kicking out demons left and right in order to clear the way for revival in that nation. She is a living legend and one of God's heroines of the faith.

Many Women Do Noble Things (Proverbs 31:29)

The last but certainly not the least great woman I want to share about in this chapter is my own mother, Eleanor Johnson Lindsey. I dedicated this book to her because I am what I am and who I am due to her prayers and belief in me. I went through some dark trials—though never deep rebellion—and she was always there for me.

Mom met my dad while she was a Presbyterian. When he told her that he was called of God to be a minister, she cried. Being a pastor's wife was not her idea of a fun life, but the problem was that he wanted to be a *Baptist* minister, which meant she would have to leave the Presbyterian Church and be rebaptized. The news was overwhelming.

Mom was a spunky lady, though, and the tears were short-lived. She and Dad went to Southwestern Seminary in Fort Worth, Texas, after Dad graduated from Baylor. I lived on "seminary hill," and, as I have mentioned, times were tight. In fact, the house we lived in was eventually torn down. (It was not in the greatest shape even way back then!)

As Dad and Mom pioneered churches under the Home Mission Board, money was always tight, but I never heard Mom complain. She just prayed.

For years, Mom had a list of people's names from her church and others to pray over. She helped me clean up my first draft of *Possessing the Gates of the Enemy*, and I still have her old typewriter. I never knew a day that went by without her praying through my schedule. She stepped over into glory from room 222 at Baylor Hospital on February 22, 2016, when she was nearly ninety years old, and I miss her and her prayers every day.

SEVEN

Gender to Gender

Have you ever noticed that women are different from men? Every woman called of God to make a change in her world needs to understand how to work with men!

Men Who Bark and the Women Who Love Them

One day while driving to the store, I began listening to my five-year-old son, who was sitting in the backseat. At first I thought he was talking to himself out loud. Then, as I really tuned in, I realized that most of his conversation was not with words; rather, he was simply making sounds—such as "urrrrrr, bang, bang, uh-uh-uh-uh, vroom, vroom, vroom" and the like.

Puzzled by this, I wondered if imitating sounds could be a pattern in little boys. I found to my utter amazement that it is. I wondered further if perhaps this surprising discovery would not have caught his dad off guard at all. So I expanded my research to men, in general, and my husband, in particular. As I listened, I was intrigued to find that even grown men are sometimes prone to this peculiar behavior.

When we first married, I would watch Mike open the door and bark like a dog to rattle the various pets in houses up and down the alley of our neighborhood. Then Mike would shut the door with a grin on his face as the uproar of responding barks ensued. I realize that not all men do this. (But I do think that quite a few men would either relish this thought or at least enjoy it.) My husband's friend David, who lived directly under our upstairs apartment, loved to do the same. In fact, occasionally they would bark in chorus! It seemed to be a form of that mysterious thing called "male bonding."

Born to Be Different

Females, on the other hand, are more prone to speak words—lots of them. Little girls dote on long conversations over tea parties. They talk to their dolls and pets. And when they grow up, so does the need to talk. A noted marriage therapist said that a wife needs at least one good hour of conversation with her husband a day.

When I was teaching about the differences between men and women to a group of pastors' wives in Latin America, the women laughed and gently protested that their husbands needed lots of words. Although this may be true, there is a major difference between talking and communication. Pastors in general may be more prone to talking, but it is heartfelt communication on a more intimate level that women need—not just words. Women generally have a greater need for this kind of intimate interchange than men do.

The gender gap is so broad that it is even evident in small children. Books have been written that attribute the problem to men and women coming from different planets! (And if you have had a problem communicating gender to gender, this may not seem out of the realm of possibility.)

A part of the gender gap is physical in nature. Gary Smalley and John Trent have this to say about it:

> Medical studies have shown that between the 18th and 26th weeks of pregnancy, something happens that forever separates the sexes. Using heat-sensitive monitors, researchers have actually observed a chemical bath of testosterone and other sex-related hormones wash over a baby boy's brain. This causes changes that never happen to a baby girl. Here's a layman's explanation. . . .

> The human brain is divided into two halves, or hemispheres. . . . The sex-related hormones that flood a baby boy's brain cause the right side to recede slightly, destroying some of the connecting fibers [between the hemispheres]. One result is that, in most cases, a boy starts life more left-brain oriented.
>
> Because little girls don't experience this chemical bath, they leave the starting blocks much more two-sided in their thinking. And while electrical impulses and messages do travel back and forth between both sides of a baby boy's brain, those same messages can proceed faster and be less hindered in the brain of a little girl.
>
> Well, not exactly. What occurs in the womb merely sets the stage for men and women to "specialize" in two different ways of thinking. And this is one major reason men and women need each other so much.
>
> The left brain houses more of the logical, analytical, factual and aggressive centers of thought. It's the side of the brain most men reserve for the major portion of their waking hours. It enjoys conquering 500 miles a day on family vacations, favors mathematical formulas over romance novels, stores the dictionary definition of love and generally favors clinical, black-and-white thinking.
>
> On the other hand, most women spend the majority of their days and nights camped out on the right side of the brain. It's the side that harbors the center for feelings, as well as the primary relational, language and communication skills. It enables them to do fine detail work, sparks imagination and makes an afternoon devoted to art and fine music enjoyable. Perhaps you can begin to understand why communication is difficult in marriage.[1]

I know that some of you women readers will be tempted at this point to get into what we in America call "male bashing" and make a comment such as, "I always knew that men were brain-damaged!" Resist this at all costs or you may create a need for gender reconciliation.

It All Began in the Garden

Although it is true that men and women have many physical differences, I believe the breakdown in their spiritual communication began way back in the Garden of Eden, as recorded in the book of Genesis.

In order to understand God's original intention for the sexes, we need to recognize one very important point: The only thing God said was not good in all of creation was man's aloneness (see Genesis 1:4, 10, 12, 18, 21, 25, 31; see also Genesis 2:18). It stands to reason, therefore, that Satan would want to wound the relationships between men and women—not only in the home, but also in the workforce and the Church—so that man would once again be in the only state God called "not good." (I want to make it clear to all unmarried readers that this affects you, too. You can be unmarried and still not be alone.)

In the beginning, God created mankind (or *humankind*, as is now the more common term) in His image, male and female (see Genesis 1:26–27). It is a mistaken belief that Adam had both male and female attributes. Although Eve was "bone of my bones, and flesh of my flesh" (Genesis 2:23), God put something in her that came straight from heaven, which Adam had not been created with. I believe God looked around and knew, in the context of His purposes, that something was still missing upon the earth. If He left man in his present state, then the full image of who He is as God would not be represented upon the earth—so He created woman. The full image of God, therefore, is not fully displayed through only one gender, but it happens on every level as men and women complement each other, side by side. When this happens, all things created seem to breathe a sigh of relief and somehow express, "This is right. This is good. This is how God intended the earth to be."

Sadly, men and women have so wounded each other that we see extreme forms of anger displayed. At one end are women who turn to lesbianism and feminism, and say to men, "We don't need you. The only good man is a dead man." Almost invariably at the root of this rage is a father who was abusive. It would be interesting to check out whether or not this pattern exists in the lives of leading women within the most extreme feminist movement.

On the other hand, men's views can also be distorted concerning women. Many men who are strongly against women in ministry in the Church have often had big problems with a controlling woman somewhere in their lives, and the women they know suffer because of the way their mothers, sisters, lovers or other females abused them.

This breakdown in communication began in the Garden. Satan's strike against the man and woman seems to have occurred at the Tree of the Knowledge of Good and Evil. A fascinating aspect of this interchange between the snake, the woman and the man is that the sin involved the mouth.

Note that Satan approached the woman with food. Perhaps he worked on a natural desire of hers to prepare food for her husband. Here was a different and appealing tidbit they had not eaten before. Sadly, if they had partaken deeply enough of the fruit of the Tree of Life, they would not have had any desire for this forbidden fruit.

Likewise, it is possible that the man was used to receiving food from the woman, and this weakened his defenses against eating that which the Lord had said, "You must not." Immediately after they partook, their eyes were opened and death came into their lives. I also believe that a veil was placed between them, inhibiting their ability to communicate, because the only way a man and a woman can truly relate is through God. Before the Fall, a supernatural anointing existed that surpassed the differences in their brains and gave them oneness of heart.

Created to Complete, Not Compete

Norm Wright wrote a fascinating book titled *What Men Want*. In chapter 2, "The Dialogue," he relates an imaginary conversation between God and a man. It goes like this:

> "So You purposely made them (male and female) different as they are?"
>
> "Yes, I did. You're suggesting it was accidental?"
>
> "Oh, no . . . no, not at all. But, sometimes . . ."
>
> "You know the story. Satan, clothed in the form of a serpent, came to them and spoke to Eve. He convinced her to disobey Me. She invited Adam to join her, and instead of saying, 'No, we need to obey God,' he caved in. This was the first sign of passivity. The man-woman relationship

> and everything else became disordered. He then began to blame. First he blamed his wife, and then he blamed Me for giving her to him. Ever since Adam's time, men have tended to be defensive. They often interpret innocent questions as accusations. And the blame that started in the Garden . . . oh, men have cultivated that ability well! The role I assigned to Adam has been distorted."
>
> "Ah, wait a minute. Men are defensive by nature? I don't think we're so defensive."
>
> (Silence.)
>
> "Well, perhaps some men are, but we do get accused a lot. . . ."
>
> (Silence.)
>
> "All right, we're defensive. Okay, please continue, or is that it?"
>
> "There's much more. In the Garden, both Adam and Eve could relate emotionally. They were able to give one another the gift of understanding. Not now. Now, if a woman wants understanding from a man, what does she get?"
>
> "Solutions, answers, advice . . ."
>
> "A relationship that was meant to be complementary became competitive. Eve's desire was to control Adam. What I created to be a perfect balance resulted in a deteriorating imbalance and a clash of wills."[2]

Wright goes on to share other deep insights about male-female relationships that resulted from the Fall, such as power struggles, domination, emotional nakedness, lack of trust, fear, anger, control and the like.

It does not take a very perceptive person to look at the relationships between men and women today and see that he is accurate in his assessments. Painfully accurate.

God looked down through time and already had a remedy prepared: Jesus, the Lamb of God, slain from the foundation of the world. He came and died so that the terrible rip in gender relationships, which came in through sin, could be healed through His own blood on Calvary. Only the power of the cross can fill the gender gap and create the bridge we so desperately need to restore us to Eden.

Without men and women working side by side, the Church will be ineffective. The complete image of God will be manifested in its full expression only when men and women stand side by side in the Church. Is there any wonder that the devil fights gender reconciliation at all levels? Satan cannot afford to have Eden restored and man and woman standing together as they did in the Garden. This would bring order to the home and order to the Church.

Commissioned to Subdue—But Not Each Other

The Bible says that one day there will be a restoration of all things that God has spoken by the mouth of all His holy prophets since the world began (see Acts 3:21). One of these prophecies was that in the end times, He would pour out His Spirit upon the sons and daughters (see Joel 2:28–29).

Jane Hansen Hoyt and Marie Powers's excellent book, *Fashioned for Intimacy*, gives us an in-depth study of Creation and the role of men and women. (I highly encourage you to read it. It will fill in many of the blanks I am not able to cover in this one chapter.) One of the points the authors make is that humanity was made to have authority upon the earth.[3] This was the job description given to God's image bearers—initially the man, and subsequently man and woman together. At the moment of Adam's creation, an evil force was already loose in the earth that Adam was instructed to guard against in order to protect his sanctuary. Ultimately, Adam and Eve together were commissioned to subdue and be in authority over all the earth. The enemy they were to subdue was God's enemy, Satan.

Satan cannot afford to have Eden restored and man and woman standing together as they did in the Garden. This would bring order to the home and order to the Church.

Satan simply cannot afford for men and women to reconcile on a gender level. I personally believe that no power of agreement on the earth is stronger than a husband and wife who touch heaven together in their prayers. When healing happens on this level, God's created sons and daughters will come into a level of authority that Satan has not had to deal with since the beginning of the world. He has, therefore, built up generations of strongholds to prevent gender reconciliation.

Numbers of Christian leaders today feel that the gender gap is the final pioneer area in need of healing. Pastors and leaders are meeting together for prayer, but the sexes remain separated in the meetings. I would even go as far as to say that I believe a cultural gender bias is at work. Many male leaders who agree mentally that men and women need to work together in ministry show little evidence of their belief by their words or actions.

Purging Our Patterns of Denial

I hesitate even to bring up the topic of denial, but when a stronghold is exhibited in a culture, the mindset is often so ingrained that godly people who are caught in its grip have no idea they are participating. I have often seen this form of denial in relation to racial reconciliation. (Which, by the way, is another area in which we still have a long way to go.)

One day when Mike and I were meeting with leaders in another country, we were discussing the need for racial reconciliation on a national level. These godly leaders looked at us and said, "We don't have a problem with racism in our country."

I turned quietly and looked at a black friend (I might add, the *only* black person in the meeting) and said, "Elan [not his real name], are you always the worship leader and never the speaker?"

Elan looked rather uncomfortable, gazed at the floor and in a downcast voice answered, "Yes." The white leaders were absolutely shocked and proceeded to plan a time of national repentance.

I bring this up because I have seen similar instances with women leaders in meeting after meeting. A number of years ago, I attended a prayer breakfast for American leaders on our National Day of Prayer in Washington, D.C. At one point, the master of ceremonies asked all the ministers in the room to stand. As I looked around, not one woman stood up. Why? We were too embarrassed to face the possible criticism our standing might evoke. I would stand if asked today, but I simply did not have the strength of spirit to do so back then.

Another time, I spoke at a major meeting for pastors and leaders. At the end of the meeting, the seventy leaders had a discussion about how they were going to take their city for God. The conversation was full of comments such as, "We men have to do this. We guys need to be more united." As I sat quietly on the side, I watched the faces of the three or so women ministers in the group. Their eyes reflected sadness, and I felt a deep sense of sorrow for them. The insensitive statements of the male leaders did not really matter that much to me; I was flying out of the city the next day. They, however, had to remain, feeling extremely marginalized in their call to minister in that city.

A word of caution to women leaders reading this chapter: It is very important that we not allow a root of bitterness to spring up in our souls over this need for gender reconciliation (see Hebrews 12:15). You can always identify a woman minister who has unforgiveness toward men in her heart—it affects the purity of her message. Little slurs against men will come out in her speech. This is not healthy, and it needs to be dealt with.

There may be women readers who need to stop and make a list of the men who have hurt them, and simply forgive. Likewise, some men need to make a list of the women who have hurt them. I am greatly concerned about the number of militant female Christian leaders who are making sweeping statements in anger that say, "It's our time, and we are going to do what God calls us to do no matter whom we run over." This will only create a bigger breach between the genders.

Mike and I once went to a church where the pastor so hated women that his Mother's Day message was simply an opportunity to berate women. He finally got so angry that he jumped up and down on one of the metal chairs until it bent! Needless to say, women never preached in that pulpit. I am grateful to report that he has since changed his opinion.

Getting God's Perspective

Why is gender reconciliation necessary? Because God wants us to see clearly in our walk with Him:

> "And why do you look at the speck in your brother's eye, but do not consider the plank in your own eye? Or how can you say to your brother, 'Let me remove the speck from your eye'; and look, a plank is in your own eye? Hypocrite! First remove the plank from your own eye, and then you will see clearly to remove the speck from your brother's eye."
>
> Matthew 7:3–5

One day when I was airplane hopping in Dallas, to my surprise, my good friend John Dawson was on the same flight. (John is international president of Youth With A Mission.) We were able to sit across the aisle from each other, and the conversation came around to this issue of the need for gender reconciliation. John has often mentioned that he believes gender-to-gender reconciliation is one of the pioneer areas in relationships.

I shared with him that some men ministers are actually very positive about releasing women into ministry, but they are put off by pushy, loud and controlling women. It should not be a mystery to anyone that men hate pushy women.

(As a side note to this, I have often found it difficult with my prophetic gift not to overwhelm a meeting. Many times, I have gone away kicking myself for opening my mouth so much. People with a prophetic gift can be pushy whether they are male or female. You need to strike a balance and discern when it is appropriate to share prophetic insight and when it is best to keep your mouth shut. It is an ongoing growth process.)

John grinned and said, "That's interesting. Do you mind if I share that in my meetings?" He then proceeded to explain that, while women bond through affirming one another, men bond through razzing (a mild to not-so-mild form of teasing). I have to admit that a light bulb went off in my head at that moment. Memories of meetings where I was the only female leader in a crowd of guys poured through my mind. (You see, sometimes I am the token woman. I really do not mind. They say, "Well, we'd better get a woman, so let's ask Cindy Jacobs." Actually, I take it as a compliment that they love and trust me.)

The point is that there were times when I thought the men were being hostile to me, but they were actually showing that they liked me! I was "one of the boys," so to speak.

What a revelation! What does this mean? When women get together, one of the first things they will say is something like, "Oh, Susie, I really like your dress. Is it new?" or "What have you done to your hair? It looks great." Whereas, a man would say something like, "Where did you get that tie—from the garbage can?" or "Hey, old man, I heard you huffing and puffing up those stairs. Getting old, aren't you?" (I personally believe men have a lot to learn from women about affirmation, but then, I think I just got myself into trouble!)

Lord, Help Us to Understand Each Other

Communication breakdown—that snake's intrusion between men and women—has far-reaching effects today. Saint Francis of Assisi prayed some wisdom on this centuries-old problem: "Lord, grant that I may seek more to understand than to be understood." One passage of Scripture that is particularly applicable to gender-to-gender relationships came from Paul:

> Fill up and complete my joy by living in harmony and being of the same mind and one in purpose, having the same love, being in full accord and of one harmonious mind and intention. Do nothing from factional motives [through contentiousness, strife, selfishness, or for unworthy ends] or prompted by conceit and empty arrogance. Instead, in the true spirit of humility (lowliness of mind) let each regard the others as better than and superior to himself [thinking more highly of one another than you do of yourselves]. Let each of you esteem and look upon and be concerned for not [merely] his own interests, but also each for the interests of others.
>
> Philippians 2:2–4 AMPC

Some excellent resources are available today to help men and women communicate more effectively. And even though many of these books are geared toward marriage, the principles, in most cases, can be applied to any gender relationship. One of the best books I have found is *Communication: Key to Your Marriage* by Norman Wright (Bethany, 2012). Another good source of help is Alfred H. Ells, founder and director of Leaders that Last Ministries in Mesa, Arizona. The following numbered list is his "Nine Proven Steps to Resolving Conflict":[4]

1. Don't *stuff* conflict issues—pray about them—then *talk* about them.
2. One person starts by *openly* and *honestly sharing* with the other (see James 1:19; Proverbs 15:32; Ephesians 4:15, 25).
3. The other person is to *listen, understand and respond* to what is being said (see Proverbs 18:13; Philippians 2:1–4; Ephesians 4:2; James 5:9).
4. Mutual restating.
5. *Stick to the topic* and look for *areas of agreement*, not just disagreement.
6. If the discussion escalates, *withdraw*, but *not before scheduling* the next discussion.
7. Mutually identify a *biblical plan of action* that will resolve the problem and *restore unity.*
8. Humble yourself and take ownership for how you have *accidentally or purposely offended* the other person *or contributed to the problem.*
9. Control your spirit (see Proverbs 16:32; Colossians 3:12–13).

I found excellent advice on relationships in an article titled "Advice You Can Bank On" by Gary Smalley. Although the focus of the article is marriage, the principles can be used across the board for both sexes:

> To divorce-proof your marriage [or relationships], be sure you are making more "deposits" to the well-being of your spouse [or other person on some kind of relational level such as family, church, business, etc.] than "withdrawals."[5]

Smalley goes on to say that a "withdrawal" is anything that drains energy from your mate: a harsh word, a promise not kept, or being ignored, hurt or controlled.

In essence, to keep good accounts in "relational banking," we need to give more positive input than negative. I once heard that it takes ten positive comments to make up for every one negative remark. I think that is quite probable. This leads me to what I call a "spirit of affirmation" in relationships.

Accentuate the Positive, Eliminate the Negative

Many times, we in the Body of Christ tend to be extremely negative. Some cultures and generations are much more critical than others. I once mentored a young lady who came from a country where people spoke their minds much more freely than we did in Texas. She was always in hot water for things she would say at church. She would, for instance, walk up to a woman and say, "You look really fat in that dress." This kind of brutal honesty would be bad in any case, but in our Southern culture, it was almost unpardonable!

We worked and worked with her until she began to see what a critical person—both personally and culturally—she was and finally became a much more gracious, loving individual.

We should "fast" from criticism for three days to see if we are capable of refraining from speaking negatively about others.

I sometimes think we should "fast" from criticism for three days to see if we are capable of refraining from speaking negatively about others. When I tried this, I was amazed at how many critical thoughts I had to slay in my mind so they did not come out of my mouth. Actually, I work at this regularly, as do many believers.

Releasing a spirit of affirmation is a very important concept for both males and females to understand. It is often difficult for us to verbalize praise for one another, even when we want to.

Many people in my parents' generation (World War II era) held an unspoken philosophy that you did not praise your children to their faces because it would spoil them. I started comparing notes with others of my age and found that their parents would compliment them to their siblings but would not pass those positive words along to them personally. At times when I have mentioned this unspoken philosophy to different members of my parents' generation, they usually look surprised at first, but then they begin to change this unhealthy mindset.

Some cultures are not very good at praising people. Their thinking is, *Why should I praise people just for doing what they should be doing?* It is important, however, for everyone to receive words of encouragement and gratitude. The Bible has so much to say about thankfulness (see, for example, 1 Chronicles 16:8; Psalms 7:17, 50:14, 68:26, 142:7; Isaiah 12:4; 2 Corinthians 9:11; Ephesians 5:4; 1 Thessalonians 5:18).

Women especially need verbal affirmation. This is why men are told four times in Scripture to love their wives. If women do not receive enough affirmation, especially by their husbands (if they are married), they can become quite vulnerable to the attention of other men. This is not to say that men do not need affirmation; of course they do. But women, in general, have a greater need for affirmation than do men.

When Gender Bonds Lead to Bondage

In studying why people fall into adultery, I have found that Christian women are most often hooked through the spirituality or sensitivity of men rather than through physical attraction. This creates a bond in the emotions or the soul realm that often leads to spiritual adultery.

Spiritual and emotional adultery is when two people, either of whom is married to someone else, form a bond in which they think more about each other than they do their spouses (this could happen in a business, church or school). Is this a possibility in your life? A good test is to check your thought life. How much of your time do you spend thinking about a person of the opposite sex who is not your mate?

Years ago, I related on a regular basis with a male leader from another ministry. After a few months, I found myself looking forward to his calls. We had so much in common. Each conversation was spiritually and intellectually stimulating. In the meantime, Mike was busy working at a job that took him away from home from seven in the morning until around eight or nine at night.

Please understand: I never held this man's hand, kissed him or even considered it. The pull, however, was strong—very, very strong. I slipped into a mode in my thought life where he filled a space in my emotions that only my husband was supposed to fill.

Mike and I have always had the kind of relationship where we can be open about anything with one another. One day, Mike said, "Honey, this guy calls and asks about you when you're on the road. He wants to know if you have arrived safely and how the ministry is going. I think he cares for you a little too much."

At that moment, I was hit by a huge reality check. You see, if I had consciously realized that the relationship I had with this ministry leader had gone that far emotionally, I would have pulled out long before. I was blindsided because of the distance Mike's job and our busy lives had put between us, and I was, frankly, emotionally needy for conversation.

I then shared with Mike that I felt I was somewhat wrapped up with this other man in my emotions, and I was shocked to come to that realization. We prayed together, and I asked God to forgive me. Mike and I then discussed how we could improve our communication.

What I had not understood was that intimate conversation breeds intimacy. When having conversations with those of the opposite sex, it is very important to maintain a brother-to-sister relationship. This is especially important with prayer partners. Prayer partners of the opposite sex should never become confidants greater than your spouse. Nor should you have private one-on-one meetings with them. Phone conversations are okay, but I would limit them and involve the person's spouse as much as possible.

After Mike and I talked, I thought it would be quite easy to break the tie I had formed with the other guy. Wrong! Although I stopped talking to this man on the phone, the pull I felt toward him was tremendous. Some days it was all I could do not to pick up the phone and call him. Thoughts of his voice and how he looked haunted my mind.

Finally, one day I cried out to the Lord for help. The Lord gently spoke to me in my spirit that a major reason I was so emotionally entangled with the other guy was that I had lost my first love for *Him*. The Lord could have kept me emotionally pure and disentangled if I had spent more intimate time in worship and prayer. Wow, was that a revelation!

The Holy Spirit then instructed me to appropriate the fear of the Lord upon my life concerning that relationship. I closed my eyes and imagined myself in the throne room of heaven and gave God all my needs and empty places and asked Him to fill them with His presence and love. Immediately, I sensed a sweet presence of the Lord, and His answering touch permeated my soul.

What happened next took me by surprise. Suddenly, I had a vision of Mike and me dancing together, and a song that was special to me when we first fell in love poured from my memory. . . . "The First Time Ever I Saw Your Face." At that moment, all the first-love emotions I had for Mike poured through my heart. I fell in love with my husband all over again.

Spiritual adultery. It sounds really ugly, doesn't it? Actually, it can happen in other kinds of relationships, too. I have even heard of a Christian leader to whom God spoke that he was in spiritual adultery with the ministry. Things were definitely out of order in his home.

Soul Ties: The Good, the Godly and the Ugly

Another type of bond is a *soul tie*, which also occurs in our emotions. Unlike spiritual adultery, this affects married and unmarried alike, and can be healthy or unhealthy. A soul tie forms between two people who are in some kind of covenantal relationship. A well-known example of a godly soul tie in the Bible is the friendship of David and Jonathan. First Samuel 18:1, 3–4 tells us about their bond:

> Now when he had finished speaking to Saul, the soul of Jonathan was knit to the soul of David, and Jonathan loved him as his own soul. . . . Then Jonathan and David made a covenant, because he loved him as his own soul. And Jonathan took off the robe that was on him and gave it to David, with his armor, even to his sword and his bow and his belt.

According to *Strong's Concordance*, the word *knit* means "to tie or bind."[6] David's and Jonathan's souls were knit together in covenant. This can be a wonderful thing. A dark side can surface, however, that can bind you in an unhealthy relationship, such as the one I had with the other ministry leader. These ties can be quite strong, so it is very important that you not enter lightly into covenant with other people.

Healthy Soul Ties

Healthy, covenantal relationships can be a tremendous strength and blessing. Mike and I, for example, have such relationships with a number of couples. I have mentioned that we learned a lot from Peter and Doris Wagner. In addition, Ed and Ruth Silvoso, Chuck and Pam Pierce, Bob and Susan Beckett, Dutch and Ceci Sheets, Russ and Julie Zylstra, Jim and Becky Hennesy, Hal and Cheryl Sacks—the list can go on and on of people who are like family to us. We have wept, prayed and endured great crises together. They are "until death do us part" relationships, unless the Lord should tell us otherwise.

In addition to David and Jonathan, another instance of a godly soul tie in the Old Testament is that between Ruth and Naomi. In fact, we sing about their covenantal relationship at weddings: "Entreat me *not to leave you*" (Ruth 1:16, emphasis added). Their relationship was quite a healthy one between an older and a younger woman.

Unhealthy Soul Ties

Unhealthy, dysfunctional soul ties are dangerous. Counselors might call them codependent relationships. One way these ties are formed in a negative way is through sex outside of marriage. The Bible tells us that in a sexual union the two become one flesh (see Matthew 19:5; 1 Corinthians 6:16).

I have often counseled people—both married and unmarried—who are plagued by thoughts of former boyfriends or girlfriends with whom they had sexual relationships. These memories might linger even though the individuals have asked for forgiveness for their sins. Married individuals often feel deep guilt because of these betraying thoughts and emotions. You see, they are supernaturally tied to those old relationships. Thank God that His power can break those kinds of ties! Other covenantal relationships that cause hindrances can be traced to former church memberships where people made vows to join the church but never asked to be released from those vows to go to a new place.

How do you break an ungodly soul tie? Well, God might give you a supernatural plan such as He did in the case of my deep emotional tie with the ministry leader, or you can pray one of the following prayers with me:

> *Father God, I now ask forgiveness for the sin of breaking covenant and/or forming an ungodly soul tie outside of marriage. Please forgive me. In Jesus' name, Amen.*

A variation of the prayer is:

> *Father God, I recognize that I have an unhealthy soul tie with ____________. Please set me free today. Free my thoughts and my emotions. I now break any tie that I have had with this person, in Jesus' name, Amen.*

I must admit that being so vulnerable about my personal life is not easy. After counseling many, many people who had problems with spiritual adultery and ungodly soul ties, however, I felt the best way to set you truly free was to open my own heart and share my experience with you. I pray that the truth will set you free. It could save your marriage, or the marriage of someone near you, or help you walk away from a codependent relationship that keeps you from finding all that God has for you.

The Healing Balm

Although these truths I have shared can run on many levels, the deepest wounding in need of the healing balm of the Lord's power in most relationships begins with gender issues. John Dawson says in his book *Healing America's Wounds*, "The wounds inflicted by men and women on each other constitute the fundamental fault line running beneath all other human conflict."[7]

A few years ago, I sat in the audience of an Aglow International conference in Orlando, Florida, while John Dawson was speaking. Toward the end of his session, John simply and humbly made a confession and asked forgiveness of the nearly ten thousand women representing about eighty nations. John asked forgiveness as a male for the multitude of hurts inflicted on these women by men.

How can I describe what happened? A torrent of tears poured out of many, many women. Most of them—some who were victims of incest, physical and/or emotional abuse—had never dreamed they would ever hear such words from a male. As I looked around, I noted women holding each other and weeping. The power of forgiveness was at work on a scale that few in the Body of Christ understand.

A supernatural release of God's love and power came from those simple words. Who could ever have dreamed that John Dawson's words would produce such a profound, deep effect on this gathering of women? John stood in the gap for those wounded women to bring them to a place of release from their emotional prisons.

Several years later, I sat down to read *Healing America's Wounds*, in which John puts his confession into writing, and was touched once again by memories of that moment:

> Dear female reader, I may not be the guy that hurt you, but I look upon your hurt with shame and embarrassment, nonetheless. There have been times when I have had to ask forgiveness of mother, wife, sister and female associate. One woman in particular I would beg for forgiveness if I knew how to contact her. I am no stranger to masculine pride and male appetites. Maybe I haven't committed rape or some other loathsome offense, but it is really just a matter of degree.
>
> Some of you were molested by your father—the ultimate parental betrayal. Some of you experienced other forms of incest and you haven't felt whole since. Most of you know what it's like to be the plaything of a teenage boy, emotionally if not physically, and nearly all of you carry some wound of rejection from a broken teen relationship or a troubled marriage.
>
> You know what it's like to be ogled like a side of beef by someone of greater strength; to be condescended to and joked about in the presence of men. You also know what it is like to be treated tenderly but never taken seriously, your gifts spurned and your advice unheeded.
>
> Please forgive me, forgive us. You were never meant to experience these things. They represent a gross distortion of the part of the character of God that was to be revealed to you through father, brother, husband and male friend. These things broke God's heart along with yours.[8]

Possibly John's confession has deeply touched you. If so, I would encourage you not to move on too quickly with this chapter. Why not stop and forgive any hurt done to you, either by a man or a woman? Women can be controlling and dominating and wound the men they relate to. This gender issue is a two-way street; both have deep sin issues that need to be addressed. The power of the cross is here even through the written Word. You might even call a friend and ask for prayer. James 5:16 says, "Confess your trespasses [faults] to one another, and pray for one another, that you may be healed."

I once spoke at a conference in Brisbane, Australia, with John, when he decided there needed to be repentance between the sexes. We worked on this concept for three days before true confession and repentance fell. At one point a Baptist pastor called the women in the church forward and asked their forgiveness for not releasing them into ministry.

The response was startling. Some of the most reserved, somewhat quiet women fell to their knees and wept almost to the point of wailing. Their pain levels must have been enormous! Later, as I studied the history of Australia, I found out why the women of this country particularly suffer. The first white women who ever came to the shore of this former penal colony were repeatedly gang raped and suffered other unspeakable outrages.

After our visit, Jim Nightingale, Robyn Pebbles and other Australian leaders went to the very place where this atrocity had occurred and reenacted the arrival of the women in the costumes of the day through a prophetic act. The difference was, instead of being horribly abused, the women were received with a godly welcome, and a proclamation of repentance was read to them. I believe that the ax was laid to the root of female abuse that day through a loving, prophetic act.

Vive la Différence!

God has purposes not only for the genders, but also racially *within* the genders. Let me explain. When God created the races, He also placed redemptive purposes or strengths within the females or males of different ethnic groups. As I was pondering this one day, I meditated on the fact that God chose a Jewish woman to raise His Son on the earth.

Although Jewish women are often stereotyped as controlling, smothering females, this is only a perversion of the wonderful gift of nurture that Jewish women have for their children. For those of you who are mothers, or nurturers through teaching Sunday school, I believe there is a great possibility that we can learn from the Jewish culture. (Of course, I realize there are great moms in every culture.)

One of my good friends who is Jewish, Hal Sacks of Bridge Builders Ministries in Phoenix, Arizona, has suggested that Jewish males have special gifts of faithfulness to wives and family, as well as perseverance in the face of great adversity.

Other cultures have an emphasis on hospitality, such as the Italians and Arabs. Italian women in general cannot stand having people come into their homes without feeding them. Italian men seem to me to have a gift of leadership. I have heard of ex-Mafia men who made the best head ushers or administrators for churches. Why? For one, they understand authority.

Much will be gained from the healing of the genders and races. This is really a pioneer area we are just beginning to understand in the Body of Christ. I personally believe that we are much further along in the area of racial reconciliation than gender reconciliation. Conferences in which the people in leadership are quite comfortable dealing with the race issue have not even begun to touch the issue of gender.

While speaking at a large gathering for a women's conference, I received an unusual prophecy from the Lord. It went like this:

> If My Body begins to release gender-to-gender reconciliation and healing, there will be a day when divorce in the Church will be abnormal. For I desire healing between the male and female. My people have bought into a lie that there will always be large numbers of people divorcing. I desire to heal those broken through divorce and those who were victims, but I also desire to break down the walls that have caused relational breakdowns and divorce. Only believe, says the Lord, for all things are possible if you will only believe.

The next several chapters took me quite some time to write as I read stacks of books and pored through many translations of the Bible. I have also been working with some theologians who have been prayerfully studying the Greek and Hebrew concerning the question of women and the Church. Actually, what I have found is quite exciting, and I pray that it will cause a great release of women into many areas of ministry.

EIGHT

The Woman Question

Since the Lord is calling godly women all over the world to *rise up*, to be transformational in their communities and fierce lovers of God, it is important to have a strong theological understanding of their roles. This is foundational. Many professional women have trouble finding their places—not only outside the church but also inside its walls.

God is calling many women in this hour to follow Him and use all their talents, gifts and abilities. Understanding how to do this in a biblical way that pleases the Lord is stressful and confusing to many women.

As I have intimated earlier, I was amazed to read the accounts of women ministers from a century ago whose struggles paralleled those I wrestled with in the early 1980s, when I finally submitted to the call of God. And, amazingly, I still hear these same unresolved issues voiced by young women today.

But, Lord, What Is a Woman to Do?

What are the reasons for trepidation in the hearts of women called by God? Although the reasons vary, the following are the most frequent:

Women in General

1. What about those difficult passages? (Is it true that women should be silent in church?)

2. Is God really calling me?
3. What is He calling me to do?
4. How will saying yes impact my family or relationships?
5. What will my pastor and church think?
6. Am I having grandiose hallucinations in thinking that God wants me to be a woman minister?
7. How do I find the answers to all these questions?

Married Women

1. How should I, as a woman in leadership, relate to my husband?
2. What about the question of "submission"?
3. How will I handle my duties at home if I go into the ministry? (Who will wash the clothes and go to the grocery store?)
4. What will my husband think? Will he be mad, supportive or think I have lost my mind? Have I lost my mind?

Single Women

1. If I accept the call, will the man I fall in love with be happy about it?
2. How will I support myself financially if I go into ministry on a full-time basis?
3. What will people think of a single woman ministering alone?
4. How do I explain the call of God on my life to the people of my local church?

These questions can tend to buzz around and around in your brain until you are brought to a point of desperation and tears. Believe me, I have been there and lived it. Many voices bombard a woman trying to sort out her place, not only in ministry but also in life in general. For the woman sensing a call of God, the decision-making process is greatly compounded by the fear of missing His will for her life, as well as the fear of being labeled unbiblical.

If the woman is raised in a part of the world where women are repressed or oppressed, or the culture frowns upon women doing any kind of work outside the home, a compound fracture often occurs that can cripple her ability to hear the voice of God.

Major prophetic voices are prophesying all around the world that this is the time to find a way to release women into ministry.

Restoring God's Truths about Women

So how do you answer these questions and find God's will for your life? I wish I had all the answers. I can only tell you that I have personally sorted through volumes of resources, met with highly respected theologians and listened intently to the Holy Spirit's leading as I researched this subject.

Of one thing I am certain: *God is calling women today in a greater way than He ever has before.* Major prophetic voices are prophesying all around the world that this is the time to find a way to release women into ministry. Some prophets say: "God is raising up a new generation of women ministers in the anointing of an Esther or a Deborah." Others announce: "Make way for the women, for God is pouring out His end-time anointing on the women."

Dr. Bill Hamon often talks about what he calls "restored truth," or the fact that God emphasizes certain truths at different times down through the ages. Luther's ringing affirmation that "the just shall live by faith" was a restored truth that began the Protestant Reformation; today most Catholics agree that Luther's insight was valid. Part of the role of the prophet is to announce to the Church the truths that God is restoring, or truths that have been neglected. Such is the case with the role of women in the Church.

One Commission for Two Genders

No issue in the Church today is more controversial than the roles of women in ministry. A good friend of mine, who was the editor of a major Christian magazine, said, "Just put *woman* and *minister* in the same sentence, and you won't believe how many angry letters we receive."

One extremely insightful comment came to me from Gary Kinnaman, who pastors the pastors of Arizona. During breakfast with Gary and his wife, Marilyn, one morning, he brought up Galatians 3:28. "Cindy," he said, "the Body of Christ has come a long way in recognizing that there is neither Jew nor Greek, neither slave nor free, but we haven't begun to understand that there is neither male nor female."

I wrote a whole chapter on the gender issue, but I feel I need to write this chapter as the foundational stone upon which I will build the remainder of the book. Many leaders believe, as I have already mentioned, that bringing resolution to the conflict over gender roles in ministry could be likened to the "final frontier" for the Church. Some prophets have even gone so far as to say they believe that in five years many of us will feel as though we were in the Dark Ages concerning women in ministry.

Before she died in 2015, Vonette Bright of Campus Crusade for Christ made the following statement in an address to both men and women at the "Latinoamerica 2000" meeting in Panama, which drew about four thousand delegates: "There are not two commissions—one for men and one for women."

She went on to describe how Bill (her husband), the founder and president of Campus Crusade for Christ (now Cru), always treated her as an equal partner in the ministry. She wanted only to be Mrs. Bill Bright, but he urged her to develop her capacity for leadership. As a result, she was often a peer with men on committees and was one of three women on the original fifty-member Lausanne Committee for World Evangelization, which helps mobilize evangelical leaders. Her views changed through the years as she traveled the world and saw how often women are pushed down. Her voice rang out so that all could hear her warning clearly: "I feel that God may judge some men for limiting women and not allowing them to develop their leadership skills."

Vonette shared evidence of how women's perspectives enhance committee decision-making: A feminine point of view can help balance masculine tunnel vision, which tends to focus on results without consideration for how those results will both help and hurt people.[1]

The Woman Question: Determining Your Position

As I have studied the so-called "difficult passages" about women, I have concluded that the differing interpretations are rather like those relating to end-time eschatology: Throughout the years, I have heard excellent sermons on just about every position—all using Scripture, and all sounding as if they have merit! When this kind of impasse happens, we must arrive at a position through personal study, prayer and seeking God's face.

I have had to work through my own cultural and denominational grids in order to discern what is from the Holy Spirit and what is simply my "own stuff." Here are a couple of my personal filters:

1. How is my cultural or denominational background coloring my beliefs? (I was raised in a Texan and Southern Baptist culture. Regardless of our backgrounds, we all have cultural biases, whether we want to admit them or not.)
2. How is my personal "baggage" causing me to refuse to look at Scripture in a new way? (For example: Am I biased against men or women because of my family of origin, or because of fear of being in error or disloyal to my denomination?)

As I have considered my own background, I have had to ask myself, *Have I ever sincerely studied the opposing view while prayerfully seeking the Lord to give me His heart and mind on the matter rather than simply relying upon what I have been given?*

When God began to deal with me about preaching the Gospel, as I wrote in chapter 1, I had to move from the extreme position that it was unbiblical for women to preach at all, to saying yes to becoming a woman minister.

Many women throughout history and today have brought and are bringing great blessing to the Body of Christ through their teaching ministries, missionary work or pastoring of churches. Jesus said, "By their fruit you will recognize them" (Matthew 7:20 NIV). One of the ways to judge whether or not God is working through a person's ministry is by measuring its fruitfulness and blessing. Women in numerous different ministries teach both men and women and are producing godly, lasting fruit for the Kingdom. Would that be happening if God had not sanctioned their work? Would not their ministries simply be dead and lifeless if God were not anointing them? This question alone should compel us to rethink some of the traditional positions the Church has taken regarding women.

Truth Does Not Change; Beliefs Do

Many times, throughout the years, the Lord touched my life through an experience that went beyond my theological beliefs and caused me to do serious searching in the written Word. I remember when I did not believe that God spoke to His children other than through Scripture. (I had been taught that, since the canon of Scripture is closed, God does not speak anymore as He did in Bible days.) My understanding has so changed that I wrote a whole book about how to hear the voice of God.

My pastor father, who has been with the Lord since 1973, helped me immensely in my spiritual journey. I once asked him, "Dad, what would you do if you found that what you believed wasn't the truth?"

He looked me straight in the eye and replied, "Honey, I'd go where the truth was taught." His answer was very freeing to me. It has allowed me to examine and judge the doctrine I am hearing from the pulpit in light of Scripture. Dad always wanted me to have a *personal* relationship with Jesus Christ rather than a secondhand one, and a *personal* rather than secondhand understanding of truth.

Why have I explained all of this? For this reason: If you are not willing to reexamine your belief system and allow the Holy Spirit to expose any motives that may be causing you to be unfairly biased, this chapter will probably be a waste of your time. Please realize that I do not want to thrust my conclusions upon you, as I am aware that I can be influenced by my own biases. You may read my conclusions and come away with your same belief system. I would like, however, for us, together, to ask the Lord to *help us come to His mind on this*. Before we continue, please pray the following prayer with me:

> *Dear Father, give me eyes to see and ears to hear the truths that might be different from my own thinking. I ask You by the power of Your Holy Spirit within me to help me be open to new understanding. Show me where my culture or religious biases may be affecting my willingness to be open to what the Spirit is saying to the Church today. In Jesus' name, Amen.*

We are about to grapple with the two most controversial issues surrounding women in ministry:

(1) whether or not women can teach men in the Church, and
(2) whether or not in teaching men, women must still be "in submission."

I will discuss more about authority structures in the home in chapter 9 and more about spiritual authority outside the home in chapter 10. *Please bear with me!* These are *extremely* sensitive areas to address. In fact, many of my friends have grinned and said, "Cindy, I'm so glad God hasn't asked me to deal with the woman question." I have prayed that the Lord will help me present the different sides of the issues so that you can pray and find the answers that bring peace within your own heart. I am grateful for the movements and teachers that have emerged since I first was dealing with these Scriptures. Many, such as Bill and Beni Johnson, Ché and Sue Ahn, John and Carol Arnott, John and Brenda Kilpatrick, and others, have come such a long way in their release of women in leadership that this subject is rather a nonissue. Believe me, however, that there are many churches and denominations where it is still a very big deal.

Formulating Your Bias for Interpretation

While researching this subject, I was given a paper titled "Gender and Leadership" by Dr. J. Robert Clinton, professor at Fuller Theological Seminary. This paper reveals Dr. Clinton's own journey concerning women in leadership, one that led to his paradigm shift (i.e., a change from one model of explanation to another) concerning women in ministry. His shift came partly as a result of receiving a personal blessing from the Lord through the ministry of women leaders.

In this insightful paper, Clinton states the six axioms (i.e., established rules or principles of self-evident truth) he has learned throughout his years of Bible study. These axioms, he points out, form part of his framework for doing biblical interpretation. They include the injunction to "Interpret unclear passages in the light of clear ones—not the other way around" and the realization that "Controversial passages lacking consensus from godly people of different persuasions usually mean that the passages are not clear enough to resolve with certainty. Therefore, we must be tolerant on different views on those passages."[2]

Adding to Clinton's points, several facts are clear to me from Scripture:

- God used women to further the spread of the Gospel.
- Women were used by God in leadership positions in both the Old and New Testaments.
- God chose women as leaders in the Old Testament, which put them in roles that affected the whole nation of Israel (such as Deborah, Esther and Miriam). In the New Testament, we could liken this choosing to that of leadership in the Church if we think

of ourselves as "Jews inwardly" (see Romans 2:28–29); "the Israel of God" (see Galatians 6:11–16); and a "chosen," "royal" and "holy nation" (see 1 Peter 2:9–16; cf. Deuteronomy 7:6). There is never any indication in Scripture that using women in leadership will "pass away" in New Testament times.

- Both the Old and New Testaments tell us that God is going to pour out His Spirit upon His handmaidens as well as the servants (see Joel 2:28–29; Acts 2:17).

Deborah and Esther: Called to Save Their Nations

Now, I realize that a segment of the Body of Christ will disagree with me over women having a place of leadership in the Church; however, an even larger segment will agree. Using Deborah and Esther as examples, we see that these two women leaders were given high governmental positions that affected the entire nation (by God's choosing, of course, but would we want it any other way?). Deborah *ruled* the nation as the senior judge of all the judges (see Judges 4:4–5; cf. Deuteronomy 16:18–20; 17:9–12). She was the top authority. She instructed and prophesied, and commanded Barak to go to war (see Judges 4:6–7). There is even a hint of rebuke when she said the honor would be given to a woman, not to Barak, for the victory (see Judges 4:9). Some people today would accuse Deborah of being totally out of her place by instructing a man. Perhaps she would even be branded a Jezebel!

Esther called a whole nation to a solemn assembly to fast and pray to save God's people (see Esther 4:16). I have heard it said that this is "only one exception." Calling Esther's action "only one exception," however, reflects a bias against women. Why not say that it "set a precedent"?

Are we not all "exceptions" in one way or another by the grace and calling of God? I certainly believe that I am, because I see my own weaknesses and frailties, oftentimes like neon signs flashing before my eyes.

A Closer Look at the Roles of Women

Dr. A. J. Gordon, founder of Gordon College and Seminary, was a Baptist pastor in the 1880s and '90s who advocated for women in ministry. He was a historical mentor for Robert Clinton, whom I mentioned above. I was fascinated to study Dr. Gordon's article on "The Ministry of Women" written in December 1894. (This article is reprinted in Appendix A.) It is so relevant to today that I was amazed it could have been written such a long time ago. One of the reasons this paper is so important (as pointed out by Clinton) is that Gordon's arguments cannot be disqualified because he was biased by the women's liberation movement. On the contrary, Dr. Gordon's arguments are firmly grounded in Scripture and guided by the same interpretational principles that traditionalists use.

Let's take a look at some ways that women were used of God in Scripture. I am aware that in this area disputes may arise; what is clear to me may not be clear to you. (Do you remember that prayer we prayed earlier? Even if something makes you angry, read to the end and then prayerfully seek God about it.)

We will discuss in chapters 10 and 12 the view that Jesus had of women in general and how He elevated the societal status of women. Now we examine the ministry of women in the New Testament and the early Church to help lay a foundation for moving from those passages that are clear (or more clear) to those passages that are unclear.

Deacons

According to various translations of Romans 16:1, Phoebe is classified as a "servant" or "minister"[3] of the church at Cenchrea. The word used to describe her, *diakonos*, is in a masculine form. I found a number of different explanations regarding her office. The 1894 article by Dr. Gordon that I mentioned earlier is particularly enlightening:

> The same word, *diakonos*, here translated "servant," is rendered "minister" when applied to Paul and Apollos (1 Cor. 3:5), and "deacon"

> when used of other male officers of the Church (1 Tim. 3:10, 12, 13). Why discriminate against Phoebe simply because she is a woman? The word "servant" is correct for the general unofficial use of the term, as in Matt. 22:[10]; but if Phoebe were really a functionary of the Church, as we have a right to conclude, let her have the honor to which she is entitled. If "Phoebe, a minister of the church at Cenchrea," sounds too bold, let the word be transliterated, and read, "Phoebe, a deacon"—a *deacon*, too, without the insipid termination "ess," of which there is no more need than that we should say "teacheress" or "doctress." This emendation "deaconess" has timidly crept into the margin of the Revised Version, thus adding prejudice to slight by the association which this name has with High Church sisterhoods and orders. It is wonderful how much there is in a name! "Phoebe, a *servant*," might suggest to an ordinary reader nothing more than the modern church drudge, who prepares sandwiches and coffee for an ecclesiastical sociable. To Canon Garratt, with his genial and enlightened view of woman's position in apostolic times, "Phoebe, a deacon," suggests a useful co-laborer of Paul, "travelling about on missionary and other labors of love."[4]

We noted above that the ending of the word *diakonos* when it describes Phoebe's office is masculine. Yet, Phoebe is clearly a female. It seems that there are occasions in Scripture where the "offices" in the Church are given male endings, even though the person filling the office may be a woman!

Charles Trombley provides insight concerning what Romans 16:2 says about Phoebe:

> Paul uses an interesting word concerning Phoebe in Romans 16:2. The *King James Version* used the word *succourer* in this verse, but the word *prostatis* isn't translated that way anywhere else in the Greek Scriptures. It was a common, classical word meaning "patroness or protectorship, a woman set over others." It's the feminine form of the masculine noun *prostates*, which means "defender" or "guardian" when it refers to men. In 1 Timothy 3:4–5,12 and 5:17, the verb *peritoneum* is used of the qualifications for bishops and deacons when Paul charged the men to "rule"

> well their households, which included caring for their needs. Whatever it means for men, it must mean the same for women. Whatever these bishops and deacons did for their households, Phoebe did for the Church and Paul. The positions were identical.
>
> If we refuse to admit that Phoebe "ruled" or "led" or was a "defender" or "guardian," then we must reduce the male deacons to whatever level Phoebe was ministering. If Phoebe just *succored*, then that's all the male deacons did. It's quite inconsistent to translate the word as "ruler" when it refers to men and *succourer* when it refers to women.[5]

Another place where the role of women as deacons has apparently been minimized is in the English translation of *gunaikas* ("women" or "wives") in 1 Timothy 3:11. Paul has just outlined the requirements for bishops and deacons (see verses 8–10). Many translators have assumed that "likewise, *gunaikas*" in 1 Timothy 3:11 could refer only to wives of the male leaders; to support their translation, they added the word *their* to the text. In 1 Timothy 3:11, however, there is no definite article in the sentence construction, nor are possessives used. Furthermore, identical language is used for both the deacons and the women who "likewise" must be "grave" (see verses 8, 11). This means, therefore, that the translation "their wives" must be rejected. Paul is clearly referring to women in important leadership positions.

Clearly, Paul held Phoebe and other female fellow-workers in high esteem. In fact, of the 29 people Paul greets in Romans 16, ten are women (if we count Junia, which I do).[6]

Another source for the importance of women in leadership in the early Church is from the testimony of a governor of Bithynia, called Pliny the Younger (AD 52–113). He also indicates that women were deacons in the early Church. In a letter seeking advice regarding how to handle the large numbers of all classes from both sexes turning to Christ, Pliny states:

> I thought it the more necessary to inquire into the real truth of the matter by subjecting to torture two female slaves who were called *deacons*, but

> I found nothing more than a perverse superstition which went beyond all bounds.[7]
>
> (emphasis added)

Even though women were recognized as leaders in the first-century Church, during the second century, women's positions in leadership began to fade. An early third-century writing called the *Didascalia* (teaching) said that persons being baptized came up from the water and were received and taught by the women deacons, so such women were still teaching during the third century. By the time the Council of Orange convened in 441, however, the office of women deacons had been almost completely abolished. The Council directed, "Let no one proceed to the ordination of deaconesses anymore."[8]

I often wonder about the adding of the "*ess*"—the ministry terms that we use to describe a woman's function in the Church. Often it applies a standing less than that of a man who is doing the same job. In fact, historically, when the change was made from *deacon* to *deaconess*, that is exactly what happened.

It is great to note that there are an increasing number of women deacons being appointed, both in evangelical and charismatic churches.

Elders

Traditionalists who argue that the biblical apostles were men, exclusively, also claim that the elders were always male. From the book of Hebrews, however, we see that sometimes the term *elder* included women. In Hebrews 11:2 we read: "This [faith] is what the ancients were commended for" (NIV). The word *ancients* comes from the Greek word *presbuteroi* (plural of *presbuteros*) and has traditionally been translated into English by the terms *elders* (KJV, NKJV) and *men of old* (RSV, NASB). Yet among these elders mentioned, we find Sarah (see verses 11, 13); Moses' mother (see verse 23); the women among "the people" who crossed the Red Sea (see verse 29); Rahab (see verse 31); possibly Deborah, one of the judges who "administered justice" (see verse 33);

possibly Esther "whose weakness was turned to strength" and saved her people from destruction by foreign armies (see verse 34); and possibly the woman of Zarephath (see 1 Kings 17:7–24) and the Shunammite woman (see 2 Kings 4:8–36) who received back their dead, raised to life again (see verse 35).

In addition, the line "others were tortured and refused to be released, so that they might gain a better resurrection" in Hebrews 11:35 (NIV 1984) strongly reminds us of the mother of the seven brothers martyred by Antiochus Epiphanes during the Maccabean rebellion (see 2 Maccabees 7). This woman urged her sons to be courageous in light of the resurrection to come, and, ultimately, she herself was martyred.

These elders are the same ones who surround us as the "great cloud of witnesses" in Hebrews 12:1 (NIV). Clearly, in biblical usage the term *elder* does not exclude women.

In fact, because the Old Testament was the Bible for the New Testament Church and, thus, precedent setting, it certainly would not have seemed unusual for women to hold responsible positions of eldership alongside Moses' mother and Rahab and Deborah.

We also find the feminine form of *presbyter* or *elder*—*presbytera*—occurring in nonbiblical early Christian literature. The word is often translated simply as "old woman"; however, at times the term refers to women who were part of the clergy. Basil the Great (AD 330–379), for example, bishop of Caesarea and one of the Cappadocian fathers, uses *presbytera* for a woman who is head of a religious community. Also applied to women is the term *presbutis*, "older woman" or "eldress." This usage of the word for *eldress* appears in Titus 2:3 and is often translated here as "older woman."

Apostles

A troublesome passage that often limits women's ministry in the Church is 1 Timothy 3:1: "This is a faithful saying: If a man desires the position of a bishop, he desires a good work." At first reading, it would seem clear that a woman cannot be a bishop because the text reads, "If a man . . ." In fact, Christian tradition has leaned heavily in the direction of male bishops throughout history. The word translated "man," however, is actually the Greek word *tis*, a gender-neutral pronoun meaning "anybody" or "anyone." Thus this verse should read: "If anybody or anyone desires the office of a bishop . . ." This seems to leave room for women.

Archaeological evidence supports the position of women in high positions of leadership in the early Church. According to the late Dr. Catherine Clark Kroeger, fresco work in the Priscilla catacomb in Rome shows one of the many *orant* (praying) women depicted in the catacombs as having an amazingly authoritative stance, such as that of a bishop. The shepherds on either side may represent pastors, in which case the woman could be in the role of bishop, blessing pastors in her charge.[9]

Still, for some, the thought of a woman ever being included among the highest levels of authority in the Church—including the fivefold ministry offices named in Ephesians 4:11—is simply too big a stretch. Let's look at a woman who many believe held the office of apostle, and then see if, experientially, we can conclude that God is anointing women to do the work of apostles in more recent times.

As I have noted, many traditionalists voice the opinion that Jesus would have chosen a woman in the original Twelve if He had wanted to establish women as apostles. Here is Trombley's answer to this objection: "Christ ministered primarily to the house of Israel (see Matthew 15:24). He preached to Jews who were governed by both civil and religious matters."[10]

Although the original Twelve were male, we need to keep in mind that Jesus took the radical step of having female disciples. And even if the early women disciples were not explicitly called apostles, this does not mean they were not exercising authority in the early Church. Many leaders in the early Church—both men and women—were unnamed.

I like the statement David Cannistraci begins with in the section of his book *The Gift of Apostle*, titled "Can Women Be Apostles?" He says:

> This is a truly complicated question, but as Gilbert Bilezikian has pointed out, "Every generation of Christians needs to examine its beliefs and practices under the microscope of Scripture to identify and purge away those worldly accretions that easily beset us, and to protect jealously the freedom dearly acquired for us—both men and women—on the hill of Calvary."[11]

There are times when we have to look around and say, "If God is possibly using women in powerful ways in the Church, maybe we need to reevaluate our thinking, *for they are either tools of the devil or blessed by God* to fulfill a place that we didn't think they could fulfill."

I discussed this with a theologian friend who stressed the point that people sometimes have imperfect motives, but God blesses their efforts anyway, such as when Moses struck the rock (see Numbers 20:10–12). We must ask, though: Just because a woman feels called to minister, does that mean she is doing so out of impure motives? The ones I know certainly are not. They feel a genuine call to preach, and they display the character and nature of Christ in their motivation.

In the passage in Romans we looked at earlier, Paul mentions Junia and Andronicus together as being "of note among the apostles" (Romans 16:7). There is much controversy as to whether the gender of the name in Scripture is the female *Junia* or the male *Junias*.[12] The reasons I believe Junia was a woman are: (1) Andronicus and Junia were likely a married couple. (If Junia is female, the pairing of her name with a masculine name recalls the only other pairing of female and male names, Priscilla and Aquila in Romans 16, whom we know to have been married [see Acts 18:1–2]); and (2) early Church father John Chrysostom praises Junia, the woman apostle.

Trombley summarizes:

> John Chrysostom (337–407), bishop of Constantinople, [said this] about Junia. "Oh, how great is the devotion of this woman that she should be counted worthy of the appellation of apostle!" Nor was he the only church father to believe Junia was a woman. Origen of Alexandria (c.

> 185–253) said the name was a variant of Julia (see Rom. 16:15), as does *Thayer's Lexicon.* Leonard Swidler cited Jerome (342–420), Hatto of Vercelli (924–961), Theophylack (1050–1108), and Peter Abelard (1079–1142) as believing Junia to be a woman.[13]

This passage is fascinating indeed. It includes three prominent early Church fathers, *Thayer's Lexicon* and three medieval theologians who all agree with the premise that Junia was a woman. Surely we have accepted other stances in Scripture to be true with much less supportive historical evidence than this one! Then why the struggle? For one, because the office of apostle is believed to be the highest spiritual authority of those listed in Ephesians 4:11. If Junia was a woman, then the entire theology barring women from holding leadership roles in the Church would have to be changed. The paradigm shift would be massive.

Incidentally, some of my friends and I have a saying about our spiritual journey in the last few years. It goes like this: We have made so many fast paradigm shifts that it has stripped our gears five times! Probably our brakes, too! We are, however, quite recovered as of this writing. Who knows how many more paradigm shifts we might make if the Lord tarries?

So we see the question about whether or not Junia was a woman, although vigorously debated, is part and parcel of the bigger controversy in the Body of Christ about the roles of women in the Church and home. The Church is in a major transitional time in our thinking on this subject, and we are all in process and doing the best we can before God to state our beliefs.

I discovered a fascinating tidbit of information in the book *Woman in the Bible* by Mary J. Evans concerning the English translation of Chrysostom's *The Homilies of Saint John Chrysostom*:

> It is interesting that in spite of Chrysostom's clear statement, the editors of the English translation of his works felt bound to add a footnote pointing out that Chrysostom must have been wrong on one of the two points for "it is out of the question" for a woman to have been an apostle![14]

In order to apply the title of apostleship to modern-day leaders, it is important to examine the criteria for apostleship. David Cannistraci gives the following seven demands that define apostles:

1. Apostles are required to have a definite and personal call from God in their lives.
2. Apostles are required to have a special intimacy and acquaintance with Jesus Christ. In 1 Corinthians 9:1, Paul qualifies himself as an apostle by citing his contact with Christ: "Am I not an apostle? Am I not free? Have I not seen Jesus Christ our Lord?" Clearly, personal acquaintance with Christ was considered a requirement for apostleship among the Twelve (see Acts 1:21–25). Although today's apostles are of a different category, we can be sure that intimate knowledge of Christ is vital for fruitfulness in apostolic ministry (see John 15:4–5).
3. Apostles are elders and must meet the biblical qualifications of an elder.
4. Apostles are ministers and must function as such. The work of a valid apostle will always be in the areas of equipping, training and leading others into mature ministry.
5. Apostles are required to have the recognition and confirmation of peers.
6. Apostles must have specific fruit to which they can point to demonstrate their apostleship.
7. Apostles must maintain their apostleship by complete submission to Christ, or they will fall from apostleship and lose their office as did Judas (see Acts 1:25).

Cannistraci ends this section by giving the following definition of *apostleship*:

> An apostle is a person who is called and sent by Christ and has the spiritual authority, character, gifts and abilities to successfully reach and

establish people in Kingdom truth and order, especially by founding and overseeing local churches.[15]

Cannistraci is a "New Apostolic Reformation" leader, to use a term coined by Peter Wagner. The New Apostolic Reformation movement consists of churches that are not affiliated with a certain denomination, but rather have relational covenants with other churches of like beliefs. We are still learning about the role of the apostle in the Church today. In general, the New Apostolic churches are in consensus that someone who holds the office of bishop in the Church is also an apostle. Not all apostles, however, are bishops. Bishops generally have more than one church under their leadership.

Today, apostles are beginning to be recognized in such areas as prayer, worship networks, evangelism and so on, which interface with the local churches. Their work affects a much broader base than, for instance, one particular denomination.

Let's consider some women who have greatly affected the face of the Church in apostolic roles.

Aimee Semple McPherson (1890–1944)

In the light of our study, I propose that Aimee Semple McPherson, founder of the Foursquare Church, was an apostle. Although traditionalists might object on the grounds that she had no apparent "male covering," history records that God did a work through her that affected her generation and generations after. The doctrine of the Foursquare Gospel that she proposed is embraced by thousands of people around the world.

Catherine Booth (1829–1890)

I believe that Catherine Booth, who, along with her husband, William, founded The Salvation Army, was also an apostle. Indeed, when her husband had to stop his work due to a complete breakdown in health, Catherine took charge of the entire ministry.

As one biographer notes: "It was she, and not William Booth, who laid the first stone of the Salvation Army." Though Salvation Army letterheads and news stories today declare "William Booth, Founder," the title of her biography is more accurate: *Catherine Booth, the Mother of the Salvation Army*. Before her death in 1890, she had preached to millions.[16]

Henrietta Mears (1890–1963)

There are other women who would not have thought themselves to be apostles to the Church, but who, to my thinking, fit the definition given earlier. One of these is Henrietta Mears. Miss Mears was the founder of Gospel Light Publishing Company. (By the way, Regal Books, which was created under Gospel Light, published the first edition of this book.)

Some of Miss Mears's most outstanding accomplishments occurred during the time she was director of religious education at First Presbyterian Church in Hollywood, California. Within three years of her arrival, she had built a dynamic Christian education program with a Sunday school enrollment rising from a quite respectable Presbyterian 450 to an absolutely awesome 4,500; it was the talk of the West Coast. In the class she taught for college students, weekly attendance ran to 500 young men and women who were devoted to "Teacher," as she was called. Her enthusiasm for the Lord Jesus Christ was contagious.[17]

Miss Mears had a profound impact on the Reverend Billy Graham when he was a speaker at the Forest Home camp she founded. At the time, Mr. Graham was a thirty-year-old college president who was having deep personal struggles over the inerrancy of Scripture (i.e., that the Bible is without error, being written under the inspiration of the Holy Spirit). Miss Mears talked personally with Graham and prayed with him until he experienced a tremendous breakthrough in faith concerning God's Word.

Graham gives insight into her quick wit, humor and transparency in his book *Just As I Am*. He shares how he invited her on a moment's notice to a very fancy dinner held in his honor in England. She accepted. When he and his wife, Ruth, went to greet her, they both commented on how lovely she looked. In his own words, "She smiled and pulled us closer. 'I didn't have a formal thing in my suitcase and had no time to shop,' she whispered. 'I'm wearing my nightgown!'"[18] Miss Mears was not at all "religious." She was as real as can be and displayed genuineness in her personhood that few have reached.

I wrote in *The Voice of God* how Henrietta Mears's biography has affected my own life. She led both Bill and Vonette Bright to the Lord. The couple lived with Miss Mears for ten years of their married life. Bill Bright said, "Her life was one of spiritual multiplication."

Former chaplain to the United States Senate, Dr. Richard C. Halverson had the following to say about this great saint of God:

> In my mind, Henrietta Mears was the giant of Christian education, not only in her generation, but in this century. She was an extraordinary combination of intellect, devotion and spirituality; an administrative genius, a motivator, an encourager and a leader.
>
> I thought of Henrietta Mears as *a female apostle Paul*; in fact, I often referred to her as the "Epistle Paul." There is simply no way to exaggerate her effectiveness as a teacher, communicator and inspirer.
>
> In a very real sense Miss Mears is responsible for my family. Not only had she been counselor to Doris and me through the years, but she introduced us in her office. I understand that she predicted the introduction would turn out the way it did. There is not an area of my life that her influence has not touched with great significance. Philippians 1:3 expresses my sentiments perfectly concerning her.[19]
>
> (emphasis added)

While I believe Miss Mears to have fulfilled the work of an apostle, she also exemplifies that of a teacher, so her name could be placed in the next section as well.

Teachers

As far as I can find, the most powerful example of someone teaching another person the way of Christ is that of Priscilla. I cannot find a better model. We are told that Priscilla, along with her husband, Aquila, taught the great orator Apollos "more accurately" (Acts 18:26), and in spite of Paul's words in 1 Timothy 2:12, "I do not permit a woman to teach," there is no indication that this was in any way condemned either by Luke, the author of Acts, or by Paul.

Some fascinating issues swirl around Priscilla and Aquila. When Paul first met this couple, Luke recorded the meeting by stating Aquila's name first, and then Priscilla's (see Acts 18:2). By Acts 18:18, however, the order was reversed. Why? It was customary in Paul's days to give the more prominent name first.

Ben Witherington III says:

> We can now discuss Priscilla's part in these matters. It is stated that both she and Aquila instructed Apollos and that her name is mentioned first, so that if anyone is indicated by Luke as the primary instructor, it is Priscilla. By "more accurately" (see Luke 18:26, RSV), Luke depicts Priscilla as expanding the matter further than basic Christian teaching, or at least in a way that involves the whole panorama of Christian teaching, so that the piece of the part would be seen in relation to the whole. Apollos is depicted as already having a correct framework and knowledge about "the things concerning Jesus." Further, Apollos is not just any convert to the faith, but a man "well versed in Scripture" and this presupposes that Luke wants his audience to see that Priscilla and Aquila were also knowledgeable enough about Scripture to teach Apollos in such a fashion that he would accept it from both a woman and a man.[20]

Chrysostom said of Luke's naming Priscilla first: "He did not do so without reason: the wife must have had, I think, greater piety than her husband. This is not simply conjecture; its confirmation is evident in the Acts."[21]

Note that the King James Version as well as the New King James Version *reverse* the names in their translations of Acts 18:26 from the Greek. According to Dr. Bruce Metzger, eminent scholar of New Testament textual criticism, this is only one of the places where there is a blatant tampering with the original text by scribes with a bias against women.[22] Almost every other version of the Bible translates this verse following the literal order.

Let me mention here that another place where a clear mistranslation concerning women appears, because of cultural bias, is Psalm 68:11. The NASB and a number of other versions translate it accurately: "The Lord gives the command; the *women* who proclaim the good tidings are a great host" (emphasis added). Both the KJV and the NKJV leave out the word *women*: "The Lord gave the word; great was the company of those who proclaimed it" (NKJV).

Why was this done? Any reputable translator would know that the Hebrew is referring to women because it uses the feminine gender. If one puts the translation of the King James Version in its AD 1611 context, it is not too hard to figure out. The translators simply could not believe that women could publish the Good News, so they "doctored" the passage according to their paradigm or worldview.

Priscilla and Aquila must have left Paul at some point and established a church in their home, because 1 Corinthians 16:19 says, "The churches of Asia greet you. Aquila and Priscilla greet you heartily in the Lord, with the church that is in their house."

Note that in this passage, Aquila's name is mentioned first. It is quite possible that he had a higher anointing to lead a local house church than she did, and her gift was used more in teaching, or perhaps even in a traveling ministry.

Katharine Bushnell (1856–1946), a medical doctor, missionary to China and advocate for women's rights, offers in her book *God's Word to Women*[23] a suggestion in this regard for the wording of 1 Corinthians 9:1–5, in which Paul addresses certain critics. She notes that Paul is responding to those who not only dispute his right to be called an apostle (see verse 1), but who also criticize him because he travels in the company of women. He answers their objections in this manner: "Have we not power to lead about a sister, a wife, as well as other apostles, and as the brethren of the Lord, and Cephas?" (verse 5 KJV).

It is interesting that the KJV uses the word *sister*. The NKJV and the NASB translate the word as "believing wife." Bushnell believes that the "sister" in this passage is Priscilla, who is traveling with Paul along with her husband, Aquila. If you recall the worldview the Jews held about women, you can imagine how distasteful it would have been to the Judaizers (those who wanted to put Christianity under the legal system of the Law) for a woman disciple to be in Paul's company and how they would have expressed their objections.

I hope that the example of Priscilla and Aquila (or Aquila and Priscilla, depending on whether they were in the local house church or traveling) working together as team ministers is going to be the norm one day rather than the exception.

Who in modern times is fulfilling the role of a Priscilla? For one, her namesake Priscilla Shirer. She is a powerful motivational speaker, her books and life have changed thousands, and she has touched millions through her film debut in *The War Room*. I am thankful for this beautiful woman and her role not only as a teacher but also as one who releases the power of intercessory prayer on a worldwide scale.

Pastors

As I began to meditate on the topic of women pastors, it occurred to me that it might be interesting to find out who the *men* pastors were in the Bible.[24] I decided to call a few friends who have seminary degrees and pose the question. After I asked the question the first time, silence fell for a moment on the other end of the line, and then, "Well, I don't know. Was Timothy a pastor?" Actually, no. He was an apostolic legate. Timothy represented the apostle Paul and did apostolic work himself, appointing elders and establishing church order in Ephesus and Asia Minor.[25]

It is amazing how many people are pastors but, for the most part, have just learned about pastoring from mentors or seminaries without thinking about what was probably going on during New Testament days.

This really started me thinking: *Who were the New Testament pastors? How did they function? How were they structured?* Although this book is not meant to go into these issues in depth, it is pertinent to our study to address them.

The churches during this time period were house churches. The basic social and economic unit at the time of the early Church was the *oikos* (Greek for "house" or "household") or extended family, which consisted of husband, wife, children of that marriage, grandparents or other relatives, apprentices and artisans connected to the economic basis of the house, and servants with their spouses, children or relatives.

Obviously the *oikos* was very different from what we consider to be a nuclear family: husband, wife and children from that marriage. The lives of the people in an *oikos* were connected in many ways; they saw each other every day and knew each other well. The early Church spread like wildfire "from house to house" (Acts 2:46; see also 5:42; 20:20). If the head of the household believed and got baptized, often so would the whole household, as in the cases of Cornelius (see Acts 10:1–2, 25–27, 44–48), the Philippian jailer (see Acts 16:30–34) and Crispus, the synagogue ruler (see Acts 18:8). Sometimes, as appears to be the case with Lydia, the head of the household was a woman (see Acts 16:13–15).

Peter Wagner says the following in his commentary on the book of Acts:

> It is easy for us in the twentieth century to forget that no such things as church buildings, as we now know them, existed in the Early Church. Bradley Blues says, "The gathering of Christian believers in private homes (or homes renovated for the purpose of Christian gatherings) continued to be the norm until the early decades of the fourth century when Constantine began erecting the first Christian basilicas."[26]

Mary J. Evans has the following to say about New Testament pastors in her book *Woman in the Bible*:

> In dealing with the subject of pastors in the Bible, it is important to note that we have, in fact, very little information about the precise relation between "office" and "function" in the New Testament Church. The

> Pastoral Epistles make explicit what is apparent elsewhere, that there were those who were appointed to a specific office. However, while we learn much about the characteristics required in those who aspire to office, we are told very little about the particular responsibilities and tasks assigned to the holder of any individual office. For example, some, but not all, elders labored in preaching and teaching (1 Tim. 5:17) and certainly not all preachers and teachers were elders (cf. Col. 3:16; 1 Cor. 14:26, etc.). There is no clear distinction made between regulated offices and unregulated ministry by those with no official position in the New Testament.[27]

Dr. Gary Greig, former associate professor of Old Testament at Regent University School of Divinity, makes this interesting point:

> As far as I can see from studying and praying through the evidence in the New Testament and from the popular and scholarship books and articles on the topic, the Early Church "elders" were like senior pastors or bishops, and the "deacons" like associate ministers.[28]

We might surmise, therefore, that, among others, male "deacon" ministers would include Stephen, Philip, Prochorus, Nicanor, Timon, Parmenus and Nicolaus (see Acts 6:5), and the most evident female "deacon" ministers would have been Phoebe and possibly Priscilla and Lydia.[29]

Thus, the "caregivers" of the Church, or those to whom we might attribute a pastoral function, could very well have been the presiding elders of the local house churches. No men or women are actually referred to as pastors per se in the Bible; however, they functioned as shepherds or pastors.[30]

The strong possibility that the "elect lady" of 2 John 1 is, in fact, the gatekeeper of orthodoxy for a house church means that we cannot be absolute in our assumption that women never held these kinds of leadership positions. That John, the "elder," is writing to the "elect lady" who led a house church is supported by the fact that John did not write to the male elders or leaders of that house church, but to her. As the person responsible for orthodoxy in her house church, she would have been responsible for at least some teaching and exercising of authority in the Church. It is unlikely that the "elect lady" was merely a woman with a big family, because *children* is a common New Testament term for *disciple*, especially in John's writings.[31]

Peter Wagner has some excellent points about the gift of pastor in his book *Your Spiritual Gifts Can Help Your Church Grow*. Although he is not arguing pro or con for the ordination of women in the book, he believes that the gift of pastor is not exclusively for men. He says:

> I believe that the gift of pastor is given to both men and women. My lifetime observation of churches in many cultures leads me to believe that this is usually another of the gender-biased gifts. More women, I think, have the gift of pastor than men do. Take as a starter, Yonggi Cho's Yoido Full Gospel Church in Seoul, Korea. It is the largest local church in the world and has more than 700,000 members. Women perform more than 80 percent of the pastoral work in the church.[32]

Dr. Cho often tells how he was not able to mobilize workers for his cell ministry, and the Lord spoke to him to go to the women—they would do the work. When he did not see the breakthrough in Japan that he desired, he sent a woman pastor to establish the church. God blessed her work tremendously, and a powerful church was raised up under her ministry.

This brings me to an observation I have made about the spread of the Gospel in the book of Acts. A great possibility exists that Paul placed women over many of the house churches, just as Cho did, because he knew they would get the job accomplished. He could rely on them. (I am not saying that men cannot be relied upon, but the female gender does have a more natural nurturing disposition that lends itself to hospitality as well as discipleship. This

Even when they are not naturally suited to be leaders, the Holy Spirit will sometimes use those who may not seem as gifted but are more willing.

combination works well in the establishment of house churches.) Even when they are not naturally suited to be leaders, the Holy Spirit will sometimes use those who may not seem as gifted but are more willing. After all, it is His anointing that works in and through us to accomplish His purposes.

Given the social standing of heads of households, we can reasonably assume that often the "presiding elder" (a modern name some churches give their senior pastors) of a house church was also the head of the household where the church met. Lydia and Mary, the mother of John Mark, and others, very possibly functioned as presiding elders (or at least deacons) of the churches in their houses. In fact, if this is so, most of the house churches listed in Scripture were "pastored" by women! It is quite probable that some of the leaders of these house churches began as deacons and progressed to become presiding "elder-like" figures. Either way, it is highly likely there would have been women at the "Pastors and Elders Seminar" held by Paul, as mentioned in Acts 20:16–17.

Evangelists

Women were also evangelists in the Scriptures. Consider how the Samaritan woman in John 4:28–42 went back to her village to proclaim, "Come, see a man who told me everything I ever did. Isn't this the Messiah?"

This same woman encouraged people to go meet Jesus:

> And many of the Samaritans of that city believed in Him because of the word of the woman who testified, "He told me all that I ever did." So when the Samaritans had come to Him, they urged Him to stay with them; and He stayed there two days. And many more believed because of His own word.
>
> verses 39–41

One could also say that Mary Magdalene and another Mary were evangelists, as they were the first ones commissioned to tell about Christ's resurrection (see Matthew 28:5–7).

Prophets

A number of women prophets are named in Scripture. Some verses are not clear as to whether or not the individual stood in the office of the prophet. (Note: Peter Wagner told me that he did not believe we should call a woman a *prophetess* and a man a *prophet*. He referred to the point that a woman pastor is not called a *pastorette*. We should, therefore, use the term *woman prophet* when writing and simply call a female a *prophet* when introducing her.)

Deborah ruled Israel as both prophet and judge (see Judges 4–5). Miriam was a prophet of music and dancing (see Exodus 15:20–21). Huldah is mentioned in the Old Testament twice (see 2 Kings 22:14–20; 2 Chronicles 34:22–28). She was sought after by King Josiah himself. Huldah and Jeremiah are thought to be relatives. Isaiah's wife was a prophet (see Isaiah 8:3). (That must have been some marriage! Two prophets in one family!)

According to Jewish tradition, there were 48 men prophets in the Hebrew Bible and seven women prophets. The women were Sarah, Hannah, Miriam, Abigail, Deborah, Huldah and Esther.[33]

Women in the New Testament are cited, like Anna in the Temple (who was probably more than a hundred years old). Also, Philip had four daughters who prophesied (see Acts 21:8–9).

There are numbers of modern-day women prophets such as Jane Hamon and Barbara Yoder.

The Call to Couples

The Body of Christ is fortunate to have had leaders such as Dr. Bill Hamon and Dr. C. Peter Wagner who knew that teams working together are a wave of the future. We see the value of partnership in the apostle/prophet teaming that is growing within the Church. We also see this particular partnership in marriages. Of course, not every married couple will function in this manner. There are all kinds of different gift-mixes possible in a marriage. But, whatever the gifting, if couples want to be ordained as a team, I believe it is wonderful!

Dr. Hamon writes about what he foresees as restoration coming to the Body of Christ through couples teaming in ministry:

> Immediately after the birth of the Prophetic Movement a multitude of prophets began prophesying in the nations. As a result the Berlin wall was torn down, the Iron Curtain ripped apart and the mountain of Communism was leveled. Many dictators throughout the world were dethroned. While God was shaking the dictatorial "one man rule" in the nations, He was also working in the Church. The day of the "one great man" ministry started coming to an end. God began to emphasize the "*team ministry*" principle as never before since the first-century church. The apostle-prophet teams were restored. The husband and wife teams were activated so that the wife, instead of just serving as a helper to her husband, became a co-laboring minister. We at Christian International Network of Churches ordain the husband and wife equally. If one of the mates does not know his or her calling, then we believe for it to be made known in the prophetic presbytery that we give with each ordination. *This is the day and hour when God is bringing forth His women to be the ministers that God ordained them to be. Husband-and-wife teams are one of the highest orders of team ministries.* The activation of "team ministry" is definitely a work of the Holy Spirit for this day and hour (see Rom. 12:3–8; 1 Cor. 12:12–31; Lev. 26:8; Deut. 32:30).[34]
>
> (emphasis added)

This is certainly the case among some of the Latin American churches I have observed. Vision de Futuro in Argentina, one of the largest churches in the world, with a membership of about ninety thousand, has a practice of placing couples in the ministry as a team. Reverend Omar and Marfa Cabrera, who founded the church, were an excellent example to their young leaders. They have both gone to be with the Lord, and their son, Omar, and daughter-in-law, Alejandra, are doing an excellent job of taking the movement to an even higher level as a team.

Another example of this was Marilyn and Wally Hickey and their ministry and pastoral roles. The presentation of their names would, following biblical example, be dictated by the setting.

Even though the person of the couple with the stronger anointing and public ministry gifts might be the visible leader, the combined strengths of both are needed to fulfill the work God has called them to in order to complete the purposes of God for their lives. It is certainly this way with Mike and me. Many people do not realize the extent of the ministry of Generals International and the amount of work it takes—not only administratively but also in other ways—to fulfill the vision of God. As of this writing, the *GI News* is distributed to 42 nations, and we are working to assist numerous organizations in setting up their prayer structures.

In the future, churches will call both the husband and wife to pastor the church. The one with the stronger anointing will be the prominent one, but both will be necessary for the church to function as it needs to. Many men leaders, who thus far have only allotted to their wives certain ministries to women and children, will seek their wives' counsel and endeavor to work as teams. For some, while their children are small, the team approach may be on a limited basis; it will increase as their children get older. Others will function together even when the children are small, as do the ministers in Argentina. Some wives may not feel comfortable with a visible role, or vice versa, but each will be valuable for insight and counsel.

I have observed different churches that have already taken this step and positioned the wives as pastors. Dr. James Marocco, for instance, of King's Cathedral in Maui, Hawaii, ordained his wife, Colleen, to be a pastor. She now serves on the church staff with a number of other pastors. Another example is Bob Beckett of Hemet, California, who ordained his wife, Susan, to be a pastor of the Dwelling Place Church. My own church, Trinity Church of Cedar Hill, Texas, is pastored by Jim Hennesy and his wife, Becky, also a gifted pastor.

How did the people in the churches respond when Colleen and Susan were finally recognized as pastors? They were utterly delighted. Both of these women had functioned in their roles for some time before they were officially recognized as such, so the people already loved them and looked up to them. Their ordinations were like celebrations, and it was easy to begin to call them "Pastor Colleen" and "Pastor Susan."

It is sad to me after extensive theological study, consulting scholars on this subject, that major evangelical leaders still believe that women are never supposed to teach men or even a mixed audience of men and women. While some of us find their conclusion to be surprising, we cannot be so insulated from reality that we do not recognize the deeply entrenched belief that "women in leadership" is heretical.

Although many leaders would say that "experientially" they see women in leadership, they stumble over those difficult passages. In the next two chapters, we will look further at Scriptures regarding women in the Church. Pray hard and keep your mind and heart open, and let's plunge in together!

NINE

Domestic Authority (Headship and Submission)

Even though it sounds as though this chapter is directed exclusively to married women, it is also a crucial chapter for singles, as it addresses abuses against women stemming from the misuse of Scripture, and the benefits of appropriate godly authority for all women. So if you are single, please do not skip it!

Years ago, I studied eschatology—the theology concerning the end times—extensively and would listen with fascination to Bible prophecy teachers. Whenever Mike and I joined a new church, it would have a slightly differing end-time view from the previous one, and each believed it was absolutely right.

Because this study of the end times was so interesting to me, I attended seminars and avidly read the passages and interpretations given by the teachers. They used words such as *pre-Trib*, *mid-Trib*, *post-Trib*. They all seemed to have degrees of validity. My father used to say he was a "pan-millennialist," which meant he believed everything would "pan out" in the end. I know this must sound appalling to those who are very sure about what they believe about the end times!

As I compiled research for this chapter on headship and submission, at times I felt much the same as when I was considering eschatological issues: Each position I study seems to have strengths. One reason end-time prophecy teaching is not absolutely the same across the board is that the Bible simply is not totally clear on the subject. Of course, we all have our interpretations of the symbolism and typology used and can have strong opinions, but this alone leaves room for me to believe that when we get to heaven, none of us will have had perfect interpretations.

Earlier, I alluded to the fact that I have felt much the same way as I have studied the "difficult passages" concerning women at home, women in the Church and related topics. I wrote in chapter 8 about women and the Church, hoping to bring to light the often-overlooked fact that Paul enlisted women in various aspects of the New Testament Church. Although we will now deal mostly with domestic issues, some commonalities exist between domestic (i.e., home-related) and spiritual (i.e., Church-related) issues dealing with authority structures.

In this chapter, we will discuss passages that are much disputed today related to married women and the home—what I will call "domestic authority." In chapter 10 I will deal more with spiritual authority outside the home. I have tried to distill the main points for you on this subject. Whole books have been written about these passages of Scripture; I can provide only a snapshot or condensed version here. For your further study, the Recommended Reading list at the end of this book gives many of the titles that I used in my research. A number of these have greatly divergent viewpoints.

We Are All One in Christ Jesus

As we study these difficult passages, please note that there are foundational Scriptures that affect the way I look at the verses we will examine. One such passage is Galatians 3:26–28:

> For in Christ Jesus you are *all* sons of God through faith. For as many [of you] as were baptized into Christ [into a spiritual union and communion with Christ, the Anointed One, the Messiah] have put on (clothed yourselves with) Christ. There is [now no distinction] neither Jew nor

> Greek, there is neither slave nor free, there is not *male and female*; for you are all one in Christ Jesus.
>
> AMPC (emphasis added)

There are words used in this passage (chosen by the writers under the inspiration of the Holy Spirit) that we need to think about. First, *all* believers, men and women, are called *sons*. Why was the word *sons* used instead of *daughters*? If we explore the setting of this writing, we understand that culturally, the sons were the inheritors, not the daughters. What a strong and powerful message! We are *all* sons, *all* inheritors. This is not saying that He looks on all of us as males, but as having the rights and privileges attributed to a son at that time.

Then, we see a very wonderful statement about those who are baptized into Christ: "There is neither *male nor female*" (NKJV, emphasis added). This is particularly important as we delve into the matter of headship and spiritual authority versus domestic authority. For in the Church, there is neither male nor female; but, of course, in relationships, gender is an issue. We do not stop being male and female when we become born again.

Such noted authors as Jessie Penn-Lewis have referred to Galatians 3:26–28 as the Magna Carta for women. Webster's dictionary defines *Magna Carta* as "a document constituting a fundamental guarantee." Essentially, although we have been given this wonderful Magna Carta, a couple of practical issues still have to be discussed. As I mentioned above, I will divide these into two basic categories: *spiritual authority* and *domestic authority*. Let's begin our study with the issue of headship and submission as it relates to domestic authority. It is one of the most controversial subjects I can think of in the Church today.

My Viewpoint

As I have explored these categories, I have tried to delve into them with an open mind and heart regarding the theology of women in the Church and home that I adhere to as a minister. I have read the works of both *ultratraditionalists* (who believe that women should not teach adult men in the Church or hold governmental responsibilities, and that headship in the home falls to men) and *egalitarians* ("biblical feminists" whose stance is that there is neither male nor female headship in function in the home or the Church).[1]

After researching both positions, I find that I do not fit into either one. Regarding the Church, I demonstrated in the previous chapter the biblical precedent for men and women functioning according to *anointing and spiritual gifts* rather than according to *gender*. Regarding the home, I will deal with that in the rest of this chapter.

Some might be asking, "Cindy, I am single. Where do I fit in this? Since I am not married, am I subject to every man?" I will talk about this later in the book, so read on!

As I have prayerfully threaded my way through this subject, I have had numerous dialogues with theologians. We have been challenged and stretched as we have studied, sought the Lord and reexamined our belief systems.

Heirs to a Corporate Destiny

To understand headship and submission more fully, it is important to revisit what happened in the Garden of Eden and the Fall. In doing so, we will take a look at the role of the couple in the Garden, the subsequent Fall and its effects on the Church and on both the sexes.

As I wrote earlier, for man to be alone was the only thing God declared "not good." What made the situation good or complete was the formation of the woman from his "side" (Hebrew, *tsela* [see Genesis 2:21–23]).[2] The woman was to be a "helper" (Hebrew, *ezer kenegdo*) to her husband.

> She was an *ezer kenegdo*—a helper exactly parallel to him (see Genesis 2:18)—not an exact replica of him, but a perfect complement to his imperfect reflection of the image of God. She had equal rational capacities

to the man, as shown by the fact that she understood and was held fully accountable for her sin by God (see 3:2–3, 16). Whatever else she was, she was not inferior to the man.[3]

God created the man and woman to be a team with a corporate destiny bigger than either of them. This was God's intent for marriage. The two becoming one flesh causes them to be able to accomplish something higher than either of them could do alone.

Adam and Eve's first role was teamwork in ruling the earth (see Genesis 1:26–28). And yet, it is common for teamwork to be a missing ingredient in today's marriages. For years while Mike pursued his career with American Airlines, he lived with traditionalist expectations regarding male headship and women in ministry. Mike says that in his family growing up, male headship meant that the woman was basically supposed to pour herself totally into her husband's destiny, regardless of her own giftedness. The thought that the woman had a role as "helper" such as described in the Garden was relatively unknown.

God created the man and woman to be a team. . . . The two becoming one flesh causes them to be able to accomplish something higher than either of them could do alone.

To embrace the ministry God had given me required a significant shift on both our parts, but especially his. Yet as difficult as the adjustment has been for both of us, the peak years of the Generals International ministry came only as we began to learn how to work as a team in our destiny. (More about this in the next chapter.)

The Fall: The Mighty Gender Bender

The introduction of sin and the fallen nature of the human race brought a polarization not only to married couples working together, but also to males and females relating in the Church. Genesis 3:16 records the results of this fallen nature: "To the woman He said: 'I will greatly multiply your sorrow and your conception; in pain you shall bring forth children; your desire shall be for your husband, and he shall rule over you.'"

Katharine Bushnell, a scholar whom I mentioned in the last chapter, challenged the prevailing traditionalist interpretation of this verse and others in *God's Word to Women*,[4] namely, that the woman's "desire" for her husband was sexual or psychological (or both), and that a man was to subjugate his wife under him. She argued, based upon early translations of the Hebrew Bible into Greek, Syriac, Latin, Coptic, Armenian and Ethiopic, that the word *desire* (Hebrew, *teshuqah)* should have been translated "turning" (Hebrew, *teshubah*, a difference of one letter).[5] According to Bushnell, Genesis 3:16 explains that the woman's "turning" is "toward" her husband. In other words, she "turned away" from God for fulfillment, meaning and direction, and instead "turns toward" the man.

While I agree with Bushnell that women have often inappropriately "turned toward" men instead of God for fulfillment, meaning and direction, I want to point out as well that the word *desire* (*teshuqah*) used here is found in two other passages that further clarify the meaning: Song of Solomon 7:10 and Genesis 4:7. Although Song of Solomon 7:10 uses *desire* in a positive way, in Genesis 4:7 we see sin's desire to control Cain and cause him to do evil. Genesis 3:16 also bears this negative meaning in the woman's desire to influence and control her husband. Both Genesis verses, related closely by grammar and context, indicate inappropriate desire.[6] Essentially, the woman's fallen nature will desire to control the man in her life.

The next phrase of Genesis 3:16 then says that the fallen nature of man shall *rule* over the woman. It is important to understand this word *rule* (Hebrew, *mashal*). Coming from opposite sides of the fence, both traditionalists and egalitarians (biblical feminists) define this term as "rulership" or "mastery."

Bushnell objected strongly to the idea that man "must rule" over woman in an authoritarian way. I agree with her. This verse has been used for centuries as a club against women, either to subjugate them totally or to restrict their gifts and talents. When *rule* is misunderstood as "authoritarian mastery," it makes for big trouble. Why?

In marriage the spirit of competition between husband and wife will be huge because the sin nature of both will want to control the relationship. The sin nature sets up a cycle of judgment as each person in the marriage desires to "rule" out of selfishness. This is why both submission of the woman to her husband *and* mutual submission are so very crucial in a marriage (see Ephesians 5:21–25). Without both kinds of submission, there is World War III. (Have you ever noticed that?)

There is a much better way of understanding the word *mashal* than the dead end of subordination and domination. The immediate context of Genesis 1–2 provides us with several good operating definitions of *mashal*:

- The man was to *abad* ("work, serve") and *shamar* ("watch, guard, protect") the Garden (see Genesis 2:15). In this case, the highest being of all creation, the one created in God's very image, was to serve, protect and care for lower living organisms within creation, the plants.
- The man was to enjoy the fruit of the Garden (see verse 16), but there were definite limits to what he could and could not do (see verse 17). He was never an absolute, despotic lord.
- The man was to receive the gift of a wife gratefully (see verses 23–24), someone who stood on equal footing with him. Together they were to bring glory to God by "ruling" the earth (see Genesis 1:26–28).

In addition, the Bible teaches that God rules over creation with wisdom and compassion (see Psalms 104:10–32; 105; 106; 107). His rule is not despotic or authoritarian. Jesus Himself, the Son of God, could have ruled as a dictator, but He did not (see Philemon 2:6–8). In short, Adam was to rule with gentleness, humility and servanthood, just as Christ loved the Church and gave Himself for her (see Matthew 20:25–27; Ephesians 5:25).[7]

Not Every Man Is Over Every Woman

This brings us to an important point: Ephesians 5:21–31 concerns a married couple, not every male and female. This is crucial to understand: *Not every man is over every woman*. My husband, for instance (not every male I meet), is my head. If every man had headship over me, the effects would be far-reaching and devastating.

A woman is not under every man in the church. If she is married, she will be under her husband's authority at home, and they both should be under the authority of the church. This does not negate, but enhances, the domestic authority.

If she is single, to ensure her completeness (so she will not be in the condition of being alone), it is good to have those to whom she relates in spiritual authority over her (either male or female—authority by anointing, not gender). All of us need someone that we submit our lives to. This is not to be in a controlling way, and it is totally voluntary. Mike and I, for instance, go to Trinity Church of Cedar Hill, Texas, as of this writing. We go to our senior pastor for advice and counsel. We also have a board of directors for Generals International that protects us and gives counsel into our lives.

The fact that not every woman is under every man's authority is important to every woman minister, prophet, evangelist, teacher—whatever her gifting—married and single.[8] How could a woman minister or teacher operate in her anointing if every man in the listening audience had a greater authority over her than, let's say, her husband or pastor? Her hands would be tied as to the release of her gift.

Saying that there has been misuse of authority in the Church against women is an understatement. Whole movements, such as the *discipleship* or *shepherding* movement, were particularly abusive to women in general. This movement sprang up in the 1970s and finally broke up in the 1980s. One teaching and practice of the movement was that a woman could not marry unless the elders of the church (who were all men) said they had heard from God prophetically regarding who her mate was to be. Some of its teachings were more rigid than others, giving husbands such sweeping rights as to refuse a woman the right to buy a dress unless he chose it. This sounds like the profile of a cult.

I know a number of women who were deeply wounded by this movement and its abuses. It largely affected the charismatic community. This is one area where a great need for gender reconciliation still exists. In fact, many Christian women today simply cringe when they hear the word *submission* because of all the negative connotations it has for them.

If you, as a woman, have been through the more extreme forms of religious abuse associated with distortion of headship and submission, please make sure you have prayed and forgiven your pastors, your father, your husband or ex-husband, your boyfriends and so on—anyone who has hurt you in this area—so you can read this chapter as a whole person.

If you are a man, please take a moment to reevaluate your heart to see if you have any issues regarding control or manipulation of women. I am going to talk about some pioneer areas concerning submission that caused pain for both men and women so that you can *respond* rather than *react*. This will allow you to rethink some of the ways you might have related to your wife, to any women under you (or over you) in ministry, as well as to women in general.

Mutual Submission in the Fear of God

With the understanding that this issue is surrounded by much woundedness in both of the sexes, let's look again at Ephesians 5:22–31 and 1 Corinthians 11:3. I will key off in this chapter with this pertinent Ephesians passage:

> Wives, submit to your own husbands, as to the Lord. For the husband is head of the wife, as also Christ is head of the church; and He is the Savior of the body. Therefore, just as the church is subject to Christ, so let the wives be to their own husbands in everything. Husbands, love your wives, just as Christ also loved the church and gave Himself for her,

> that He might sanctify and cleanse her with the washing of water by the word, that He might present her to Himself a glorious church, not having spot or wrinkle or any such thing, but that she should be holy and without blemish. So husbands ought to love their own wives as their own bodies; he who loves his wife loves himself. For no one ever hated his own flesh, but nourishes and cherishes it, just as the Lord does the church. For we are members of His body, of His flesh and of His bones. "For this reason a man shall leave his father and mother and be joined to his wife, and the two shall become one flesh."
>
> Ephesians 5:22–31

This passage on submission is preceded by the idea of *mutual* submission: "submitting to one another in the fear of God" (verse 21). The word for *submitting* here is *hupotasso*, which means "to subordinate, to obey, to be under obedience, to submit self unto."[9] It is amazing how little the Church focuses on a married couple submitting *one to another*. Much has been preached to women about submitting to husbands, but when was the last time you heard a sermon pointing out that for husbands to love their wives as Christ loves the Church means *placing oneself under* to serve as Jesus did when He washed the disciples' feet (see John 13:4–9)? Or when was the last time you heard a sermon asking husbands the question, "Are you submitting to your wife in the fear of the Lord?" In fact, it has been so little emphasized that it almost sounds like heresy!

The Issue Is Love, Not Submission

In preparation for this chapter, I polled some close friends with good marriages. I posed this question: "Does the subject of submission come up in your marriage?"

Each of them said an emphatic, "No!" At the time I polled them, my sampling was a couple in their twenties, one in their thirties, another in their forties and the last in their sixties.

While each of them believes in not only mutual submission but also the headship of the husband in the home, it seems that each of them in a practical sense submits to the other's strengths as well as roles in marriage.

The Gradys

My good friend Lee Grady, for instance, notes that his wife, Deborah, is the home manager. Because she homeschooled their children, which was a mutually agreed-upon decision, the brunt of the work in the home rested upon her. She was with the children more, so she naturally knew more of their needs. They prayed about this home-management decision together, but ultimately she made the day-to-day decisions. My theory is that the best marriages function this way.

The Duncans

Kyle Duncan and his wife, Suzanne, are very much a couple of the 21st century. They split the household chores and work together as a team. In fact, this seems to be the norm for modern generations. Young married men of the Duncans' age group, for the most part, do not feel that it lessens their masculinity to help their wives around the house. (In some parts of the world, including the United States, men often consider themselves to be too "macho" to adhere to this. I have friends in Argentina of this age group, however, who share in the housework mutually, so even this is changing.)

The Wagners

I watched the relationship between C. Peter Wagner and his wife, Doris, whom Mike and I, for years, considered to be our spiritual parents. They had one of the best marriages I have seen. Even though Peter was clearly the head of the house, he was so secure in his identity and position that it was utterly nonthreatening to him to have Doris suddenly yell across the house, "Peter, would you please take out the trash?" He would hop right up and go do what she had asked, knowing that it did not threaten his manhood to submit mutually to his wife's needs. Nor did it take away from his position as head of the home. Peter is now home with the Lord, and Doris still says they had the best marriage one could ever imagine.

The Sheetses

I also talked to my friend Dutch Sheets about this subject of headship and submission. One of the points he made, which I think is tremendous, is that even though he is the head of his wife, Ceci, he does not make a decision until they have mutual consent. By this, he means that if they cannot agree upon an issue, even if he knows he is right, he takes time and prays with her and by himself until they reach a compromise. He said that the Lord has never failed to bring them into agreement.

The Jacobses

As for Mike and me, we lead an extremely complicated life, as you can well imagine, so these issues can get quite complex. I am going to discuss our struggles and some of the things we have experienced in the chapter "Anointed to Serve," where I will deal with submission in a marriage where the woman is the more visible leader.

Modern-Day Foot Washing

I gained a fascinating piece of insight while doing research for this book that may get me into big trouble with male readers. Please do not skip over this section, however, because I know you want to be the kind of servant that Christ is to the Church.

When Jesus washed the feet of the disciples, He was making a huge societal statement. You see, only women and slaves ever washed anyone's feet. This is why Simon Peter objected so vigorously to Jesus wanting to wash his feet. Jesus was taking the lowest possible position and essentially doing women's work. You will get a better sense of the full impact of this in chapter 12, "The Cultural Reformation." Women were near the bottom of the list in society—right near slaves.

How does this translate in modern-day society? A wife might need her husband to mop the floor or dust the furniture or offer to babysit one night a week so she can go out with the girls. Now that is certainly modern-day foot washing!

I am chuckling as I write because, immediately after I thought of these potential examples of foot washing, I called one of my good friends, Cheryl Sacks, to share this tidbit, and she started laughing. Evidently, she had just asked her husband, Hal (they co-lead Bridge Builders International in Phoenix, Arizona), if he would help her mop the floor! He groaned when she coaxed me into telling him what I was learning about servanthood, but he was good-natured about the whole thing.

While I very much believe in the special place of responsibility God has given the husband in the family, it seems that this kind of working together is what our Creator envisioned in the Garden. It is our fallen nature that refuses to submit and wants to compete and control.

Headship—Not Subjugation

Returning to Ephesians 5:22–23, we come to the words pertaining to the wife's submission to her husband, the "head of the wife": "Wives, submit to your own husbands, as to the Lord. For the husband is head of the wife, as also Christ is head of the church; and He is the Savior of the body." (Note that Scripture does not say that he is over the household here but that he is head of his wife. I believe it pleases the Lord when couples who have children work as teams to raise their families.)

Our understanding of the word *head* (Greek, *kephale*) has significant impact on our understanding of *submission.* Two main interpretations regarding the word *head* are being advanced today: "authority" and "source."

Gilbert Bilezikian argues well for the "source" interpretation, gleaned from his survey of nonbiblical writings, as well as the Greek translation of the Old Testament and the New Testament. Bilezikian found that *kephale* is not a legitimate metaphor for "ruler, authority" in the New

Testament because of scarcity of evidence in first-century Greek writings.[10] "Source" or "source of life," he argues, is the idea it conveys in texts such as 1 Corinthians 11:3 and Ephesians 5:23. Katherine Haubert summarizes Bilezikian's conclusion that *kephale* is used metaphorically in the New Testament "in a variety of settings that give it some conceptual flexibility, but always with the notion of serving the Body in a creational, nurturing or representational dimension."[11]

When used figuratively, the word *kephale* or *head* means "fountainhead or life source."[12] The concepts of "mastery" and "dominance" are simply not present in the meaning of *headship*. Likewise, "subordination," "subjugation" and "being ruled" are not included in the meaning of *submission*. These kinds of distortions come from the fallen nature of humanity. On the other hand, however, the concept of the authority of the husband in the role of servant leadership, modeling Christ's headship over the Church, comes shining through in this whole passage (see Ephesians 5:21–31). What does a good "head of the home" do? He protects, nurtures and releases his wife to become everything God created her to be and do. A husband can either be a fountainhead of life and encouragement to his wife or bind her from reaching her full potential.

One time when I was being interviewed over the radio in Argentina, I was asked about men and wives submitting. I answered with a rather strong statement: "I believe God is going to hold some men accountable on Judgment Day for holding their wives back from fulfilling their destinies." The interviewer looked shocked! This certainly was not in the Latin American male mindset. I must say, however, that some major strides have been made in Latin America since that time.

A missionary friend who was in a country in South America told me how he was once in a pastors' meeting where the discussion turned to whether or not it was all right to beat your wife. He said that the general consensus was that it was permitted as long as no one knew. Bible collector Duane Chapman, who has produced a video entitled *The Amazing History of the Bible*, owns an original copy of *The Wife Beater's Bible*. I find that no godly counselors would suggest that a woman stay in a home where she is being beaten, but I am still amazed at how many women are afraid of their Christian husbands. Domestic abuse is a big problem in countries around the world.

Florence Littauer has written an excellent book titled *Wake Up, Women! Submission Doesn't Mean Stupidity* (W Publishing Group, 1994) that can help you discern whether or not you are in an abusive situation in your home.

Two Brains, One Head

Years ago, I had the false impression that I could not offer my own opinion about anything Mike wanted to do, because he was the head. This thinking got us into big trouble from time to time, as sometimes my opinions would have brought a good counterbalance to his ideas. I would feel greatly disturbed over some of his decisions but never say anything.

One time a man asked us to lend him what was to us a lot of money. I felt terribly uneasy about it but felt I could not counter Mike's decision. We loaned the man the money without as much as a signed paper that he would repay us. To this day we have never received that money back. Sadly, we suffered financially because of it, and I dealt with hurt and anger when we had no money to pay for necessary items. What a hard lesson! I had not been a good *helper* to Mike by my silence.

Some wives are angry at the thought of proper headship in the home and want to take away leadership responsibilities from their husbands. I feel just the opposite. I feel more fulfilled, protected and released than stymied because of Mike's headship. I should not be any more upset about the fact that God made me a woman and my husband the head than the fact that He made me five feet two and three-fourths inches tall, and Mike five feet eleven inches tall!

I do believe that my husband is responsible before God for being a spiritual leader in our home. This does not in any way negate my role as a spiritual leader. It does, however, mean that Mike needs to make sure he is right before God in his decisions and actions on our behalf.

Mostly, I find that women *want* their husbands to take more of an active role in praying with and for them and, if they have children, teaching them the Word of God. Somehow the passivity of men that began in the Garden still holds true today.

I do not believe personally that it is biblical to call men "the priests of the home." While I understand the positive connotations intended, in actuality there is only one High Priest and mediator between God and His children, and that is the Lord Jesus Christ. Each of us can approach Christ individually; women do not need men to hear from God on their behalf.

In studying books both by traditionalists and egalitarians, I find many points on either side that I heartily agree with. I mentioned earlier the book *Recovering Biblical Manhood and Womanhood* by John Piper and Wayne Grudem, which gives an extensive response to evangelical feminism. Though I differ with them on some points concerning the role of women in the Church, I do find that they have much to say that is excellent. Piper and Grudem clearly believe that headship involves authority and the word *head* does mean "source" in a few passages, but it means "authority" in others.

Piper has an interesting insight in his chapter "A Vision of Biblical Complementarity":

> If I were to put my finger on one devastating sin today, it would not be the so-called women's movement, but the lack of spiritual leadership by men at home and in the Church. Satan has achieved an amazing tactical victory by disseminating the notion that the summons for male leadership is born of pride and fallenness, which in fact pride is precisely what prevents spiritual leadership. The spiritual aimlessness and weakness and lethargy and loss of nerve among men is the major issue, not the upsurge of interest in women's ministries.[13]

The pastor in one church Mike and I attended said to me, "We are going to push you back in your gifts so your husband can come forward." It seems to me that instead of trying to suppress the gifts, such as prophecy, that the Lord has given me, he should have said, "Cindy, I see the Lord wanting to increase your husband's ability to flow in his gifts, and I'm going to work with him to see that it happens." (Of course, that situation gave me a great opportunity to grow in forgiveness and grace.)

Dennis Lindsay is president of Christ for the Nations Institute in Dallas, Texas, where he teaches a class on marriage. He says that the wife submits to the God-given position of the husband while the husband submits to the person of his wife. He also makes the following comments on submission or subjecting ourselves to one another:

> It is the art of learning to lose when you could easily win. One of the best illustrations of subjection in everyday experience concerns boats. The crews subject themselves to the commands of the captains. But there is another rule that is being observed. The craft that receives the greater advantage of maneuverability must give way to the craft with the lesser. A fishing boat with a motor must give way to a sailboat, for power gives way to sail. Aircrafts do the same—the more power and maneuverability a craft has, the less right-of-way it has. Christians, like sailors and pilots, should learn to give way to one another to avoid collisions in their lives together.

I remember my dad writing me a letter about marriage when I was dating Mike. He said, "Honey, you must give one hundred percent of yourself to Mike, and he must do the same for you. If you do this, each of you will have one hundred percent of your needs met."

Somehow, I do not think any of us has this subject of headship and submission totally figured out. Dr. Gary Greig once said to me, "Cindy, there is such a need for gender reconciliation in the Body of Christ that I am not sure any of us will see this subject clearly until the Lord does a deeper work in healing the woundedness both in men and women."

I have to say "Amen, Gary!" to that. And a day may come when the Lord shows me that what I have written in this chapter is not exactly right—I am very open to that, but He knows I have studied hard, prayed and done the very best job I can do at expressing what I have determined to be the heart of God on this issue.

While this chapter deals mainly with passages of Scripture relating to the home, the next chapter will delve into the issues stemming from women functioning inside the Church and in full-time ministry.

TEN

Oh, Those Difficult Passages!

Several years ago, my husband was interviewed by *Charisma* magazine about our ministry, Generals International. When asked how he achieved peace concerning God's call upon my life, Mike replied, "Barring all the theological questions, it came down to the basic question of whether Cindy had an anointing from God or not. Once I recognized that she did, I had the responsibility to trust God with it. He's the One who put it there."

I wish that just such a statement could settle issues of controversy within the Church concerning whether or not a woman can hold spiritual authority or teach men. Recently, a male leader told me, "Experientially, I have received greatly from women ministers, but theologically, I just can't see it in Scripture."

Numerous groups are really struggling with these issues. Pastors' associations are grappling with the woman question, and women leaders have been deeply wounded by the male leaders who, on one hand, say that the Church will never advance until it is in unity, but, on the other hand, refuse to invite women leaders to pastors' and leaders' summits.

A friend called recently after a discussion by a group that was planning a prayer summit in her state. The question on the table was whether or not women leaders should be invited to participate. She said the group was torn. What made it especially disturbing was that the male/female issue revolved around who was—and was not—going to be allowed to lead the gathering in prayer. This same group no longer stumbled over the fact that the proposed leaders had been divorced or differed in view about the rapture.

Building on Common Ground

It is vital that we find common ground when working toward unity in the Body of Christ. What are the two points we need to consider?

First, what are the absolutes that we all have in common? These should be the focus for our unity. An example is our salvation through the cross of Christ.

Second, we must respect each other's differing beliefs that do not take away from the centrality of the Gospel. Examples of these are ways of baptizing and ways of taking Communion.

Why do I believe this is important? Unity is built around those verses of Scripture that are clear in their interpretation. Plus, it seems that the issues that once caused major division, such as tongues, healing, divorce, how to baptize and other related points of doctrine, no longer stop us from coming together in unity.

But there is one issue that continues to divide and wound many in the Body of Christ. As I wrote in chapter 8, alongside the question of submission, the main issue of division today is this: Can women teach men?

Some churches believe women can teach men; others do not. Both types of churches might strongly adhere to the absolutes of the Gospel message of salvation, while also respecting differences in viewpoint regarding various Scriptures that are open to interpretation. Yet, at citywide leadership meetings, many of these same churches will exclude women leaders both physically and verbally (by verbally, I mean that the nouns and pronouns used by the leadership are all male; for example, "We *men* are going to take this city for God!").

In spite of the wall of division in the Church about women leaders, Scripture presents the prophetic promise in Acts 2:17 that God will pour out His Spirit upon male and female alike. Surely Satan wants to stop this end-time move any way he can—even to the point of using well-meaning Christians who put human limits on the Holy Spirit by forgetting that He can use whomever He chooses, in whatever way He chooses, for His purposes at any time He sees fit. God may choose a Deborah or Esther, as well as a David or Daniel.

> *Scripture presents the prophetic promise in Acts 2:17 that God will pour out His Spirit upon male and female alike. Surely Satan wants to stop this end-time move any way he can.*

With God's sovereignty and His prophetic promises in mind, we need to look at the most difficult passages in Scripture before we get to chapter 11, about women who feel that God is calling them into full-time ministry. The two passages that have brought the greatest confusion and restriction of women's ministry in the Church are 1 Corinthians 14:34–35 and 1 Timothy 2:11–15.

As we delve into these passages, I will weigh various interpretations I have studied and present comments about what I think the passages are *not* saying.

There are four essential principles for interpreting Scripture. I have tried not to make this so heavy and boring that you cannot enjoy reading it. Instead, I have endeavored to "fillet" and distill piles of research for you in terminology that is user-friendly. The four principles are:

1. Determine the author's intent.
2. Determine the context within the chapter, the book and the rest of the Bible.
3. Determine the historical or cultural setting at the time it was written.
4. Interpret unclear passages in light of passages that are clear.

In the remainder of this chapter we will study these two difficult passages by using these principles.

1 Corinthians 14

Let's begin with 1 Corinthians 14:34–35:

> Let your women keep silent in the churches, for they are not permitted to speak; but they are to be submissive, as the law also says. And if they want to learn something, let them ask their own husbands at home; for it is shameful for women to speak in church.

How this passage is interpreted often depends less upon what Paul meant by *keep silent* and *not permitted to speak* and more upon the reader's belief system regarding the scope of what a woman can do in the Church. Some groups read here that women should not be allowed to so much as talk out loud in church; other groups use this passage as blanket admonition that women are not allowed to preach. Neither interpretation takes into account Paul's practice of using women in ministry or his intent in this particular context.

Paul's Actual Concern

In general, very few churches believe that women should not talk at all in church. (This would severely limit a woman's interest in going to church, because we women, as a rule, love to talk.)

We see that Jesus went against the cultural grain and encouraged women to "go tell"—from the Samaritan woman who preached to the whole city (see John 4:28–30) to the two Marys leaving the tomb whom He sent forth with the message that He is alive (see Matthew 28:1, 8–10).

Paul's letters to the Corinthians and to Timothy address specific problems within certain churches. His two letters to Timothy deal quite extensively with false teaching and teachers who were leading women astray. And his two letters to the Corinthians are intended to correct serious breaches of moral conduct and order. These problems were causing confusion in the Church, as we can see in 1 Corinthians 14:33: "For God is not the author of confusion but of peace, as in all the churches of the saints."

What was the problem in Corinth? We know that Paul established the church at Corinth in about AD 50, that some prominent Jews were among the first believers (see Acts 18:4, 8) and that probably most of the church had come out of paganism and was of a lower class (see 1 Corinthians 1:26). Also, at the time, most women were illiterate and did not have the privilege of an education, which men did have. One of the most amazing things about this passage is that women are told to learn. Most of us today do not understand the impact of this statement because our cultural standards do not prohibit a woman from having an education. This, however, was a groundbreaking statement during Paul's time.

Rebecca Merrill Groothuis gives the following insight in her book *Good News for Women*:

> The context of this passage concerns the maintenance of order in the worship service. The same word used of women's silence is commanded of those who would speak in tongues without an interpreter. Paul's intent is evidently to silence only disruptive speaking. The particular type of disruptive speaking that is mentioned with respect to women probably has to do with interrupting the public speaker with questions—a practice that was common at this time. Paul says that women should save their questions to ask their husbands after they get home (1 Cor. 14:35). This indicates that he is primarily concerned with women interrupting teaching, not women engaged in teaching. Apparently, women had been asking questions out loud and disrupting the order of the church service.[1]

The word *silent* has the connotation of "holding one's tongue," which fits with this interpretation.[2] The word *women* (Greek, *gune*) in this passage is not "women" in general, but "wives," because 1 Corinthians 14:35 specifically mentions husbands.[3] Another word in this passage translated "shameful" means "disgraceful," or not conforming to what is right or fitting for the situation.[4]

It is easy to misread what was happening in the early Church if we view it through the filter of our modern-day church buildings and auditoriums. The early Church meetings were mostly in home settings because, as I mentioned earlier, basilicas or church buildings were not built until the fourth century. Even if the homes were large, it would still be quite disruptive for anyone to be voicing questions out loud during the meetings. If the practice of men sitting separately from the women was being followed (as still is practiced in many churches outside the Western world), the problem would only be amplified.

Defining "The Law"

An interesting perspective on this passage comes from Katharine Bushnell's *God's Word to Women*. She begins her section (lesson 25) by mentioning that women were only to be veiled when praying or prophesying; therefore, women were clearly not silenced from doing these things (see 1 Corinthians 11:4–5). On this point, even many traditionalists agree that women can pray and prophesy in the Church, while at the same time forbidding women to teach men.

Bushnell then quotes 1 Corinthians 14:34, where Paul writes, "For they [the women] are not permitted to speak . . . as the law also says." This leads to an interesting question: Where does the Law say that women are not allowed to speak? The Old Testament says absolutely nothing, from Genesis to Malachi, about forbidding women to speak. No such "law" can be found anywhere in the Bible, unless it be this one utterance from Paul. Besides, we know perfectly well the Old Testament explicitly permits women to speak in public (see Numbers 27:1–7). Jesus also encourages women to speak, without rebuking them (see Luke 8:47; 11:27; 13:13).[5]

Bushnell continues her objection to the notion that women must remain silent by saying we do not know, by comparison, if men were allowed to interrupt a speaker to ask questions. Bushnell also points out that, although Paul speaks here regarding the wives, not all of the listening women would have been married; some would have been single, widowed or divorced. Others might have been living with unbelieving Jewish or even pagan husbands whom they could not consult on matters involving believers.[6]

Some traditionalist theologians say that the "law" against women speaking in public was given in Genesis 3:16: "Your desire shall be for your husband, and he shall rule over you." Some, but not all, interpret this as a restriction on women in general and infer from this verse that every male has rule over every female in the Church. We discussed this fallacy earlier, noting that this Genesis passage is talking about domestic authority in the home and not spiritual authority in the Church, because women with husbands are being addressed, not women in general.

So what could Scripture mean by "as the law says"? Bushnell goes on to explain this, beginning with 1 Corinthians 7:1. Paul was working from a list of questions the Corinthians had previously sent. With each new question, Paul would either restate the question or quote from the letter, then give his response.[7]

Bushnell believes 1 Corinthians 14:34–35 was a new question that Paul was addressing and that his answer comes in verse 36: "What? came the word of God out from you? or came it unto you only?" (KJV). What follows, to the end of the chapter, are guidelines concerning prophesying and speaking in tongues.[8]

Bushnell suggests further that the Judaizers were trying to put the Church under their extrabiblical Jewish traditions, which state that a woman is not allowed to speak in a synagogue. Paul would actually have been rebuking the Corinthian church for not releasing the women and for putting them under the legalism that the Judaizers were trying to impose on the Church.

Getting Priorities Straight

To repeat, I believe the strongest interpretation is the one concerning disruption in the Corinthian church caused by wives asking questions during the services. I do not believe that Paul meant women were not to speak at all, because 1 Corinthians 11:5, Acts 18:26 and 21:9 make it clear that they did. I do, however, realize that reasonable people may come to differing conclusions.

Dr. Jim Davis and Dr. Donna Johnson raise some interesting points on the ambiguity of this Corinthian passage in their book *Redefining the Role of Women in the Church*:

> It is always difficult to identify the historical context into which Paul was writing. He wrote to address problems in the churches. Without knowing the local situations it is difficult for us to understand his responses. We cannot always be certain whether Paul's teaching applies only to that particular local church situation or whether it is to be applied universally.
>
> Second, the passages about women are full of ambiguous expressions and sometimes contain words which are difficult to translate. In 1 Corinthians 11:10, Paul writes, "For this reason, and because of the angels, the woman ought to have a sign of authority on her head." What does this mean? Why does he mention the angels? Is he referring to the role of the angels in worship? In 1 Corinthians 14:34, he writes, "Women should remain silent in the churches."
>
> Why did Paul not make it clearer? What exactly did he mean? One would suspect that it is not more clear because it was not that important in the Early Church. It is unlikely that the first-century church shared our preoccupation with ecclesiastical structures and status. Undoubtedly, they were too busy spreading the gospel to be concerned about precise job descriptions for women in their churches.[9]

This last statement is a powerful one. As I have traveled around the world and seen great revivals in places such as Colombia and Argentina, I have seen churches in major revival so busy trying to get the converts discipled that they are happy for laborers—either men or women! One young pastor in his twenties in Bogotá, Colombia, moaned to Mike and me that he was hardly doing any service for the Lord because he alone was responsible for 130 or so cell groups. Amazing, is it not?

I find it interesting that 1 Corinthians 14:34–35 and 1 Timothy 2:11–15 cause us so many problems when other obscure passages in the Bible seldom bother us, even though we do not completely understand them. Few Christians, for instance, spend lots of time trying to interpret the verse that deals with baptism for the dead (see 1 Corinthians 15:29).

I believe a day is coming when we will look back at the controversy over women teaching in the Church and simply shake our heads in wonder that it ever was such a big issue. I do not want any young women leaders to have to deal with rejection of their ministries based solely upon their gender. Actually, as I alluded to in the introduction of this book, this is one of the major reasons I am writing about this subject.

Years ago, when I was lonely and struggling to be a woman leader in the midst of rejection and misunderstanding, I made a vow to the Lord that I would do what I could to see that other young women leaders did not have to suffer as I had. This is why the next chapter will be one of practical sharing from my heart to those women (and the people who love them) with a call of God on their lives.

Examining 1 Timothy 2

Probably the most controversial and puzzling passage concerning women in the Church is 1 Timothy 2:11–15:

> Let a woman learn in silence with all submission. And I do not permit a woman to teach or to have authority over a man, but to be in silence. For Adam was formed first, then Eve. And Adam was not deceived, but the woman being deceived, fell into transgression. Nevertheless she will be saved in childbearing if they continue in faith, love, and holiness, with self-control.

In my study of this passage, I have found Richard and Catherine Clark Kroeger's book *I Suffer Not a Woman* to be particularly enlightening for understanding the historical and religious setting of Ephesus at the time 1 Timothy was written. Their study reveals a world of idolatrous paganism based upon a matriarchal society and goddess worship.

The city of Ephesus, the fourth largest in the Roman Empire, lay on the western coast of modern Turkey, in ancient Asia Minor. It was not an easy place in which to bring the Christian message. In pre-Hellenistic times, a famous shrine was built to the "great mother goddess," and tradition held that the original image had been brought by Amazons, women warriors from the land of the Taurians on the Black Sea. This idol was placed in an oak tree but was later removed to a sanctuary, about which the rest of the temple grew.[10]

The "great mother goddess" later came to be revered as Artemis, or Diana of the Ephesians. Her crown represented the walls of the city. Countless pilgrims made their way each year to worship her in this city, and they poured so much wealth into her treasury at the Artemisium that it became an enormous banking and finance center for all of Asia Minor.

New Testament scholar William M. Ramsay (1851–1939) insisted that it was no coincidence that the virgin Mary was first called *theotokos* ("Bearer of God") at Ephesus, where Artemis herself had earlier borne the same title.[11]

Another important aspect of our study is understanding the predominant reason Paul was writing to Timothy: heresy infiltrating the Church. We see that three people are mentioned who opposed sound doctrine: Hymenaeus, Alexander and Philetus (see 1 Timothy 1:20; 2 Timothy 2:17; 4:14). The Kroegers suggest that at least one of these individuals was a woman and that 1 Timothy 2:12 forbids her to teach a heresy that was creating serious problems in the Church.[12]

The main heresy causing problems was an emerging philosophical and religious system called Gnosticism (from the Greek word *gnosis*, meaning "knowledge"). Gnosticism is a particularly wicked deception that taught the following, among other things:

> Eve was the "illuminator" of humankind because she was the first to receive "true knowledge" from the Serpent, whom gnostics saw as the "saviour" and revealer of truth. Gnostics believed that Eve taught this new revelation to Adam, and, being the mother of all, was the progenitor of the human race. Adam, they said, was Eve's son rather than her husband. This belief reflected the gnostic doctrine that a female deity could bring forth children without male involvement.[13]

The "Silence" of a Teachable Student

Now, let's go back to 1 Timothy 2:11–15 in light of the historical and religious background. We see a similar admonition for women to learn in silence as we did in the 1 Corinthians passage. This time, however, the Greek word used is different from the 1 Corinthians 14:34 word translated "be silent." Although in the Corinthian passage *be silent* means "to hold peace," this word *silence* (Greek, *hesuchia*) used in 1 Timothy means "stillness" or "quietness" or even "agreement." It expresses the attitude of the learner.

This teachable attitude is the same attitude of humble submission that any male rabbinic scholar possessed in that day. What a beautiful thought! Paul was saying to these women, who were never allowed to be taught in a scholarly way in the Jewish synagogue system, that they could be full-fledged disciples.

Why was this especially important for women? Their culture worshiped Diana, or Artemis, and was greatly influenced by the emerging Gnosticism. These women needed to know the truth so they would not be influenced or deceived by false teachers, and so that they could separate themselves from the deception of the society all around them.

Translators' decisions to render the Greek word *hesuchia* as "silence" in the KJV, NKJV, RSV and NRSV is another place where a clear anti-woman bias exists. When *hesuchia* is used of women, these translators chose "silence." When *hesuchia* is used of men, these translators chose "quietness" (see 1 Timothy 2:11; 2 Thessalonians 3:12).

Not to Teach, or Not to Teach Heresy?

So what does this passage mean? Rather than a complete prohibition of women teaching, it is possible that what they were not to teach was heresy. After all, it was in the very same city of Ephesus that Priscilla and Aquila, whom Paul calls co-workers with him (see Romans 16:3), taught Apollos (see Acts 18:26). Other admonitions in 1 Timothy suggest that women were going from house to house (or perhaps house church to house church) leading others astray. Paul writes about this in 1 Timothy 5:13, where these women are described as "busybodies," saying things they ought not. In verse 15, Paul warns that some have already turned aside after Satan because of the error of their teaching.

The word *busybodies*, which seems to suggest that women are idly gossiping, is actually referring to persons doing something that could be considered a form of witchcraft. The Greek word for "busybodies," *periergos*, is the same word that is translated "practiced magic" in Acts 19:19. These so-called "busybodies" were dispensing something much more deadly than old wives' tales.

David Joel Hamilton has written an excellent master's thesis for his course work at the University of the Nations (Youth With A Mission University in Kona, Hawaii). He also suggests that Paul was not addressing all women, in general, but a particular woman who was teaching heresy, because Paul speaks of "women," plural, in 1 Timothy 2:9–10, switches to "a woman" in 1 Timothy 2:11–15a, and then to women, plural, again in 1 Timothy 2:15b.[14]

One of the most difficult sections of this passage is the verse 1 Timothy 2:12, because it seems to say that allowing women to teach men would "usurp authority" (KJV) or take the teaching positions that only men should have. Part of the difficulty arises because the Greek word *authentein* occurs here and nowhere else in the New Testament. Let's look at this word *authentein* to try to determine its meaning.

The most prevalent interpretation of *authentein* seems to be "to dominate." Traditionalists use this passage to demonstrate that women should not teach men because they would be "dominating them" or "usurping their authority." John Piper and Wayne Grudem write from this viewpoint in their book *Recovering Biblical Manhood and Womanhood*.

There is, however, remarkable inconsistency in how the various traditionalists prohibit women from teaching. Piper, for example, gives a list of the ministries he believes a woman can participate in, which includes teaching up to college-age groups.[15] Other traditionalists say that a woman missionary may serve as a leader and teacher, but she may not pastor a church. Some allow a woman to "share" testimonies of great moves of God seen on the mission field as long as she does not stand behind the pulpit. In this situation, the prohibition is not violated because the woman is not "teaching" but "sharing." Other traditionalists say that a woman is teaching if she opens the Bible to read a Scripture in her time of "sharing." The line between "teaching" and "sharing" can become very gray indeed.

Those who draw artificial lines around teaching and authority are doing "hermeneutical gerrymandering," making distinctions in levels of authority in ministry that are not delineated in Scripture.[16]

Furthermore, the traditionalists' viewpoints that limit the setting and audience for women do not seem consistent with other Pauline writings. Consider, again, Priscilla who taught Apollos; he was not just an ordinary churchgoer but a Christian leader. Another point that some may not have considered is the testimony of Mary Magdalene regarding the resurrection (see Luke 24:10; John 20:17–18). Men the world over for millennia have been taught the glorious fact that *He has risen just as He said*, from the testimony of this woman. The Holy Spirit entrusted the greatest message of all time to her, knowing that men everywhere would learn from it. God knew what He was doing and the precedent it would set for the Church thereafter!

Another problem with the traditionalists' position is that it sometimes assumes that Timothy and the New Testament Church knew about a prohibition against women teaching men. Groothuis has the following to say:

> Paul does not state the prohibition in the form of a reminder, and it is not mentioned elsewhere in the New Testament. How can traditionalists be so certain that it was "Paul's position in every church that women should not teach or have authority over men," and that he was giving "explicit teaching on the subject here simply because it has surfaced as a problem in this church"? Craig Keener observes that what is most significant about the wording of the passage is that Paul does not assume that Timothy already knows this rule. . . . Paul often reminds readers of traditions they should know by saying, "You know," or "Do you not

> know?" or "According to the traditions which I delivered to you." But in this case, there are no such indications that Paul is merely reminding Timothy of an established rule that Timothy would already have known about. Moreover, there are no parallel texts in the New Testament to support the view that New Testament churches normally denied women teaching authority. Since this passage is related so closely to the situation Timothy was confronting in Ephesus, we should not use it in the absence of other texts to prove that Paul meant it universally.[17]

If Paul did not mean for these texts to prohibit women from teaching men, then what could he have been saying in these passages? What else could he have been trying to correct in the Church? In order to find this out, we need to study in greater depth the meaning of the word *authentein* at the time of the first century. Words can take on different meanings even within one generation. Imagine how they can change down through many centuries!

A Closer Look at Gnostic Heresy

What did *authentein* mean at the time of the writing of Paul's letter to Timothy? While it has been translated by the word "authority" in nearly all the English Bibles, *authentein* is not the same word as *exousia*, the word used for "authority" in other passages. Studies of the use of *authentein* in the literature of the day show that originally the word *authentein* meant "murder." By the second and third century AD, its connotation had changed to "having authority over." *Authentein* was also used in connection with sex and murder. Women were known to curse men to death through the use of "curse tablets."

Evidence exists for another possible meaning of *authentein* from that time period—that of "originator." We have noted the Gnostic heresy during this time period, which taught that Eve was the first virgin, the one who had no husband and the originator of all life. She was the "illuminator," full of all wisdom, and Adam was actually given life when she saw her co-likeness lying flat upon the earth, whereupon she commanded him to live. When he saw her, he said, "You will be called 'the mother of the living' because you are the one who has given me life."[18]

This Gnostic heresy is easily exposed. The Bible states that Adam was created first and then Eve. The idea that *authentein* may have the meaning of "originator" instead of one who "usurps authority" seems to fit in light of the rest of the passage: "For Adam was formed first, then Eve. And Adam was not deceived, but the woman being deceived, fell into transgression" (1 Timothy 2:13–14). Paul could very well have been addressing the Gnostic heresy that Eve was the originator.

The heresy is dealt a further blow in verse 14, which states that Eve was deceived. The Eve of Gnostic heresy could never have been deceived because she was the all-wise illuminator. Second Timothy 2:14 sets the record straight. There is only one who is all wise, and that is God Himself. As a result of this interpretation, the passage could be translated: "I am not allowing (present tense for that situation) a woman to teach or to proclaim herself the originator of man (*authentein*). . . . Adam was formed first, then Eve." [19]

In light of the prevailing mother-goddess heresy and emerging Gnosticism in the time of 1 and 2 Timothy and Titus, it seems clear that Paul was bringing correction in 1 Timothy 2:11–15. He was correcting women or possibly "a woman" or even "a wife" who was teaching some kind of heresy. (The word for "women" here can also mean "wives.")

Even if one grants the traditionalists' interpretation that *authentein* means "to usurp authority/dominate," this passage would apply to *the attitude* of the one doing the teaching. No godly Christian woman (or man, for that matter) should ever be controlling, manipulative or domineering. In other words, it could be addressing the *attitude* of humility as she teaches rather than a complete prohibition on teaching men.

Spiros Zodhiates, Th.D., editor of the *Hebrew Greek Key Lexicon Bible*, says of 1 Timothy 2:12:

> This problematic text contains two Greek words: *gune*, which means both a woman or a wife; and *aner*, which means man both as a male

> or a husband. As far as 1 Timothy 2:12 is concerned, it should not be interpreted as a prohibition by Paul for any woman to teach, but only for a wife whose teaching may be construed by those who hear her to think that she has the upper hand insofar as the relationship between her and her husband is concerned.[20]

This explanation is one that Kay Arthur of Precept Ministries, one of the most noted women teachers of our time, gives to those who ask her about her right to teach in the Body of Christ as it relates to this difficult passage.

Katharine Bushnell suggests yet another interpretation of this passage. She points out that this letter to Timothy, the bishop of Ephesus, was written about AD 67, after the awful martyrdom of the Roman Church under Nero in AD 64,[21] and may have been a warning. Nero had put thousands of Roman believers to death after he blamed them for the burning of the city, even though Nero himself had supposedly ordered the burning. Nero was exquisitely cruel in the means he used for their martyrdom. Some were covered with skins of wild beasts and left to be devoured by dogs; others were nailed to crosses and many were covered with flammable matter and set ablaze to serve as torches during the night.[22]

In his book *The Early Days of Christianity*, Archdeacon Farrar says:

> Christian women, modest maidens, must play their parts as priestesses of Saturn and Ceres, and in blood-stained dramas of the dead. . . . Infamous mythologies were enacted, in which women must play their parts in torments of shamefulness more intolerable than death.[23]

In light of these traumatic and distressing events, Bushnell suggests that 1 Timothy 2:11–15 was not an admonition that women stop teaching for all time, but simply to lie low and be cautious during this season of persecution. I find Bushnell's speculation unconvincing. For one, it is based upon an argument from silence. Against it also are Jesus' and Paul's strong words to all believers. Jesus did not say that only men should take up their crosses and follow Him (see Mark 8:36–38). Paul did not say that only men should put on the full armor of God (see Ephesians 6:10–18), or that women should not seek to have the same attitude as Christ, who became obedient to death (see Philippians 2:5–8). Further, this interpretation does not explain the rest of the passage.

In summation, I believe there is definitely room for nontraditionalist interpretations of this passage. If the admonition for women not to teach were universal, it would have been strengthened by other passages. Instead, we find many passages showing that women did indeed teach men and held significant places as leaders in the Church (see Acts 18:26; 21:9; Romans 16:1, 3, 7; 2 John 1). The Old Testament, which was the Bible of the early Church, offers clear precedent for women teaching men in a variety of settings (see 2 Kings 22:14; Proverbs 1:8; 31:26; Micah 6:4).

I believe the Lord is clearly speaking to the Body of Christ today about the need to reexamine our belief system concerning women teaching. We must open our eyes to the fact that when God anoints women with the gift of teaching, He is releasing great revelation and blessing to the Church through them.

I pray that this chapter has brought grace and understanding to the many women and men who see the hand of God upon their lives to be everything God has called and chosen them to be in this last and greatest hour of harvest before the return of the Lord Jesus Christ for His Bride.

In the next two chapters we will continue building upon the foundation we laid for the book. Chapter 11 is subtitled "Spiritual Authority." It will delve deeper into women in Church government and give practical applications for women ministering in the Church.

ELEVEN

Anointed to Serve (Spiritual Authority)

A few years ago, a young minister asked, "Cindy, what has it cost you to serve God as a woman in ministry?"

I did not have to think a second before I said, "Everything. It has cost me everything. Death to my own desires, wishes, time—giving up those precious moments with my family and children that any mother wants to participate in." I could have gone on and on. The question elicited memories of nights spent in lonely hotel rooms when it seemed as though every demon in hell had my address.

I paused for a moment as a greater wave of emotion hit me. I then went on to say, "But do you know what I have gained? Everything."

You might ask, "Is it worth it?"

As I ask myself that same question, I see mental images of hundreds of people coming to Christ in nations all around the world, tears streaming down their faces. I ask myself, "What price is one soul rescued from an eternity of hell?" Then I realize anew and afresh, *Yes, it's worth it. For one such soul, I would follow Him in the call again and again. That's why I do what I do, and it is my greatest and highest reward.*

His Grace Is Sufficient for Every Obstacle

This chapter will be a mentoring one for women called by God to ministry of all kinds—whether as leaders in the marketplace or in the

Church. It will also be useful, however, to *all* readers by providing a window into the special and unique challenges of women in full-time Christian service (and all the women in ministry reading this chapter are probably chuckling and saying, "Amen, Cindy, amen!"). I want to say that God is calling women, both young and old, to rise up and be a voice, both inside and outside the church. As hard as it is to believe, there are churches where a woman cannot stand behind the pulpit even to give an announcement!

As a woman traveling and teaching about prayer and spiritual warfare, I have faced a number of obstacles. In fact, as I stated previously, I once complained to the Lord that it was hard enough to be a woman minister without having to teach on such a controversial subject. Of course, you can see how impressed He was with my comments—my next new topic was this one on women and the Church, which is more than a little bit controversial! It serves me right for complaining! So, the lesson from this section is this: Never, ever complain to the Lord. Just tell Him, "Yes, Lord, I'd be glad to do it. Anything You ask of me, Lord, and whenever You want."

"God, You Stole My Wife!"

One initial obstacle Mike and I faced was that while Mike agreed with his head that I should preach, his heart was having quite a struggle. I guess you could distill it down to the statement, "God, You stole my wife!" You see, being the good Southern wife that I was, I had waited on Mike hand and foot. He had never polished his own shoes, washed the car or ironed his own shirts. He did not know how to cook and had only washed the dishes once or twice in our nine years of marriage. In fact, he hardly knew how to use the microwave, and using the washing machine was totally out of the question. (Our friends now in their twenties find this hard to believe.)

During those early days, I would often offer to quit the ministry, but Mike would always protest, "No, I know that is what God wants you to do with your life."

Another major problem was that our children were still quite small. Daniel was two and Mary was five. I had a number of intense wrestling matches with God over the issue of child-rearing. I begged God to let me wait until they grew up to start ministering, but each time I went to Him the answer was the same: *Take up your cross and follow Me now.*

I often wondered why God required this kind of sacrifice from me while allowing others to stay at home until their children were grown. I now believe it was because of the subjects He had called me to teach—prayer, the healing of nations and spiritual warfare. Although I have certainly not been the only one teaching on these subjects, I do know that Generals International has been used to pioneer these messages in many countries throughout the world. Repeatedly we receive letters from leaders who share how they have set up national prayer initiatives using the materials the Lord has given us.

In light of the high personal price it has cost me as a wife, mom and woman, I can see why God does not call more women at the age He called me to travel around the world teaching. But if God is making it clear that this is His will for your life, do not be afraid to say yes to the Lord. His grace is sufficient.

Another challenge I faced as a young woman minister was that I did not know any other women who were doing what I was doing at the age I was doing it. I would go to meetings where plans were made with women who, for the most part, had almost-grown or even adult children. They had more freedom than I, so I repeatedly declined volunteering for the organizations because I wanted to be home more with my children. I teasingly said that I needed God's confirmation in triplicate on my bedroom wall before I would go out and teach.

Have I ever missed God's confirmation and gone when I could have stayed home? Yes, I believe so. Although I cannot think of any specific instances, I am sure that at times, in my youthful zeal, I occasionally missed it. Mike was a good balance for me. He would pray with me when I had any doubts about going somewhere to teach. If both of us were unsure, we called our pastor and, later, our board of directors for advice.

I will never forget the day I heard "via the grapevine" (or gossip line) that some of the men and women of our church were saying that I was not "properly submissive" to my husband. Those words hurt me so badly that I felt as though someone had knifed me in the heart. These were people I had prayed for and thought were my friends.

Later that night, Mike noticed I was walking around with a sad face and asked me what was wrong. After I told him what had happened, he gathered me in his arms and said, "Why didn't they come to me and ask me if you were submissive? After all, I'm your husband, and believe me, would I have told them a thing or two!" What a wonderful release! Mike was covering me and nurturing me in just the way I needed, and it did not matter what those other busybodies said.

Peer Points and Pressure Points

One of the most difficult subjects Mike and I had to sort through was submission. At times, we would be on the same committee as ministers and would relate on an entirely different authority level than when we were at home. I mean that we were dealing with areas of spiritual authority where there is neither male nor female, rather than with issues of domestic authority (family issues of husband and wife).

As I shared earlier, we have had some rather intense discussions and struggles around these issues. Keeping the house clean was relatively easy to settle. Mike worked full-time and got home late and things piled up when I was away. (Especially the laundry!) Because my travel schedule left me consistently behind in household chores, we simply believed God for the money to hire someone to clean house for us once a week. We did not have the finances at first, but once we leapt out in faith, God provided the funds weekly.

We solved the problem of shirts by sending them to the cleaners. Rather than let the issues come to a stalemate, we learned to look for creative alternatives that would meet both of our needs.

One big revelation was recognizing our need to identify each other's roles when we had a conversation. People often unconsciously confuse their roles. They might, for example, have one level of authority at their jobs and another at church and yet another on a certain board of directors. They flow in and out of these roles all the time. We realized that when we were talking minister-to-minister, we were in the area of spiritual authority where there is no male or female. Then, the next moment, we might switch to the subject of our children or our home and transition to the domestic level of authority.

Even when we recognize our roles, things can get murky. We have had to learn to flow together minister-to-minister, even though we are still male and female. As such, we have specific gender needs, even though we are in the area of spiritual authority. I talked a little about this earlier as I described how men relate by razzing or teasing, and women relate by affirming one another.

I remember an intense moment of murkiness when my feelings had been hurt through some false accusations. Mike, who was still working at the airlines, was rushing to get out the door. I had been trying to talk to him about how hurt I felt by a pastor who accused me of having a spirit of divination (in those days not many people understood the prophetic; therefore, anything that was forth-telling was thought to be divination). Being in a rush, Mike related to me more like a man would to another man and said, "Cindy, you're just going to have to stop being so sensitive!" (Granted, prophetic women intercessors do tend to be more sensitive than other people.)

As Mike was shutting the door to leave, I looked at him and said in a crushed voice, "But I'm a woman, too, as well as your wife!" He shut the door and left. I flung myself against the door, crying, when all of a sudden I looked up to find Mike standing there with his arms open, beckoning me to come. I ran into his arms. He hugged me tightly and said, "I'm so sorry, honey. I was treating you the way I would another man." I think he saw me as being so strong that he thought I could take anything!

Throughout the years, Mike has learned to be a good covering for me both spiritually and domestically. I almost feel sorry for someone who would try to come against me, because he would be on the phone with that person immediately to set him or her straight. On a few occasions, I asked him not to intervene because I thought it would just make the situation worse, and after thinking a few minutes, he would agree. Now that our son, Daniel, is vice-president of Generals International, both he and his dad have taken on the role of my protector! Daniel cleans up the social media sites, and Mike answers the hate mail. I do not even see most of it.

Mike and I have found that we relate best when we keep our identities in Christ and not in who we are or what we are doing in life. For Mike, it has often been difficult. He held an extremely responsible position at American Airlines, but when he traveled with me, people would teasingly refer to him as "Mr. Cindy Jacobs." I cannot tell you how much it hurt me to hear people say such things. It especially hurts today, because he is co-founder of the ministry and is essentially the nuts and bolts of the organization. Mike is far from being a Mr. Cindy Jacobs. Generals International would not be able to function without him. He is the CEO of the organization and takes care of the audits and budgets, and he chairs our board meetings. As a businessman, Mike keeps GI an organization of integrity.

Mike and I have found that we relate best when we keep our identities in Christ and not in who we are or what we are doing in life.

Inevitably, situations arise concerning the ministry about which Mike and I do not agree. Usually, we pray and reach a viable compromise, or one or the other will give in on the issue. If we do reach an impasse, however, we turn to the board of directors of Generals International for advice. (Our board is a ruling board and is by no means a "yes" board. Board members are not at all afraid to give us wise, corrective counsel; on numerous occasions they have done so.) We each share our opinions as we poll the board, and we have never failed to come up with a consensus of advice from them.

In the past, when dealing with marriage issues that bled over into the ministry, we sought the counsel of our friend and then-pastor Dutch

Sheets. His wisdom has been a great blessing to Mike and me. Most domestic authority issues do not require outside counsel, but I suggest that any married couple be willing to go for mediation if the issue is important enough to impact the life of one or the other.

If you have read any other books I have written, you know how strong I feel about the subject of being under spiritual authority in a local church. Many who have traveling ministries make a big mistake by not relating on a personal level with their pastors. Some are even afraid of this kind of authority. Mike and I, however, have never found it to be anything other than a major blessing. If you do not have a pastor you can relate to, ask God to show you what church would be a good covering for you and your ministry and, if you are married, for you and your spouse. Mike and I found a new church right after we moved back to Dallas, Texas. I have mentioned that our pastor, Jim Hennesy, prays for us and gives us wise counsel. His wife, Becky, also a pastor, has become my dear friend.

I have had some major identity struggles in trying to figure out the role of a woman in full-time ministry. For one, I had a hard time calling myself a minister. Even after I was traveling and speaking quite often, it was still hard for me to admit that I was a woman minister. Finally, the Lord spoke to me and said, *Cindy, you have accepted the call of God on your life, but you have never embraced the call. You don't like being a woman minister. In your heart, you'd rather be something else in life.*

Wow, that was really hard to hear, but true—very, very true! He went on in a gentle voice to say, *If you don't love the person I made you to be, you don't love yourself, and if you don't love yourself, then how can you love others? I have made you a woman minister, and you will always be a woman minister.*

At that moment, I embraced the call. "Lord, forgive me for not wanting to be the person You destined me to be. I choose to embrace the call today." From that moment I was free and could easily tell people, with great and abundant joy, that I was a minister.

Changed by the Challenge

This book has been quite a journey for me because of the input from my special friends. My good friend and prayer partner, Quin Sherrer, who co-authored *A Woman's Guide to Spiritual Warfare* along with another friend, Ruthanne Garlock, encouraged me to write about my ordination so that people would have insight into the challenges of a woman minister. So here goes. . . .

To begin, I had quite a challenge finding anyone who would ordain me at all. I had been licensed for nearly five years when I felt it was time to seek ordination. (By the way, I had received my license in rather an odd way. After a service, I was handed the licensing card, even though male peers had been given a commission.) Anyway, I asked my pastor if he would ordain me, and, believe it or not, he ordained Mike instead.

Later, I approached my pastor again because I wanted the impartation that I knew comes from being ordained. He agreed that we would have the ordination service during a prophetic conference Mike and I were conducting at the church. Shortly before the ordination was to take place, the pastor told me he was canceling it. When I asked him why, he murmured, "Oh, there won't be time. It will crowd the meeting."

I was crushed and felt embarrassed, because I had invited friends to come for the ordination, and there was not enough time to cancel. The Lord was gracious to me, however. The night before the conference was to start, I was washing dishes when an angel briefly stood beside me and said, "Cindy, everything will be all right." Incredible peace flooded my soul, and he was right—everything was all right.

Later, the pastor asked my forgiveness and told me he had not realized he had a problem with ordaining women in the ministry.

Some time later, a new pastor at our church, the Reverend Don Connell, discovered what had happened concerning my ordination and stopped me one day after church. He let me know that they would ordain me and that he was sorry for how I had been treated. Were those ever some healing words! By that time, I was traveling all around the world speaking to thousands of people. I knew God had ordained me by

His Spirit, but I also understood that a powerful anointing comes when one is set aside for service during ordination and the laying on of hands.

It is a true saying that good things come to those who wait. My ordination service was a glorious celebration. We had special singers, worship and a beautiful processional. My ordaining committee included Peter Wagner, Dutch Sheets, Elizabeth Alves, Eric Belcher, Don and Bernadean Connell, and Mike. It was marvelous beyond words. The group did a prophetic presbytery, in which they prophesied over my life, and everything was wonderful—until an African man came forward and started "prophesying." He said I was to kiss my husband's feet and call him "Lord," and other such things. I could not believe what was happening. It was rather like a bad nightmare.

Thank God for the committee, who one by one took him aside and corrected him for the false prophecy. They explained to him that he was mixing his cultural understanding with his own emotions. Then they told him that American women do not kiss their husbands' feet! The Lord turned the end of the ordination around and brought a powerful impartation through the laying on of hands and the ordination address.

During the prophetic presbytery the Lord spoke through Dutch Sheets that I was a Deborah whose name meant "a bee," and that there would be times when my words would be sweet to the taste and times when they would carry a sting. Eric Belcher, who was vice president of Christ for the Nations at that time, also addressed the subject of Deborah as a prophet to the nations.

Let's Talk Ordination

As I study ordination, I find that quite a bit of ecclesiastical trapping is wrapped around the subject of ordination. *Ordination* is simply setting aside a person to the call of God with impartation through the laying on of hands. Spiritual authority comes through the recognition and affirmation of setting apart a person to the Gospel.

I am amazed at the glass ceiling that still exists concerning ordination of women. Many leaders who purport to be champions of women in the ministry do not ordain women as pastors in the same way they do men. In many cases, the problem is a cultural bias against women. Although ordination is not absolutely essential for ministry, a double standard should not exist. If one church ordains a man for a certain position, and a woman is filling a similar-level job, then the woman also needs to be ordained. Women have told me of the times that their male pastors have chuckled and said, "I'd ordain you if you were a man." Most men do not realize how painful these comments are to women.

I believe it is just as important to ordain those in traveling ministries—as well as those who are full-time in other spheres of authority—as it is those who are pastoring. Often, there seems to be an unspoken feeling that those who travel as itinerant ministers are second-class citizens and only those people who pastor a particular church should be ordained. Let's consider the message this sends. Is there more than one Church? Are those who travel in ministry "outside" the Church, and those who speak locally "inside" the Church? Although this may not be an intentional message, it still amounts to the same thing. There is only one Church; we are all part of the Body of Christ.

Ordination may one day be handled in a completely different way from the way it is now. Some people do not believe that ordination as currently practiced is valid for today. Personally, I do, but I also think that if we really believe there is neither male nor female in the Spirit, and that God poured out His Spirit on both the handmaidens and the servants at Pentecost, the double standard should not exist in the Church.

If you are a woman who has gone through some difficult times, please make sure you do not allow a root of bitterness against men to grow in your heart (see Hebrews 12:15). We do not wrestle against flesh and blood, but against principalities and powers of darkness (see Ephesians 6:12). Use the hard times as character-building experiences (see Romans 5:1–5).

Not Called? Do Not Enter the Battle

If you are a woman considering a call to full-time Christian service as a minister, let me say a personal word to you. Make sure that you are *called*. So many challenges exist for women in leadership that you must "know that you know" that you are following the will of God and not your own personal desires. God is able to make His call abundantly clear to you. When it is His call, it will be burned deeply within your heart. If you are not sure, you will be swayed by the storms swirling around this controversial subject, and you will certainly be weighed in the balance and found wanting.

Anne Graham Lotz, daughter of Billy Graham, tells her story in *Christianity Today*:

> I began my career as an itinerant minister in response to God's call in my life which was confirmed by Acts 26:15–18. I knew from His Word that I was to be His servant and a witness of Jesus Christ that would involve evangelism and discipleship around the world. One of the invitations I accepted was an opportunity to address approximately 1,000 pastors and church leaders. But when I stood up to speak, some of the men in the audience rose, reversed their chairs, and turned their backs to me.
>
> I went home and prayed, "Lord, you know that addressing an audience that includes men has not been a problem for me. But it is obviously a problem for them, and I can't continue to stand in the pulpit and ignore this."
>
> As I searched the Scriptures for an answer, God seemed to remind me from John 20 that, following His resurrection, Jesus had commissioned Mary of Magdala in a similar fashion. God also seemed to speak to me from Jeremiah 1:7–8, commanding me to be obedient to my call, unafraid of "their faces"—or their backs. He reinforced this in verse 17, clearly commanding me to "get yourself ready! Stand up and say to them whatever I command you. Do not be terrified by them, or I will terrify you before them." In other words, I was not accountable to my audience, I was accountable to Him.[1]

Other women have suffered similar public persecution when speaking by invitation of conference committees. Jill Briscoe, lay advisor to the women's ministry at Elmbrook Church in Brookfield, Wisconsin, where her husband, Stuart, served as pastor, tells how this happened to her when she was addressing a convention of three thousand young people:

> I introduced my subject and opened the Scriptures and read them and began to explain them. At that point, a pastor stood up and told me, "Stop, in the name of the Lord!" and said that I was out of order. He then rebuked my husband, saying that he should be ashamed to allow his wife to usurp his authority. He then took his young people out, and several other people followed. The good thing was that 3,000 rather bored kids suddenly became very attentive. But it left me feeling vulnerable and shocked.[2]

These are only two of the horror stories I have heard from women leaders in the Church. I was told that a fellow woman minister in Texas was "unordained" by her pastor after a certain apostolic group came through her city. Another friend went to church with her family on a Sunday morning after being on the road speaking to various groups and was publicly excommunicated in front of the church for traveling too much. Thank God His gifts and callings are irrevocable (see Romans 11:29), and we cannot be unordained in the Kingdom of God. (This is not to say that God never reprimands His children, but these women were disciplined unfairly according to cultural boundaries rather than biblical ones.)

Because I am being totally honest and open with you, I admit that I have had to closet myself away at times to forgive those who have hurt me—not only acquaintances but people I considered friends. Somehow, God blessed me with enormous favor, and I seemed to bounce back. I am sad to say, however, that not everyone I know has fared the same.

Marilyn Hickey: Role Model

Many of the pioneers in the Church today are women. I wrote about some of them in the chapter "Heroines of the Faith" as well as in "Moms and Other Great Women of Faith." I wanted to include one of them in this chapter because I admire her both as a woman and as a role model for my generation. Her name is Marilyn Hickey.

I called Marilyn one day to see if she would give me an interview for this book. I always enjoy talking with her. Even though more than 65 million people a day view her television program, and she has traveled and ministered in 125 countries of the world, Marilyn is always humble, warm and caring.

Marilyn's husband, Wally, was called before she was. She said that he would always compliment and encourage her for any step she took as she used her gift of teaching. Marilyn started teaching in a home Bible study for their church, which quickly multiplied to twenty. During that time, she was encouraged to start a five-minute radio show that went to fifteen minutes a day. Later, God called her to television.

Marilyn worked alongside her pastor husband at the Orchard Road Church in Denver, Colorado, (formerly "The Happy Church") for many years, but her primary call is to be a missionary evangelist and teacher. She says, "God has called me to cover the earth with His Word." Marilyn co-hosts her television show along with her daughter, Sarah Bowling. In 2004, Reese, Sarah's husband, and Sarah took over the pastorate of the church. Even though Marilyn's husband passed away in 2012, she has continued to travel the world, preach to massive crowds and hold healing meetings.

You may know that Marilyn, like myself, has had books written against what she teaches (or what she supposedly teaches). Curious, I asked, "Marilyn, do you ever read any of the critical things that are written about you?"

"No," she replied. "I have so many things to study and read that I have found I don't have time to stop and read those kinds of things."

What touched me most when I spoke with her is how unscathed she sounds in spite of some of the persecution and misunderstanding she has suffered. It caused me to get a glimpse into the heart of a great woman who has paid the price and yet remains tender and compassionate in her calling.

The Facts on Women in Ministry

In 2009, the Barna Group revealed that the number of women serving as senior pastors had doubled in the past decade from 5 percent to 10 percent. This was actually not all that encouraging to me, as 10 percent of senior pastors—when compared to the total number of women in church—is still surprisingly low. Fifty-eight percent of women pastors are affiliated with a mainline denomination.[3]

Also according to the Barna Group, women, in general, are more highly educated than their male counterparts. Seventy-seven percent have a seminary degree, as compared to 63 percent of male pastors. Yet women pastors make about $3,300 less annually than their male counterparts.[4] Some believe that this is because women tend to pastor smaller churches; however, a study of fifteen Protestant denominations conducted by the Hartford Institute found that "women only earn 91% of the salaries of men for working the same hours, in the same types of jobs, within the same denomination, in the same sized church."[5]

Dr. Vinson Synan, dean emeritus of the School of Divinity at Regent University in Virginia Beach, Virginia, reported that as of 1991, the Assemblies of God counted 4,604 women with ministerial credentials—the most of any denomination in the United States. This amounted to 15 percent of all ministers in the American Assemblies of God church. Of these, some 322 were listed as "senior pastors."[6]

As of early 2018, there were 9,142 credentialed women in the Assemblies of God, or 24.3 percent of their ministers. There are, however, only 569 women lead pastors, as opposed to more than 10,500 male lead pastors.[7] The Assemblies of God include Beth Grant on the executive presbytery, which is their highest ruling board. Looking at the disparity of women in leading roles in the denominations, Grant admonished the male pastors present at a General Council to encourage girls and young women to consider the ministry. "You can say to little girls in your churches, 'God's hand is on you,'" she said.[8]

In the Foursquare Church, founded by a woman, Sister Aimee Semple McPherson, of the 6,818 licensed U.S. ministers in 2009, 121 were female senior pastors (about 10 percent of all senior pastors),[9] and 37 percent of all credentialed ministers in the denomination were female (this includes all ministry roles).[10] Tammy Dunahoo, then interim general supervisor of the denomination, stated, "The board of directors has developed a plan to give focused attention to identify and remove all barriers that have hindered women called of God for leadership."[11]

In spite of some encouraging trends, 51 percent of churches do not allow women to become head pastors, and 33 percent of churches do not allow women to preach.[12] The glass ceiling of women as pastors or women holding authority over men seems to be the major theological sticking point, even today among some major charismatic and Pentecostal churches. There is more freedom in mainline Protestant denominations, such as Episcopal or Presbyterian, while others, such as Southern Baptist, still hold the position that women are not called to be senior pastors. Because each church is governmentally autonomous, however, some have women in pastoral leadership.

Other classical Pentecostal denominations are still grappling with the role of women in the Church. The Church of God in Cleveland, Tennessee, has debated the role of women in the Church. Some of the dialogue raised the question of whether or not recognizing women in leadership is elevating cultural concerns over biblical teaching. Dr. Cheryl Bridges John, professor of discipleship and Christian formation at the Church of God's Pentecostal Theological Seminary, "said she was shocked there was so little support for ordaining women as bishops" and that "the debate shows a doctrinal tension between the denomination's holiness and fundamentalist influences."[13] Of course, this does not mean there are not other men leaders who stand up for the role of women in the ministry.

Practical Protocol for Women in Ministry

As I prayed about what to include in this chapter, I felt that a practical section for women in ministry was needed. Some of the information will pertain more to those with traveling ministries, as I am most familiar with this kind of ministry. I could write a whole book on what I have learned about the many areas of protocol concerning women who are ministering. Let's consider a few of these areas.

An important subject we women need to learn about is how we relate to men in the ministry. I have put some practical policies in place as a traveling minister to safeguard myself from gossip or any other attack that may come from my interacting with men in general, as well as men in the ministry.

One of my first lines of defense is a personal letter sent from my office before I go any place to speak. In this letter, my office states that I am not ever to be picked up by a man alone. At times, I have had to ride with a driver from a major ministry that sent a ministry van to pick up its speakers. I try, however, to make this the exception.

Another personal policy is that I do not ever go out for lunch or dinner with a man unless my husband is there. I made an exception to this once when I had breakfast in an open room, with Mike's full knowledge. I adhere to these policies even when the man is much younger than I. It keeps both of our reputations clean and aboveboard. I believe that even women called to full-time ministry as marketplace leaders should not go out with married men. This could become the devil's playground and open doors of intimacy that should not be allowed.

We women can actually inappropriately encourage men and not understand that we are doing so. Spending long hours in intimate conversation, as I alluded to in the section on spiritual adultery, can give men the wrong idea. Never let yourself be put in a compromising situation. Do not, for instance, sit in a car talking to a man for long periods of time or have lengthy conversations on the phone. There are times when I give counsel or seek counsel from a pastor, and we might have an extended conversation, but, again, this is the exception, not the rule. If the male pastor is married, I make sure that I am also friends with his wife.

One area of concern I have is how intimately women intercessors—married and single—relate to their male pastors. While it is important to share what God has shown you, do not spend time alone together behind closed doors—particularly if you are married or the pastor is married. Sadly, this close involvement can cause a woman who is naïve to become emotionally entangled in the life of her pastor, and vice versa.

Before I speak at any local church, I ask for a letter of invitation from the senior pastor of that church. I had some problems early in the ministry when an elder or someone else from a church invited me and the senior pastor was not in complete agreement with a woman ministering. Now, I always ask for a letter of confirmation to keep on file in my office, regardless of the kind of meeting I will be going to.

For those who travel in ministry, the subject of finances can be difficult and will require clear communication. As I stated earlier, my secretary sends a letter delineating our ministry's requirements for my travel, and this includes the necessary finances. I have found that sending the letter provides clarity; plus it provides a way to make other needs known. When I first began traveling, I found that the love gifts I received did not even cover the cost of gas to drive there. Eventually, I began to resent this, believing that "the laborer is worthy of his [or, in my case, her] wages" (1 Timothy 5:18). At first, I had peace about paying travel expenses out of my own pocket. But after a while, as I found myself resenting it, I realized that God's grace for that period of my life had ended. Clear communication of your needs will also help the people who are considering inviting you to ascertain clearly from the Lord whether you are to be their speaker or not.

Today, I find that people are generous in giving to our ministry. Because of our worldwide television ministry, our expenses are quite a bit larger than those of a traveling minister who just requires enough finances for her household needs. Those who are pastors also receive a salary from their local churches. God will show you how to communicate in an ethical manner with the places to which He has assigned you.

As I have risen in visibility as a leader, I have found that there also comes an obligation to the Body of Christ to support certain major events; many times these require you to pay your own way without a love offering and often to sow into the ministries as well. This is a service to the Body of Christ. I have done this with events such as "America for Jesus" and the "Empowered21 Global Council."

In this hour, women are preaching and teaching, leading worship, working with the poor, going into prisons and doing many other valuable ministries. The Lord is uniquely calling women to be pioneers in new fields where they never used to walk. It is a privilege and honor to be a pioneer. God calls some women to do what others have never done in order to make the way easier for the next generation. I want to be like that. God has given me a heart for young leaders, both men and women. I wish I could spend time individually with the many callers who ask for mentoring, but I simply do not have the time.

During the past several years, I have convened roundtables of emerging women in leadership from those I see as my spiritual daughters in the Lord. Each is gifted and talented in her own right.

Two of the most exciting projects that many young women are being called to in this day are the ending of abortion and human trafficking. Erica Greve, of Unlikely Heroes, based in Los Angeles, California, has achieved some major rescues of women who were being trafficked in the Philippines. Her work is catching the attention of some visible people in the entertainment field as well.

Another woman, Jen Watson, goes into bars and ministers to the exotic dancers, showing them the love of Christ. She has been able to rescue many out of this lifestyle.

Laura Allred, of Back to Life and Captured, walked 240 miles from the largest abortion clinic in the western hemisphere, located in Houston, Texas, to the courthouse in Dallas, Texas, in which the first court case legalizing abortion in America took place. Thirty-nine women, some postabortive, and others who are abortion survivors, trained rigorously for this walk for life. They endured blisters, weather, exhaustion, financial challenges and other difficulties to take a stand for unborn children.

This call to bring justice to those who have no voice to speak for themselves is part of the DNA of the next generation. They are courageous and passionate. I call them the "New Justice League" who, like Wonder Woman of the fictional Justice League, fight against oppression. The generations are in good hands with women like these who are taking a stand in America and with others like them around the world.

I mentioned Sharon Ngai who, along with her husband, Jonathan, formed Radiance, a 24/7 house of prayer right in Hollywood, California, in an old motion-picture studio.

My friend Becky Hennesy, who pastors Trinity Church in Cedar Hill, Texas, alongside her husband, Jim, carried the vision for what is now Hope Mansion, a maternity home for women who do not want to abort their babies but have no place to go. Many of these young pregnant women are thrown out by their boyfriends, threatened by husbands or put out in the streets by their families because they are pregnant but do not want to abort. Champions like these are bringing justice to those who have no justice. They become a voice for the voiceless.

I am aware that you might be longing for dialogue with other emerging women in leadership. Please, I encourage older women reading this to find your "daughters." We need mothers as well as fathers for the next generation.

For the many who have asked me for help when I do not have the personal time to sit and mentor, I pray this chapter has helped you pursue your calling. It is often a great frustration to me when women ask for my help but I am not able to give them personal time, because I really do care. This is one of the major reasons I have written this chapter.

If you are called to minister, but are frustrated, please be assured that God will make a way for you where there seems to be no way. In all the years I have ministered, I have never done any self-promotion—I let it all come from the Lord. I have never had one door that I cared anything about walking through remain closed. God has opened doors that have astounded me. As I travel, many a pastor tells me that I am the first woman ever to preach the Gospel from that pulpit. These words have rung in my ears from Pakistan to Nepal to Latin America. The fact is, you simply cannot keep the Holy Spirit out of a place where He wants to go.

The next and final chapter is quite exciting and eye opening. "The Cultural Reformation" deals with the way God views women, their involvement historically in revival and their role in the Church today.

TWELVE

The Cultural Reformation

Blessed be He who did not make me a Gentile; blessed be He who did not make me a woman; blessed be He who did not make me an uneducated man (or a slave).

Tosefta[1]

A hundred women are no better than two men.

B. Berakhot (Talmud)

A woman is a pitcher full of filth with its mouth full of blood, yet all run after her.

Babylonian Talmud Shabbath 152A

When a boy comes into the world, peace comes into the world; when a girl comes, nothing comes.

Babylonian Talmud

These sayings depict a world in which women were often marginalized and despised. In the midst of this twisted thinking came One who would bring cultural reformation—the Savior, Jesus Christ. No wonder women loved Him! The women were "last at the cross and the first at the tomb." For the female gender, there never has been nor ever will be one who smashed barriers and set the captives free as He did.

As I have studied Jesus' love for the lowly, the oppressed and the downtrodden, I have been amazed and increasingly aware of how He shows Himself to be so personally relational and yet such a cultural reformer. To experience the full impact of this One who tore down the walls of partition, let's take a look at the world into which He was born.

Greco-Roman Attitudes

The following is a brief sampling of practices that characterized Greco-Roman male attitudes concerning women. The following examples come from the period leading up to the time of Christ.

Infanticide

Girl infants were exposed and left to die much more frequently than boys. Girls, after all, were an expensive and unremunerative investment, not only because of the cost of supporting them as children, but also because of the expense of providing them with dowries (Posidippus—who lived between the third and second centuries BC).[2]

Abuse

At one time in Rome, husbands greeted their wives with a kiss. This was not a sign of affection, but rather a test to see if their wives had been drinking wine. Drinking wine was thought to make a woman "loose" and sexually uninhibited. If women smelled of wine, their husbands had a legal right to kill them.

Women usually were married at age twelve to much older men and were expected to bear a child every two years.

Note Seneca's perspective on women: "Women and ignorance are the two greatest calamities in the world."[3]

Sermonides of Amorgos said this: "Zeus designed this as the greatest of all evils: women. Even if in some way they seem to be a help, to their husbands especially, they are a source of evil."[4]

And this statement has been attributed to Demosthenes: "Mistresses we keep for the sake of pleasure, concubines for the daily care of our person, but wives to bear us legitimate children and to be faithful guardians of our households."[5]

The Jewish Perspective

The historical Jewish perspective toward women is startling in its prejudice. The ancient day-to-day treatment of women belied the tone of respect used in Scripture.

Divorce

A husband's legal right to divorce his wife if she caused an "impediment" to the marriage limited a woman's security. A man could divorce his wife without her consent for reasons ranging from her chastity to burning a meal to the husband finding a fairer woman.[6]

Most rabbis repeatedly stressed the inferiority of women in their teachings.

> A certain Rabbi Yochanan, we are told, quotes the Mishnic (the Mishna is the most ancient and important part of the Talmud) rabbis as teaching that a man could do as he pleases with his wife: "It is like a piece of meat brought from the shambles, which one may eat, salt, roast, partially or wholly cooked." A woman once complained before Rav (a great rabbi) of bad treatment from her husband. He replied, "What is the difference between thee and a fish, which one may eat either broiled or cooked?"[7]

The wife's household duties included grinding flour, baking bread, washing clothes, breast-feeding the children for eighteen to 24 months, making the beds, working with wool and washing her husband's face, hands and feet.[8] Although many of these tasks are not abnormal in themselves (I made our bed this morning!), there are still places in the world where these simple household tasks are taken to extremes. When Mike and I were in Nepal last year, for example, we learned of a practice by some tribal people in which the women wash their husband's feet each night and then drink the dirty water to show respect. And that is not all! When the men travel, they wash their feet and bring the dirty water home in a jar so their wives can drink it.

The Ten Curses against Eve

Another example of Talmudic prejudice against women is found in "The Ten Curses Against Eve," the commentary on Genesis 3:16:

1. Greatly multiply refers to catamenia [discharge from menstrual cycle], and so on;
2. Thy sorrow in rearing children;
3. Thy conception;
4. In sorrow thou shalt bring forth children;
5. Thy desire shall be unto thy husband [followed by language too coarse for printing here, leaving no doubt of the rabbinical interpretation of *desire*];
6. "He shall rule over thee" [more, and fouler language];
7. She is wrapped up like a mourner;
8. Dares not appear in public with her head uncovered;
9. Is restricted to one husband, while he may have many wives;
10. And is confined to the house as to a prison.[9]

To be fair, not all rabbis were woman haters. Some, such as Rabbi Jacobs, said, "One who has no wife remains without good, and without a helper, and without joy, and without blessings, and without atonement."[10] Statements such as this one honoring women, however, were few and far between. We do have passages from Hebrew texts, however, that balance the misogynistic words of some of the rabbis. This includes

Scripture itself. Proverbs 31:10 says eloquently, "Who can find a virtuous wife? For her worth is far above rubies."

The more I have studied ancient cultures, the greater admiration I feel for what Jesus did to set precedents for treating women and children with respect. Until I completed this study, I overlooked many seemingly simple little words and actions recorded in the gospels that I now understand were huge statements in the culture of Jesus' day. Jesus brought an enormous reformation not only for women and children, but also for the whole family. The New Testament writers later built upon these actions and teachings in Scripture.

The Good News Perspective

From the very beginning of the New Testament, women are given a place of unprecedented equality and prominence. This new place is first illustrated in chapter 1 of Matthew's Gospel, where Matthew traces the lineage of Christ. Matthew mentions not only the men's names, but also three significant women ancestors in the Messiah's genealogy: Tamar, Rahab and Ruth.

The next powerful cultural statement is evidenced when the angel Gabriel first appeared not to Joseph, or Mary's father, or any other male, but to a young woman probably about fourteen years old (see Luke 1:26–38). (Today, we would call her a teenager and not a woman at all.) And what the angel said was even more amazing. . . . *You have found favor with God.*

No wonder Mary sang, "He has regarded the lowly state of His maidservant; for behold, henceforth all generations will call me blessed" (Luke 1:48)!

It is also interesting to study the way the Holy Spirit inspired the New Testament writers to include male and female pairings through the Scriptures. This is beautifully shown in the story of the infant Jesus' presentation at the Temple. Two noted and respected leaders, Simeon and Anna, were drawn by the Spirit to come and bear witness to the fact that this was indeed the Messiah. Simeon, who was waiting for the

"Consolation of Israel" (Luke 2:25), gave prophetic testimony regarding His arrival. Anna, also a prophet, spoke about Jesus to all those who were looking for "redemption in Jerusalem" (see Luke 2:38). The recognition of Jesus as Messiah was announced that day in beautiful gender equity—a foretaste of the day when the Holy Spirit would come upon both handmaidens and servants (see Joel 2:28–29).

Luke's account of Jesus' birth lists these other pairings of men and women: Zechariah and Elizabeth, and Joseph and Mary.

More male-female pairings come to the forefront in the parables of Jesus. Luke 18:1–8, for instance, tells the story of the woman who refuses to stop crying out to an unjust male judge for vindication. The setting of the story is a male-oriented society where females rarely receive the same kind of justice as men. The woman's cries are heard because of her persistence. Jesus finished the parable with the statement: "Shall God not avenge His own elect who cry out day and night to Him?" (verse 7).

Witherington says:

> Jesus' choice of a woman in need of help as an example for His disciples perhaps indicated Jesus' sympathy and concern for this particular group of people in a male-oriented society, and also because the aspect of this woman's behavior that Jesus focuses on (her perseverance or persistence) is a characteristic that in a patriarchal society was often seen as a negative attribute in a woman (Prov. 19:13).[11]

Women in the Ministry of Jesus

The second chapter of John starts with a fascinating exchange between Jesus and His mother. Mary tells Jesus there is a problem. The hosts of a wedding have run out of wine. Evidently, she believes He can remedy the situation. He replies, "Woman, what does your concern have to do with Me? My hour has not yet come" (John 2:4).

To us, the address *Woman* may seem rather disrespectful, but there is no harshness or disrespect here at all, as can be seen in Matthew

15:28, Luke 13:12, John 4:21, 8:10 and 19:26. Yet, Jesus does seem to be distancing Himself from her as His mother by calling her "Woman." The phrase *My hour has not yet come* may refer to the time when she will know Him in an entirely different way—as Savior—rather than simply as a mother knows her son.

If Jesus was ever so slightly distancing Himself from Mary as His mother, His address really makes His response to Mary much stronger. He changes the water to wine as a result of a woman seeking His help. This would have been quite unusual in His time. Not only did He literally change water into new wine, but He was also transforming the "old wine" of prejudice against women into that of a "new wine" perspective in which there is "neither male nor female." According to Jesus, both women and men equally approach the throne of God in times of need.

(A parenthetical comment on this passage: One of the gods worshiped during Jesus' time was Bacchus, the god of wine. Jesus' first miracle of turning water to wine very well could have been a direct act of spiritual warfare against Bacchus, the god of disorder and revelry. Jesus came to bring the wine of the Spirit, which sets all things into right order.)

The next major blow to cultural prejudice against women is Jesus' conversation with a Samaritan woman (see John 4:4–26). This story records the most extensive personal conversation Jesus had in all of Scripture. If Jewish men reviled anyone more than an unclean woman, a foreign woman or an immoral woman, it would have been a Samaritan woman—the very kind of woman with whom Jesus spoke at length. It is to be noted that Jesus gives this long theological discourse of who He is in this conversation with a woman.

The story of the woman at the well speaks powerfully both to gender prejudice and racial prejudice. Jesus chose to reveal Himself to a woman who was considered little better than a dog. Even His disciples were astonished at His behavior. Jesus came to reconcile races and genders.

The Samaritan woman became the first evangelist! She preached the message to the whole city, to men and women. Surely Jesus could have gone into the city and found a Samaritan man, but no, He chose a woman from the lowest class of society and gave her value as one worthy to spread the Good News.

(A final parenthetical comment on this passage: Respected rabbis were expected to keep their distance from sinners, but Jesus spoke directly to sinners about matters of the Kingdom. This was very unusual for a rabbi in His day.)

Another clear example that Jesus despised double standards of conduct for men and women is found in the story of the woman caught in adultery:

> The scribes and Pharisees brought to Him a woman caught in adultery. And when they had set her in the midst, they said to Him, "Teacher, this woman was caught in adultery, in the very act. Now Moses, in the law, commanded us that such should be stoned. But what do You say?"
>
> John 8:3–5

I can only imagine the thoughts that ran through Jesus' mind. One immediate thought would have been that the scribes and Pharisees had quoted only part of the law on adultery. Leviticus 20:10 says that *both* "the adulterer and the adulteress shall surely be put to death." The woman alone had been brought forward as "caught in the act"—the guilty man was getting off scot-free.

Many other double standards had evolved in Jewish society since the Law had been given. Of course, the eternally present Son of God and Lawgiver knew that. His next statement ripped the covers off the hidden places of their hearts: "He who is without sin among you, let him throw a stone at her first" (John 8:7).

What was Jesus saying? Whichever of you has never indulged in sexual fantasy, throw the first stone. Whichever of you has never had a problem with lust, throw the first stone. We know the woman's accusers must have had some kind of struggle, because the Bible makes it clear that His statement smote their consciences (see John 8:9).

This was absolutely incredible! Jesus saw the sin of a woman and the sin of a man as equal. He leveled the sexes and held men to the same moral responsibility for their actions as He did women.

Another strong statement from Jesus about the value and equality of women is the story of the healing of the woman with the issue of blood (see Matthew 9:20–22; Mark 5:25–34; Luke 8:43–48). What is often overlooked in this story is that a woman could not enter into the Temple precincts during her menses. She would have been considered unclean and could only have been made "clean" again through rather elaborate ritual washing. When Jesus noted the woman with the menstrual flow was healed, however, He immediately brought her into His presence. The statement Jesus was making: *There is never a time when you cannot approach Me. You can never be too "defiled" or "unclean" that I will not take you in.*

Jesus and the Children

Unlike the terribly wicked practice of exposing children to the elements at birth to die (infanticide), Jesus went out of His way to proclaim their worth. A cultural background of the terrible practice of infanticide brings a whole different slant to the story of the disciples sending the children away and the Lord becoming indignant over what His followers had done. One of the most beautiful passages in Scripture establishes a strong place for the little ones in His Kingdom: "Let the little children come to Me, and do not forbid them; for of such is the kingdom of God" (Mark 10:14).

Jesus and His Healing Ministry

Jesus broke from the rabbis and their oppressive rules concerning women. When He healed the crippled woman on the Sabbath in the synagogue, Jesus *touched* her and *spoke* to her (see Luke 13:10–17), both actions avoided by overly scrupulous rabbis. But that was not all:

The biggest slap on the face to the Pharisees came when Jesus called her "a daughter of Abraham." No woman was ever called a daughter of Abraham. Only men were to be called sons of Abraham.

Jesus also healed Peter's mother-in-law of a fever on the Sabbath, right after He healed the man with the unclean spirit in the synagogue (see Mark 1:23–31). Again, He broke precedent by taking her hand. No rabbi would take a woman's hand until sundown on the Sabbath.

Women as Disciples

It is widely known that Jesus included women with His traveling team. This must have seemed absolutely scandalous.

> Now it came to pass, afterward, that He went through every city and village, preaching and bringing the glad tidings of the kingdom of God. And the twelve were with Him, and certain women who had been healed of evil spirits and infirmities—Mary called Magdalene, out of whom had come seven demons, and Joanna the wife of Chuza, Herod's steward, and Susanna, and many others who provided for Him from their substance.
>
> Luke 8:1–3

As we have noted, it has often been claimed that Jesus chose twelve male disciples to set a precedent for men only in ministry. We must remember, however, that Jesus came to the Jews, a very patriarchal people. Jewish believers would become His bridge team to the world. To impose a first-century Jewish culture grid on all future Christians not only too narrowly defines those who could be disciples, but also sets artificial limits on Jesus' worldwide mission to the Gentiles. Jesus started with twelve men, but by Luke 8, we see that His ministry team had greatly expanded. In fact, it does not take much of a stretch to believe that by Luke 10, some of the seventy of the ministry team were also women. And we are explicitly told in Acts 1:13–14 that women were included in the company of the 120 awaiting Pentecost in the Upper Room.

Other women besides those in the Luke 8 traveling team were also among His disciples. Remember the story of Mary and Martha? Martha was worried about the meal, and Mary wanted to sit at the feet of Jesus and learn from Him. According to Witherington, "the use of the phrase 'to sit at the feet of' is significant because evidence shows this is a technical formula meaning 'to be a disciple of.'"[12]

It was unknown in those days for a rabbi to come into the home of a woman and specifically teach her. Other rabbis would have questioned Jesus' behavior of being in the home of two women alone. Witherington goes on to say: "As in the case of Jesus' relation to His mother Mary, we again see a reorganizing of traditional priorities in light of Kingdom requirements. Martha's service is not denigrated, but it does not come first. One must reorient one's lifestyle according to what Jesus says is the 'good portion.'"[13]

Paul, Women and the Family

Paul followed Jesus' lead in revolutionizing the thinking of His day concerning the family. He grounded His instructions regarding honoring mother and father (see Ephesians 6:2) in the fifth commandment (see Exodus 20:12). But as we know from His theology, He did not slavishly follow rabbinic tradition.

In Roman times, households were governed by a common understanding of "household ethics." This common understanding was the basis for Roman tax and legal codes. The tax and legal codes made it clear that the man was the undisputed ruler of the house. Similarly, the Mishnah or Jewish tradition also put women in a subordinate and subservient position, as I stated in the opening of this chapter.

In the book of Ephesians, Paul gives us the "household ethics" or rules of order for the Christian home. What he wrote under the inspiration of the Holy Spirit rocked the foundations of society with the transforming power of the Gospel. Paul writes of the wife's submission in the context of mutual submission under Christ (see Ephesians 5:21–22). The wife and husband are fully included in the Body of Christ (see verses 23–24). The husband is instructed to love his wife in order that she may respect him (see verse 33). Her respect for him is to be the fruit of his love for her.[14]

In writing these words, Paul completely redefines the marital relationship. Paul's theology engages the very fabric of society, challenging all established cultural protocols, reshaping human value systems and transforming interpersonal relationships.[15]

The power of the cross cuts through the walls of division and brings dignity to men, women and children. There is no preferential treatment here. God loves all of His children the same—no matter what their age, gender or race. The Good News of Jesus Christ wrought a cultural reformation that continues to reshape our understanding today.

Attitudes of Early Church Leaders toward Women

Seeing in Scripture Jesus' (and Paul's) restructuring of the value of all people, I was amazed to find that some of the early Church fathers had a negative attitude toward women. The following quotes give some examples:

> Having become disobedient, she [Eve] was made the cause of death, both to herself and to the entire human race.
>
> Irenaeus, Bishop of Lyons, AD 177[16]

> Do you not know that you are an Eve? God's verdict on the sex still holds good, and the sex's guilt must still hold also. YOU ARE THE DEVIL'S GATEWAY, you are the avenue to the forbidden tree.
>
> Tertullian of Carthage, a few years later[17]

What is particularly sad about Tertullian's statement is that it is far from biblical. Scripture tell us, for instance, that "in Adam all die" (1 Corinthians 15:22), and that "Adam was not deceived" (1 Timothy 2:14). Even reformers such as Martin Luther had a bias against women. He once said, "No gown worse becomes a woman than to be wise."[18]

Bible Translation

Katharine Bushnell believed that Babylonian Talmudic thinking significantly influenced the translators of the English Bible. This is how: The Babylonian Talmud had existed as oral instruction for many centuries but was put in writing and published in Babylon around AD 800.[19]

In the 1530s, an Italian Dominican monk named Pagnino translated the Hebrew Bible relying on rabbinic interpretation of certain key passages regarding women. The *Biographie Universelle* quotes the following criticism of his work, in the language of Richard Simon: "Pagnino has too much neglected the ancient versions of Scripture to attach himself to the teachings of the rabbis."[20]

Bushnell then shows that later translations of the Bible into English, such as Coverdale's and Tyndale's, depended upon Pagnino's various renderings.

An excellent quotation sums up one of my life's philosophies as I have tried to study this subject: "Interpret your Bible by what the Bible says, and not by what men say that it says."[21] All of us, including myself, have some biases. The hard thing is to put them aside and try to hear what the Lord is saying in His Word.

The Impact of Jesus' Reformation in Modern Times

As I have studied the impact of Jesus' cultural reformation, it has been both fascinating and, I must admit, sad. First I would become exhilarated in studying the history of revivals when the Holy Spirit was trying to bring "new wine" thinking into the Church; then I would become discouraged when I saw how cultural influences inhibited what the Spirit was doing.

Around the advent of the twentieth century, a substantial move of God occurred regarding the role of women in the Church. Great reformers were hearing the Holy Spirit say that it was time for the women to come forth.

Leaders such as A. B. Simpson (who founded the Christian and Missionary Alliance church) gave women a prominent place in church ministry and encouraged women's leadership in virtually every phase of early CMA life. Simpson included women on the executive board committee, employed them as Bible professors and supported female evangelists and branch officers (the early CMA equivalent to a local minister). Half of all CMA vice presidents in 1887 were women.[22]

The Evangelical Free Church provided for women preachers in its original constitution. Charles Finney allowed women to speak in his Presbyterian church to mixed audiences. Dr. A. J. Gordon published his major treatise on women in 1894. Gordon Bible College prepared women to answer any call of the Spirit. Gordon pastored the Clarendon Street Baptist Church in Boston the last 24 years of his life. A woman graduate of Gordon Bible College later went on, after being ordained in 1914, to serve as an assistant pastor of the Stoughton Congregational Church. William Bell Riley pastored Minneapolis's First Baptist Church, one of the largest in the Northern Baptist Convention, for 45 years. Like Gordon, he advocated women preaching, pastoring and doing evangelistic work.[23]

I have noted in studying many denominations that when they were still simply "moves of God," and the Holy Spirit was pouring out His power, no one seemed to mind that women were preaching. Later, when the denominations became routine, institutionalized and set in governmental structure, the women were voted out. (I wonder somehow if the Holy Spirit was voted out, too.)

A study of the Moody Bible Institute shows that under Dwight L. Moody, women served as pastors, evangelists, Bible teachers and as ordained ministers. In August 1929, the *Moody Monthly* listed Lottie Osborn Sheidler as the first woman to graduate from the pastor's course. Yet, on August 1, 1979, MBI administration published the following statement about the role of women in public ministry:

> Our policy has been and is that we do not endorse or encourage the ordination of women nor do we admit women to our Pastoral Training

> Major. . . . While there were women in the Early Church who exercised spiritual gifts, they were not given places of authority in the government of the church.[24]

The Free Methodists began licensing women as local preachers in 1873, and founder B. T. Roberts wrote on behalf of women's ordination. The Wesleyan Methodist Church, founded in 1842, promoted equality for women and for blacks. Wesleyan minister Luther Lee delivered the sermon "Women's Right to Preach the Gospel" at the 1853 ordination of Congregationalist Antoinette L. Brown, America's first fully ordained woman.[25]

Northern and Southern Baptist churches had different attitudes toward women ministers. In the North, women preached in the Free Will Baptist, Seventh-Day Baptist, Swedish Baptist, German Baptist and German Baptist Brethren churches. When the German Baptist Brethren Church split in 1883, Mary Melinda Sterling became the first ordained Brethren woman in the Brethren Church. In the South, Southern Baptists overwhelmingly restricted females' public roles to singing in the choir and public testimonies. In stark contrast, American Baptist churches in the North ordained dozens of women in the first quarter of the twentieth century.[26]

Some Southern Baptist churches today have ordained women. One of my prayer partners is an ordained woman pastor. Because Southern Baptist churches are autonomous with regard to such decisions, some churches have ordained women even though the practice is not currently encouraged by the denomination.

Early in the years of the last century, women worked in parachurch agencies such as the Young Women's Christian Association (YWCA). Other denominations such as the Quakers, the Nazarenes and The Salvation Army were pioneers in ordaining women in ministry. It is ironic that there was a greater freedom for women in some of these denominations a century ago than we see today. Why is this?

Part of the explanation may be a conservative backlash against changing social values.[27] Separatist fundamentalists such as John R. Rice wrote books against bobbed hair, bossy wives and women preachers, lumping all three together into one ominous group.

Another factor has been the rise of feminism in its most militant, anti-male state. Any woman who preaches, even if she takes a stance against the errors of extremist feminism, takes a risk of being labeled a "flaming feminist." Actually, the early feminist movement in America for the women's right to vote came from inspiration by the Holy Spirit to protect the home. I believe that today God is calling many women to be pioneers to pray and speak out against unrighteousness, to protect their homes in much the same way that Frances Willard and other early feminists did.

The Pentecostal movement, which also began around the turn of the twentieth century, recognized the anointing of the Holy Spirit upon women's lives. In the predominantly black Azusa Street Mission, charisma (or the anointing) was what counted, not race, gender or class. Those called by the Holy Spirit led the meetings. The prophetic class led the movement, rather than the priestly class. Listen to Frank Bartleman, an eyewitness of the revival:

> We had no pope or hierarchy . . . we had no human program; the Lord Himself was leading. We had no priest class. . . . These things have come in later, with the apostasizing of the movement. We did not honor men for their advantage in means or education, but rather for their God-given "gifts." The Lord was liable to burst through anyone. Some would finally get anointed for the message. All seemed to recognize this and gave way. It might be a child, a woman or a man. It made no difference.[28]

This reminds me of my husband's statement during the interview he gave *Charisma* magazine about why he believes I am called to preach the Gospel. He said that it was God who anointed and who gives the anointing. His answer was based upon an understanding of the function of the prophetic class that Bartleman referred to.

According to an article in *Evangel*, the newspaper of the Azusa Street revival, published in 1916:

> A marked feature of this "latter day" outpouring is the Apostolate of women. Men have hypocritically objected to women making themselves conspicuous in pulpit work, but thank God, this conspicuousness is of God Himself. They did not push themselves to the front, God pulled them there. They did not take this ministry on themselves, God put it on them.[29]

If Pentecostal and charismatic churches are to look at the Azusa Street outpouring as a historic milestone in their history, we need to take a hard look at the fact that half of those put in leadership as elders were women.

Sadly, after the great initial outpouring, a struggle ensued throughout the following 29 years during which the roles of women in the Church were added and then subtracted. Women were not alone in this treatment. The color barrier that had once been declared "washed away" by the Azusa Street revival reemerged. It appears quite clear to me that when the spirit of prejudice is allowed to rise in the Church, women and minorities are its focused target.

The shift from the prophetic to the priestly role for ministry took its toll on many women leaders. One of the most outstanding was Aimee Semple McPherson, who was an ordained Assembly of God minister for three years. Aimee left the Assemblies to form the International Church of the Foursquare Gospel, in 1927, partly because of the lack of consensus concerning women in ministry in the Assemblies. She stated in a lecture in one of her classes, probably in the late 1930s:

> This (the Foursquare Church) is the only church, I am told, that is ordaining women preachers. The Assemblies of God are not ordaining women, to my knowledge. . . . Foursquaredom is the only work that has given such acknowledgment to women preachers, as well as men. Even the Pentecostal work, in some cases, has said, "No women preachers." But I am opening the door, and as long as Sister McPherson is alive, she is going to hold the door open and say, "Ladies, come!"[30]

Even though the official position of the Assemblies of God today is pro-women in ministry, as I stated earlier, the number of women senior pastors is still relatively small in comparison with the men. Sister McPherson would be proud to know, however, that Foursquare still leads the way for ordained women ministers.

The Army Arising

Today the Holy Spirit wants to pour out His Spirit just as He did in the last century. The Spirit of God is declaring to the Church that God wants us to be a prophetic class of people who long for a fresh Pentecost. God is longing to pour out His Spirit upon both His sons and daughters.

I have a burning longing in my heart that we not miss it this time and that an outpouring will rain down upon the whole Church, male and female. This outpouring will take us to a new place in God, a place we have not yet known, where men and women, teamed together, will plant their feet on soil held by Satan for centuries to preach the Good News that Jesus is alive.

Psalm 68:11 is a prophetic message for the great army of women who are arising in the land: "The Lord gives the word [of power]; the women who bear and publish [the news] are a great host" (AMPC). According to personal correspondence with Dr. Gary Greig, this passage and Isaiah 40:9–10 both refer to God raising up an army of women evangelists in the last days, since both refer to the Lord appearing in glory to bring judgment on the earth and to restore His people in the land of Israel. The verb forms in both passages are in the feminine form, not the usual masculine form.

Greig goes on to say the following about Isaiah 40:9–10:

> The literal translation with the feminine verb forms in caps is . . . (9) Onto a high mountain GO UP (feminine singular form of the imperative of the verb "go up") ONE WHO PROCLAIMS GOOD NEWS (to) Zion (literally "female evangelist of Zion" using the fem. sing. form of the participle meaning "one who proclaims good news" or "evangelist"

> or "herald" derived from the verb "to announce good news, proclaim good news, herald good news") SAY (fem. sing. imperative) to the cities of Judah, "Here is your God!"
>
> See, the Lord Yahweh is coming and His strong arm (a reference from Exodus to God's power working in signs and wonders) rules for Him. See, His reward is with Him and His recompense goes before Him.

What a powerful end-time statement! The incredible thing is that these passages about the Spirit raising up women evangelists have been there all this time, perhaps hidden until this season and hour when God is calling women to come forth and preach and prophesy over cities: *Cities, behold your God!* Isaiah 40:10 tells of God working signs and wonders through this company of women in the end times.

God is speaking to the prophets all around the world that an army of women is coming who will be evangelists to their cities and who will perform mighty signs and wonders.

The gospels end with one of the most powerful and beautiful stories ever told about a woman (see John 20:1–2,11–18): She was a woman who came to the tomb to do what women did for the dead . . . anoint them for burial. Mary Magdalene went that day to the place where they had placed her Master's body. To her surprise, however, He was not there.

Suddenly, someone called her name. It was Jesus. Scripture tells us that Jesus stopped on His way to heaven to comfort Mary and tell her that He was (is) alive. Have you ever wondered why He chose Mary Magdalene? I believe it was because the men could all have gone back to their former respectable professions, but she, a faithful follower of Jesus, had nothing to go back to. Jesus was the only way out for her.

He must have known this, and in His immense love He made a stop, just for her—the woman of least value in all society's eyes—to give her a message . . . *Go tell them I'm alive!*

What a powerful first-fruit statement! Jesus entrusted a woman to preach the Gospel of His resurrection, and the record is in Scripture. Surely this is a groundbreaking, precedent-setting stamp of approval from the Holy Spirit on the role of women in the Church today!

I believe that is the message God is speaking to us as women—"Rise up, and go tell the world about Me and My resurrection." He is also saying it to men and women together as teams. Maybe you feel inadequate, the last one that Jesus would choose to speak His Word—but, you see, He is not like all the others. He does not look on the outward form as they do. He only wants you to bow your knee before the King of Glory and give Him all of yourself, and He will fill you with all of Himself. The Lord is looking for a new generation of women who will arise and be fierce lovers of God, who will give Him 100 percent of their lives.

Then you can run to the streets, and to your neighbors, and to the people in the grocery stores and proclaim with all your heart: *Come meet a man who told me everything I ever did and still loves me.* Go! Go on! Man, woman or child—He is calling all to go today. Go tell them He is alive!

Afterword

An afterword is a good place for ponderings. While writing on the subject of women rising up and being used of God both inside the church and out, I have studied the role we ladies have in society. Of course, there have been tomes written about that subject.

One thing that I have noticed is there has been huge progress made in some movements in releasing women in a whole variety of roles. They have studied the issue of women in ministry and have settled it theologically. Places like the Bethel Church headed by Bill and Beni Johnson. This has caused many women to rise up to take their places as leaders, not only in preaching and teaching, but also in media, arts, entertainment, business, writing and many other roles.

I am thankful for them and other leaders like Dr. Ché and Sue Ahn of Harvest International Ministries (HIM). Others like John and Carol Arnott have also made huge progress in this area.

There are still huge gaps, though, and places where there is still a huge struggle. In the past couple of years, I was uninvited to a prayer leader's meeting and, in another place, was walked out on when I mentioned women in ministry.

It is my belief that those times will be fewer and fewer. There are still numbers of denominations that do not allow women to stand in a pulpit and preach. As some would say, however, "The train has left the station!" Women are burning with passion to bring justice and righteousness to the earth, and we will not be stopped.

Women are speaking up about the sexual abuse they have suffered and finding their voices in what used to be solely a man's world, even though some are still persecuted.

I pray that someday both men and women will read what I have written in the former paragraph and muse aloud, "How could those things have happened?" I often tell my daughters-in-the-Lord, "Some of us have paid a high price so you can be who you are today. Don't waste it!" There will always be injustices and battles to fight in order to see God's will be done on the earth. Be a voice! Don't be silent in the face of opposition. God will give you the courage to say yes in the battle, even when your flesh is afraid. Above all, *rise up* and take your place in bringing the Good News about God's Kingdom; be like Jesus, be unashamed of the Gospel and never, never, never give up!

APPENDIX A

Gender and Leadership

I include the following article in this book for several reasons:

1. A. J. Gordon was a powerful missions-minded Baptist pastor who in the early 1880s and 1890s advocated for women in ministry. Some people today erroneously think that anyone who advocates for women in ministry is powerfully influenced by the women's liberation movement and, hence, is disqualified from speaking without bias about the issue.

2. Dr. Gordon strongly endorsed the principle of interpreting confusing passages in light of clear passages and not the other way around. He used what were, in his mind (and mine), normative passages to set the standards.

3. This article shows the difficulty of the passages being interpreted. Godly exegetes have continued to wrestle with these passages. My general observation, therefore, is that to draw a major doctrine out of a passage over which so many learned exegetes differ is not wise.

4. The tone of Dr. Gordon's spirit as he examined the issues displays wisdom and grace.

5. He shows how male biases actually influenced translation of the Scriptures, which in turn influenced views.

6. A. J. Gordon was my historical mentor for two years and has had a powerful impact upon my life. I honor him by remembering him in this way.

Unless otherwise indicated, all Scripture passages in this article are taken from the KJV.

The Ministry of Women

by Dr. A. J. Gordon, December 1894

The occasion for writing the following article is this: At a recent summer convention a young lady missionary had been appointed to give an account of her work at one of the public sessions. The scruples of certain of the delegates against a woman's addressing a mixed assembly were found to be so strong, however, that the lady was withdrawn from the programme, and further public participation in the conference confined to its male constituency.

The conscientious regard thus displayed for Paul's alleged injunction of silence in the church on the part of women, deserves our highest respect. But with a considerable knowledge of the nature and extent of woman's work on the missionary field, the writer has long believed that it is exceedingly important that that work, as now carried on, should either be justified from Scripture, or, if that were impossible, that it be so modified as to bring it into harmony with the exact requirements of the Word of God. For while it is true that many Christians believe that women are enjoined from publicly preaching the Gospel, either at home or abroad, it is certainly true that scores of missionary women are at present doing this very thing. They are telling out the good news of salvation to heathen men and women publicly and from house to house, to little groups gathered by the wayside, or to larger groups assembled in the zayats. It is not affirmed that a majority of women missionaries are engaged in this kind of work, but that scores are doing it, and doing it with the approval of the boards under which they are serving. If anyone should raise the technical objection that because of its informal and colloquial character this is not preaching, we are ready to affirm that it comes much nearer the preaching enjoined in the great commission than does the reading of a theological disquisition from the pulpit on Sunday morning, or the discussion of some ethical or sociological question before a popular audience on Sunday evening.

But the purpose of this article is not to condemn the ministry of missionary women described above, or to suggest its modification, but rather to justify and vindicate both its propriety and authority by a critical examination of Scripture on the question at issue.

In order to gain a right understanding of this subject, it is necessary for us to be reminded that we are living in the dispensation of the Spirit—a dispensation which differs most radically from that of the law which preceded it. As the day of Pentecost ushered in this new economy, so the prophecy of Joel, which Peter rehearsed on that day, outlined its great characteristic features. Let us briefly consider this prophecy:

> 17 And it shall be in the last days, saith God,
> I will pour out my Spirit on all flesh:
> And your sons and daughters shall prophesy,
> And your young men shall see visions,
> And your old men will dream dreams:
> 18 Yea and on my servants and on my handmaidens in those days
> Will I pour forth of my Spirit: and they shall prophesy.
> 19 And I will shew wonders in the heaven above,
> And signs on the earth beneath;

Blood, and fire, and vapor of smoke:
20 The sun shall be turned into darkness,
And the moon into blood,
Before the day of the Lord come,
That great and notable day:
21 And it shall be, that whosoever shall call on the name of the
Lord shall be saved. (Acts 2:17–24, R. V.)

It will be observed that four classes are here named as being brought into equal privileges under the outpoured Spirit:

1. *Jew and Gentile:* "All flesh" seems to be equivalent to "every one who" or "whosoever," named in the twenty-first verse. Paul expounds this phrase to mean both Jew and Gentile (Romans 10:13): "For there is no difference between the *Jew and the Greek*. . . . For whosoever shall call upon the name of the Lord shall be saved."
2. *Male and female:* "And your sons and your daughters shall prophesy."
3. *Old and young:* "Your young men shall see visions, and your old men shall dream dreams."
4. *Bondsmen and bondmaidens* (*vide* R. W. margin)*:* "And on my *servants* and on my *handmaidens* in those days will I pour forth of My Spirit, and they shall prophesy."

Now, evidently these several classes are not mentioned without a definite intention and significance; for Paul, in referring back to the great baptism through which the Church of the New Covenant was ushered in, says: "For in one Spirit were we all baptized into one body, whether *Jews or Greeks, whether bond or free*" (1 Cor. 12:13, R. V.). Here he enumerates two classes named in Joel's prophecy; and in another passage he mentions three: "For as many of you as were baptized into Christ did put on Christ; there can be neither *Jew nor Greek*; there can be neither *bond or free*; there can be no *male and female*; for ye are all one in Christ Jesus" (Gal. 3:28, R. V.).

We often hear this phrase, "neither male nor female," quoted as though it were a rhetorical figure; but we insist that the inference is just, that if the Gentile came into vastly higher privileges under grace than under the law, so did the woman; for both are spoken of in the same category.

Here, then, we take our starting-point for the discussion. This prophecy of Joel, realized at Pentecost, is the *Magna Charta* of the Christian Church. It gives to woman a status in the Spirit hitherto unknown. And, as in civil legislation, no law can be enacted which conflicts with the constitution, so in Scripture we shall expect to find no text which denies to woman her divinely appointed rights in the New Dispensation.

"*Your sons and your daughters shall prophesy.*" Here is woman's equal warrant with man's for telling out the Gospel of the grace of God. So it seems, at least, for this word "prophesy" in the New Testament "signifies not merely to foretell future events, but to communicate religious truth in general under a Divine inspiration (*vide* Hackett on "Acts," p. 49), and the spirit of prophecy was henceforth to rest, not upon the favored few, but upon the many, without regard to race, or age, or sex. All that we can gather from the New Testament use of this word leads us to believe that it embraces that faithful witnessing for Christ, that fervent telling out of the Gospel under the impulse of the Holy Spirit, which was found in the early Church, and is found just as truly among the faithful to-day.

Some, indeed, foreseeing whither such an admission might lead, have insisted on limiting the word "prophesy" to its highest meaning—that of inspired prediction or miraculous revelation—and have then affirmed that the age of miracles having ceased, therefore Joel's prophecy cannot be cited as authority for women's public witnessing for Christ to-day.

This method of reasoning has been repeatedly resorted to in similar exigencies of interpretation, but it has not proved satisfactory. When William Carey put his finger on the words, "Go ye into all the world and preach the Gospel to every creature," and asked if this command were not still binding on the Church, he was answered by his brethren: "No! The great commission was accompanied by the miraculous gift of tongues; this miracle has ceased in the Church, and therefore we cannot hope to succeed in such an enterprise unless God shall send another Pentecost." But Carey maintained that the power of the Spirit could be still depended on, as in the beginning, for carrying out the great commission; and a century of missions has vindicated the correctness of his judgment. When, within a few years, some thoughtful Christians have asked whether the promise, "The prayer of faith shall save the sick," is not still in force, the theologians have replied: "No; this refers to miraculous healing; and the age of miracles ended with the apostles." And now it is said that "prophecy" also belongs in the same catalogue of miraculous gifts which passed away with the apostles. It is certainly incumbent upon those who advocate this view to bring forward some evidence of its correctness from Scripture, which, after repeated challenges, they have failed to do, and must fail to do. Our greatest objection to the theory is, that it fails to make due recognition of the Holy Spirit's perpetual presence in the Church—a presence which implies the equal perpetuity of His gifts and endowments.

If, now, we turn to the history of the primitive Church, we find the practice corresponding to the prophecy. In the instance of Philip's household, we read: "Now this man had four daughters which did prophesy" (Acts 21:9); and in connection with the Church in Corinth we read: "Every woman praying and prophesying with her head unveiled" (1 Cor. 11:5); which passage we shall consider further on, only rejoicing as we pass that "praying" has not yet, like its yoke-fellow, "prophesying," been remanded exclusively to the apostolic age.

Having touched thus briefly to the positive side of this question, we now proceed to consider the alleged prohibition of women's participation in the public meetings of the Church, found in the writings of Paul.

We shall examine, first, the crucial text contained in 1 Tim. 2:8–11:

> (8) I desire therefore that men pray in every place, lifting up holy hands without wrath and doubting. (9) In like manner that women adorn themselves in modest apparel with shamefastness and sobriety; not

> with braided hair and gold or pearls or costly raiment; (10) but (which becometh women professing godliness) through good works. (11) Let a woman learn in quietness with all subjection. (12) But I permit not a woman to teach, nor to have dominion over a man, but to be in quietness, etc. (R.V.).

This passage has generally been regarded as perhaps the strongest and most decisive, for the silence of women in the Church. It would be very startling, therefore, were it shown that it really contains an exhortation to the orderly and decorous participation of women in public prayer. Yet such is the conclusion of some of the best exegetes.

By general consent the force of *boulomai*, "I will," is carried over from the eighth verse into the ninth: "*I will that women*" (*vide* Alford). And what is it that the apostle will have women do? The words, "*in like manner*," furnish a very suggestive hint toward one answer, and a very suggestive hindrance to another and common answer. Is it meant that he would have the men pray in every place, and the women, "*in like manner*," to be silent? But where would be the similarity of conduct in the two instances? Or does the intended likeness lie between the men's "lifting up holy hands," and the women's adorning themselves in modest apparel? So unlikely is either one of those conclusions from the apostle's language, that, as Alford concedes, "Chrysostom and most commentators supply *proseuchesthai*, 'to pray,' in order to complete the sense." If they are right in so construing the passage—and we believe the *hosautos*, "in like manner," compels them to this course—then the meaning is unquestionable. "I will, therefore, that men pray everywhere, lifting up holy hands, etc. In like manner I will that women pray in modest apparel, etc."

In one of the most incisive and clearly reasoned pieces of exegesis with which we are acquainted, Wiesinger, the eminent commentator, thus interprets the passage, and, as it seems to us, clearly justifies his conclusions. We have not space to transfer his argument to these pages, but we may, in a few words, give a summary of it, mostly in his own language. He says:

"1. In the words '*in every place*' it is chiefly to be observed that it is public prayer and not secret prayer that is spoken of.

"2. The *proseuchesthai*, 'to pray,' is to be supplied in verse 9, and to be connected with '*in modest apparel*;' so that this special injunction as to the conduct of women in prayer corresponds to that given to the men in the words '*lifting up holy hands*.' This verse, then, from the beginning, refers to prayer; and what is said of the women in verses 9 and 10 is *to be understood as referring primarily to public prayer.*

"3. The transition in verse 11 from *gunaikas* to *gune* shows that the apostle now passes on to something new—viz., the relation of the married woman to her husband. She is to be in quietness rather than drawing attention to herself by public appearance; to learn rather than to teach; to be in subjection rather than in authority."

In a word, our commentator finds no evidence from this passage that women were forbidden to pray in the public assemblies of the Church; through reasoning back from the twelfth verse to those before, he considers that they may have been enjoined from public teaching. The latter question we shall consider further on.

The interpretation just given has strong presumption in its favor, from the likeness of the passage to another which we now consider:

> Every man praying or prophesying, having his head covered, dishonoreth his head. But every woman praying or prophesying with her head unveiled dishonoreth her head. (1 Cor. 11:4, 5.)

By common consent the reference is here to public worship; and the decorous manner of taking part therein is pointed out first for the man and then for the woman. "Every woman praying or prophesying." Bengel's terse comment: "*Therefore women were not excluded from these duties*," is natural and reasonable. It is quite incredible, on the contrary, that the apostle should give himself the trouble to prune a custom which he desired to uproot, or that he should spend his breath in condemning a forbidden *method* of doing a forbidden thing. This passage is strikingly like the one just considered, in that the proper order of doing having been prescribed, first for the man, and then for the woman, it is impossible to conclude that the thing to be done is then enjoined only upon the one party, and forbidden to the other. If the "in like manner" has proved such a barrier to commentators against finding an injection for the silence of women in 1 Tim. 3:9, the unlike manner pointed out in this passage is not less difficult to be surmounted by those who hold that women are forbidden to participate in public worship. As the first passage has been shown to give sanction to women's praying in public, this one points not less strongly to her habit of both praying and prophesying in public.

We turn now to the only remaining passage which has been urged as decisive for the silence of women—viz., 1 Cor. 14:34, 35:

> Let the women keep silence in the churches: for it is not permitted unto them to speak; but let them be in subjection, as also saith the law. And if they would learn anything, let them ask their own husbands at home: for it is shameful for a woman to speak in the church.

Here, again, the conduct of women in the church should be studied in relation to that of men if we would rightly understand the apostle's teaching. Let us observe, then, that the injection to silence is three times served in this chapter by the use of the same Greek word, *sigao*, twice on men and once on women, and that in every case the silence commanded is conditional, not absolute.

"*Let him keep silence in the church*" (verse 28), it is said to one speaking with tongues, but on the condition that "there be no interpreter." "*Let the first keep silence*" (verse 30), it is said of the prophets, "speaking by two or three;" but it is on condition that "a revelation be made to another sitting by."

"*Let the women keep silence in the church*," it is said again, but it is evidently on condition of their interrupting the service with questions, since it is added, "for it is not permitted them to speak, . . . and if they would learn anything, let them ask their husbands at home." This last clause takes the injunction clearly out of all reference to praying or prophesying, and shows—what the whole chapter indicates—that the apostle is here dealing with the various forms of disorder and confusion in the church; not that he is repressing the decorous exercise of spiritual gifts, either by men or by women. If he were forbidding women to pray or to prophesy in public, as some argue, what could be more irrelevant or meaningless than his direction concerning the case: "If they will learn anything, let them ask their husbands at home"?

In fine, we may reasonably insist that this text, as well as the others discussed above, be considered in the light of the entire New Testament teaching—the teaching of prophecy, the teaching of practice, and the teaching of contemporary history—if we would find the true meaning.

Dr. Jacob, in his admirable work, "The Ecclesiastical Polity of the New Testament," considering the question after this broad method, thus candidly and, as it seems to us, justly, sums up the whole question: "A due consideration of this ministry of gifts in the earliest days of Christianity—those times of high and sanctified spiritual freedom—both shows and justifies the custom of the public ministration of women at that time in the Church. The very ground and title of this ministry being the acknowledged possession of some gift, and such gifts being bestowed on women as well as men, the former as well as the latter were allowed to use them in Christian assemblies. *This seems to me quite evident from Paul's words in 1 Cor. 11:5, where he strongly condemns the practice of women praying or prophesying with the head unveiled, without expressing the least objection to this public ministration on their part, but only finding fault with what was considered an unseemly attire for women thus publicly engaged.* The injunction contained in the same epistle (1 Cor. 14:34), 'Let your women keep silence,' etc., refers, as the context shows, not to prophesying or praying in the congregations, but to making remarks and asking questions about the words of others."

On the whole, we may conclude, without over-confidence, that there is no Scripture which prohibits women from praying or prophesying in the public assemblies of the Church; that, on the contrary, they seem to be exhorted to the first exercise by the word of the apostle (1 Tim. 2:9); while for prophesying they have the threefold warrant of inspired prediction (Acts 2:17), of primitive practice (Acts 21:9), and of apostolic provision (1 Cor. 11:4).[1]

As to the question of teaching, a difficulty arises which it is not easy to solve. If the apostle, in his words to Timothy, absolutely forbids a woman to teach and expound spiritual truth, then the remarkable instance of a woman doing this very thing at once occurs to the mind (Acts 18:26)—an instance of private teaching possibly, but endorsed and made conspicuously public by its insertion in the New Testament.

In view of this example, some have held that the statement in 1 Tim. 2:9, with the entire paragraph to which it belongs, refers to the married woman's domestic relations, and not to her public relations; to her subjection to the teaching of her husband as against her dogmatic lording it over him. This is the view of Canon Garratt, in his excellent observations on the "Ministry of Women." Admit, however, that the prohibition is against public teaching; what may it mean? To teach and to govern are the special functions of the presbyter. The teacher and the pastor, named in the gifts to the Church (Eph. 4:11), Alford considers to be the same; and the pastor is generally regarded as identical with the bishop. Now there is no instance in the New Testament of a woman being set over a church as bishop and teacher. The lack of such example would lead us to refrain from ordaining a woman as pastor of a Christian congregation. But if the Lord has fixed this limitation, we believe it to be grounded, not on her less favored position in the privileges of grace, but in the impediments to such service existing in nature itself.

1. The following note, which we transcribed from Meyer's Commentary, seems to be a fair and well-balanced *résumé* of the case: "This passage (1 Tim. 2:8–11) does not distinctly forbid *proseuchesthai* (to pray) to women; it only distinctly forbids *didaskein* (to teach) on their part. There is the same apparent contradiction between 1 Cor. 14:34, 35 and 1 Cor. 11:5, 13. While in the former passage *lalein* (to speak) is forbidden to women, in the latter *proseuchesthai* (to pray) and even *propheteuein* (to prophesy) are presupposed as things done by women, and the apostle does not forbid it. The solution is that Paul wishes everything in the Church to be done decently and in order, while, on the other hand, he holds by the principle, 'Quench not the spirit.'"

It may be said against the conclusion which we have reached concerning the position of women, that the plain reading of the New Testament makes a different impression on the mind. That may be so on two grounds: first, on that of traditional bias; and second, on that of unfair translation. Concerning the latter point, it would seem as though the translators of our common version wrought, at every point where this question occurs, under the shadow of Paul's imperative, "Let your women keep silence in the churches."

Let us take two illustrations from names found in that constellation of Christian women mentioned in Rom. 16:

"I commend unto you Phoebe our sister, which is a servant of the church which is at Cenchrea." So, according to the King James Version, writes Paul. But the same word *diakonos*, here translated "servant," is rendered "minister" when applied to Paul and Apollos (1 Cor. 3:5), and "deacon" when used of other male officers of the Church (1 Tim. 3:10, 12–13). Why discriminate against Phoebe simply because she is a woman? The word "servant" is correct for the general unofficial use of the term, as in Matt. 22:11; but if Phoebe were really a functionary of the Church, as we have a right to conclude, let her have the honor to which she is entitled. If "Phoebe, a minister of the church at Cenchrea," sounds too bold, let the word be transliterated, and read, "Phoebe, a deacon"—a *deacon*, too, without the insipid termination "ess," of which there is no more need than that we should say "teacheress" or "doctress." This emendation "deaconess" has timidly crept into the margin of the Revised Version, thus adding prejudice to slight by the association which this name has with High Church sisterhoods and orders. It is wonderful how much there is in a name! "Phoebe, a *servant*," might suggest to an ordinary reader nothing more than the modern church drudge, who prepares sandwiches and coffee for an ecclesiastical sociable. To Canon Garratt, with his genial and enlightened view of woman's position in apostolic times, "Phoebe, a deacon," suggests a useful co-laborer of Paul, "traveling about on missionary and other labors of love."

Again, we read in the same chapter of Romans, "*Greet Priscilla and Aquila, my helpers in Christ Jesus.*" Notice the order here; the woman's name put first, as elsewhere (Acts 18:18; 2 Tim. 4:19). But when we turn to that very suggestive passage in Acts 18:26 we find the order reversed, and the man's name put first: "Whom, when Aquila and Priscilla had heard, they took him and expounded unto him the way of the Lord more perfectly." Yet this is conceded to be wrong, according to the best manuscripts. Evidently to some transcriber or critic the startling questions presented itself: "Did not Paul say, 'I suffer not a woman to teach, nor to usurp authority over the man'? but here a woman is actually taking the lead as theological teacher to Apollos, an eminent minister of the Gospel, and so far setting up her authority as to tell him that he is not thoroughly qualified for his work! This will never do; if the woman cannot be silent, she must at least be thrust into the background." And so the order is changed, and the man's name has stood first for generations of readers. The Revised Version has rectified the error, and the woman's name now leads.

But how natural is this story, and how perfectly accordant with subsequent Christian history! We can readily imagine that, after listening to this Alexandrian orator, Priscilla would say to her husband: "Yes, he is eloquent and mighty in the Scriptures; but do you not see that he lacks the secret of power?" And so they took him and instructed him concerning the baptism of the Holy Ghost, with the result that he who before had been mighty in the Scriptures, now "mightily convinced the Jews." How often has this scene been reproduced; as, *e.g.*, in the instance of Catherine of Sienna instructing the corrupt clergy of her day in the things of the Spirit till they exclaimed in wonder, "Never man spake like this woman;" of Madame Guyon, who by her teaching made new men of scores of accomplished but unspiritual preachers of her time; of the humble woman of whom the evangelist Moody tells, who, on hearing some of his early sermons, admonished him of his need of the secret of power, and brought him under unspeakable obligation by teaching him of the same. It is evident that the Holy Spirit made this woman Priscilla a teacher of teachers, and that her theological chair has had many worthy incumbents through the subsequent Christian ages.

To follow still further the list of women workers mentioned in Rom. 16, we read: "Salute Tryphaena and Tryphosa, who labor in the Lord. Salute Persis the beloved, which labored much in the Lord" (verse 12). What was the work *in the Lord* which these so worthily wrought? Put with quotation another: "Help those women which *labored with me in the Gospel*" (Phil. 4:3). Did they "labor in the Gospel" with the one restriction that they should not preach the Gospel? Did they "labor in the Lord" under sacred bonds to give no public witness for the Lord? "Ah! but there is that word of Paul to Timothy, 'Let the women learn in silence,'" says the plaintiff. No! It is not there. Here again we complain of an invidious translation. Right the Revised Version gives it: "Let a woman learn *in quietness* (*hesuchia*)," an admonition not at all inconsistent with decorous praying and witnessing in the Christian assembly. When *men* are admonished, the King James translators give the right rendering to the same word: "That with *quietness* they work and eat their own bread" ([2] Thess. 3:12), an injunction which no reader would construe to mean that they should refrain from speaking during their labor and their eating.

As a woman is named among the deacons in this chapter, so it is more than probable that one is mentioned among the apostles. "Salute Andronicus and Junia, my kinsmen, and my fellow-prisoners, who are of note among the apostles" (v. 7). Is Junia a feminine name? So it has been commonly held. But the *en tois apostolois*, with which it stands connected, has led some to conclude that it is Junias, the name of a man. This is not impossible. Yet Chrysostom, who, as a Greek Father, ought to be taken as a high authority, makes this frank and unequivocal comment on the passage: "*How great is the devotion of this woman, that she should be counted worthy of the name of an apostle!*"

These are illustrations which might be considerably enlarged, of the shadow which Paul's supposed law of silence for women has cast upon the work of the early translators—a shadow which was even thrown back into the Old Testament, so that we read in the Common Version: "The Lord gave the word; great was the company of those that published it" (Ps. 68:11); while the Revised correctly gives it: "The Lord giveth the word; *the women that publish the tidings are a great host.*"

Whether we are right or wrong in our general conclusions, there are some very interesting lessons suggested by this subject:

Especially, the value of experience as an interpreter of Scripture. The final exegesis is not always to be found in the lexicon and grammar. The Spirit is in the Word; and the Spirit is also in the Church, the body of regenerate and sanctified believers. To follow the voice of the Church apart from that of the written Word has never proved safe; but, on the other hand, it may be that we need to be admonished not to ignore the teaching of the deepest spiritual life of the Church in forming our conclusions concerning the meaning of Scripture. It cannot be denied that in every great spiritual awakening in the history of Protestantism the impulse for Christian women to pray and witness for Christ in the public assembly has been found irrepressible. It was so in the beginnings of the Society of Friends. It was so in the great evangelical revival associated with the names of Wesley and Whitefield. It has been so in that powerful *renaissance* of primitive Methodism known as the Salvation Army. It has been increasingly so in this era of modern missions and modern evangelism in which we are living. Observing this fact, and observing also the great blessing which has attended the ministry of consecrated women in heralding the Gospel, many thoughtful men have been led to examine the Word of God anew, to learn if it be really so that the Scriptures silence the testimony which the Spirit so signally blesses. To many it has been both a relief and a surprise to discover how little authority there is in the Word for repressing the witness of women in the public assembly, or for forbidding her to herald the Gospel to the unsaved. If this be so, it may be well for the plaintiffs in this case to beware lest, in silencing the voice of consecrated women, they may be resisting the Holy Ghost. The conjunction of these two admonitions of the apostle is significant: "Quench not the spirit. Despise not prophesying" (1 Thess. 5:19).

The famous Edward Irving speaks thus pointedly on this subject: "Who am I that I should despise the gift of God, because it is in a woman, whom the Holy Ghost despiseth not? . . . That women have with men an equal distribution of spiritual gifts is not only manifest from the fact (Acts 2; 18:26; 21:9; 1 Cor. 11:3, etc.), but from the very words of the prophecy of Joel itself, which may well rebuke those vain, thoughtless people who make light of the Lord's work, because it appeareth among women. "*I wish men would themselves be subject to the Word of God, before they lord it so over women's equal rights in the great outpouring of the Spirit*" (Works, v. 555).

As is demanded, we have preferred to forego all appeals to reason and sentiment in settling the question, and to rest it solely on a literal interpretation of Scripture. Yet we cannot refrain from questioning whether the spiritual intuition of the Church has not been far in advance of its exegesis in dealing with this subject. We will not refer to the usage prevailing in many of our most spiritual and evangelical churches, but will cite some conspicuous public instances.

Annie Taylor's missionary tour into Thibet has been the subject of world-wide comment. And now she is returning to that vast and perilous field with a considerable company of missionary recruits, both men and women, herself the leader of the expedition. In this enterprise of carrying the Gospel into the regions beyond, and preaching Christ to all classes, she is as full a missionary as was Paul, or Columba, or Boniface. Yet in all the comments of the religious press we have never once heard the questions raised as to whether, in thus acting, she were not stepping out of woman's sphere as defined in Scripture.

When before the Exeter Hall Missionary Conference in 1888, Secretary Murdock described the work of Mrs. Ingalls, of Burmah, declaring that, though not assuming ecclesiastical functions, yet by force of character on the one hand, and by the exigencies of the field on the other, she had come to be a virtual bishop over nearly a score of churches, training the native ministry in theology and homiletics, guiding the churches in the selection of pastors, and superintending the discipline of the congregations, the story evoked only applause, without a murmur of dissent from the distinguished body of missionary leaders who heard it.

When at that same conference, the representative of the Karen Mission having failed, it was asked whether there were any missionary present who could speak for that remarkable work, the reply was, "Only one, and she is a woman." She was unhesitatingly accepted as the speaker; and though at first demurring, she finally consented, and had the honor of addressing perhaps the most august array of missionary leaders which has convened in this century. The clear and distinct tones in which Mrs. Armstrong told her story did not suggest "silence;" but the modesty and reserve of her bearing completely answered to the Scripture requirement of "quietness." And though she had among her auditors missionary secretaries, Episcopal bishops, Oxford professors, and Edinburgh theologians, not the slightest indication of objection to her service was anywhere visible.

We vividly remember, in the early days of woman's work in the foreign field, how that brilliant missionary to China, Miss Adele Fielde, was recalled by her board because of the repeated complaints of the senior missionaries that in her work she was transcending her sphere as a woman. "It is reported that you have taken upon you to preach," was the charge read by the chairman; "Is it so?" She replied by describing the vastness and destitution of her field—village after village, hamlet after hamlet, yet unreached by the Gospel—and then how, with a native woman, she had gone into the surrounding country, gathered groups of men, women, and children—whoever would come—and told of the story of the cross to them. "If this is preaching, I plead guilty to the charge," she said. "And have you ever been ordained to preach?" asked her examiner. "No," she replied, with great dignity and emphasis—"*no; but I believe I have been foreordained*." O woman! you have answered discreetly; and if any shall ask for your foreordination credentials, put your finger on the words of the prophet: "Your sons and your daughters shall prophesy," and the whole Church will vote to send you back unhampered to your work, as happily the Board did in this instance.

How slow are we to understand what is written! Simon Peter, who on the Day of Pentecost had rehearsed the great prophecy of the new dispensation, and announced that its fulfillment had begun, was yet so holden of tradition that it took a special vision of the sheet descending from heaven to convince him that in the body of Christ "there can be neither Jew nor Gentile." And it has required another vision of a multitude of missionary women, let down by the Holy Spirit among the heathen, and publishing the Gospel to every tribe and kindred and people, to convince us that in that same body "there can be no male nor female." It is evident, however, that this extraordinary spectacle of ministering women has brought doubts to some conservative men as to "whereunto this thing may grow." Yet as believers in the sure word of prophecy, all has happened exactly according to the foreordained pattern, from the opening chapter of the new dispensation, when in the upper room "these all continued with one accord in prayer and supplication, *with the women*, and Mary the mother of Jesus, and with His brethren," to the closing chapter, now fulfilling, when "the women that publish the tidings are a great host."

The new economy is not as the old; and the defendants in this case need not appeal to the examples of Miriam, and Deborah and Huldah, and Anna the prophetess. These were exceptional instances under the old dispensation; but she that is least in the kingdom of heaven is greater than they. And let the theologians who have recently written so dogmatically upon this subject to consider whether it may not be possible that in this matter they are still under the law and not under grace; and whether, in sight of the promised land of world-wide evangelization, they may not hear the voice of God saying: "*Moses, my servant, is dead*; now, therefore, arise and go over this Jordan."

APPENDIX B

Generals International Policies

As I mentioned in chapter 11, an important subject we women in ministry need to understand is how we relate to men in ministries. I have included the following letter, which my office sends out before I go any place to speak, to show you some of the precautions I take to safeguard myself from gossip or any other attack that might present itself from my interactions with men.

Purpose of This Letter

The purpose of this letter is to inform you of the policies of Generals International regarding Cindy Jacobs's speaking engagements, including information on travel and hotel accommodations, honorariums and any special requests that may pertain to your scheduled event.

Meeting Location

Please send us the address and phone number for the location of the conference meeting(s). We will be keeping this information in our office records in case of emergency and we need to contact Cindy immediately. If there is a contact person at this location that we should ask for, please include that person's name and position if applicable.

Transportation Arrangements

I will be sending you Cindy's itinerary shortly, as arrangements have been made. Please make arrangements for her to be transported to and from the airport and the meeting(s). The policy of G.I. is for Cindy to be picked up by a woman or a man escorted by a woman, in order to avoid any questionable appearance. On all trips Cindy will be traveling with a companion; please be prepared to lodge this person as well as cover the travel cost for his or her ticket. As a policy, while our office will make the travel arrangements, we ask that you cover the price of the tickets up-front. Please write the check to Generals International. Thank you for complying with our policies on these points.

Hotel Accommodations

We do require that Cindy's hotel expenses (other than personal) be covered. Since you are familiar with the geographical area where Cindy is speaking, please make hotel accommodations accordingly for her. It is necessary for the accommodations to provide a quiet and pleasant atmosphere for Cindy (and any additional traveling companions). When these arrangements have been made please contact our office. We need to have the hotel name, address, phone/fax number, and confirmation number in our records.

Honorarium

Generals International requests an honorarium of $5,000, as this covers one day of the ministries' expenses. When sending an honorarium or reimbursement check, please make it payable to Generals International. G.I. is a nonprofit, tax exempt corporation; therefore, please don't issue a 1099 at the end of the year. A board sets Cindy's salary, and she doesn't take personal funds. If a check is inadvertently made payable to "Cindy Jacobs," we will not be able to process it, and it will have to be returned to you. Thank you for your kind understanding in this matter.

Materials

Many times our office sends materials for resale (books, tapes & videos) to the meeting place where Cindy is scheduled to speak. For overseas meetings this is optional. Please let us know what is needed to be done as far as customs and shipping so we can decide what should be done. If we decide to send materials please be prepared with the following: For the purpose of sending materials, please let us know how many people are expected to attend. It would be appreciated if you would have a person assigned to handle receipt of the materials, as well as facilitate the sale and accounting of funds collected. An inventory/ instruction packet will be sent with the materials to assist in keeping account. Please provide us with this person's name and the address to send the materials to. If you have any questions, please do not hesitate to contact me at 972–576–8887 or write me at ea@generals.org.

APPENDIX C

Women and Justice Issues

Women and children have long faced oppression, abuse, violence, neglect and exploitation. The blotter of crimes could fill many pages in this book, and the locations where injustices have occurred literally crisscross every nation on earth. While some governments and a few men have stood against these atrocities, throughout history it has primarily been women who have fought for the rights of other women. Their voices have been heard, and we have seen breakthroughs that have altered the course of history forever. We should celebrate these victories of the past.

But the fight is not over. Today, crimes continue to be perpetuated against women and children. More than 27 million people are trapped in slavery of all types throughout the world, and many of the enslaved are women and children.[1] Human trafficking is now the second largest international organized crime, generating more than US $31 billion annually—a figure surpassed only by the sale of illegal drugs.[2]

Although modern-day slavery is a civil rights violation that affects everyone, it is of critical importance to women. Not only are women and children the ones most frequently trafficked for labor and sex, but throughout the world women are coming forward to fight on behalf of the oppressed. While the media, churches and politicians have taken up justice causes, it is primarily women who are giving their lives to rescue and rehabilitate children who were kidnapped from their homes and forced into brothels. It is also women who are most often on the front lines of defense to help to rescue the most vulnerable in our society.

These are the shocking facts, and they should cause us to pray, reflect and take action. But behind every statistic is a story of someone who has been the object of oppression, and behind every act of rescue or healing there is the story of someone like you who has responded and fulfilled her destiny. One such woman is my friend Erica Greve. Here is the story of how she responded when she came face to face with human trafficking in America.

Erica's Story

I was working as an emergency department social worker intern at a children's hospital in the San Francisco Bay area, there to help hurting children, when my life changed forever. I had known that I would hear shocking stories of how young lives had been shattered by the trauma of all sorts of abuse and neglect, but I am not sure that I was ready for Sarah's story (name changed).

Sarah looked to be sixteen years old, but she was only twelve. She was unable to read or write. Her speech was slow and thick, and as she talked, she cradled a red crayon in her right hand. A coloring book on her lap was opened to a page filled with horses. It took only a few moments to realize that she was what we call mentally challenged.

Sarah told me about a man she had met when she was ten. She was walking home from school and noticed him staring at her from a car. The next day, he was back and asked her name. Soon enough, the thirty-year-old man became her boyfriend, and she fell "in love." She told me his name and recalled how he was the first man ever to say "I love you" to her. He gave her marijuana, and they began to have sex. But soon enough, physical beatings started. Sarah's "boyfriend" introduced her to her "cousins," other girls around her age. Because Sarah "loved" her boyfriend, she was expected to make money so they could survive. That's how she ended up walking the streets of Oakland, alongside her "cousins."

Sarah's story had a profound impact on me, and it changed my life forever. Although I did not encounter many trafficking victims in the emergency room where I was working in Oakland, seeing the exploitation of some of the most vulnerable in our society firsthand stuck with me. Kids like Sarah simply do not have the ability to see through the manipulations of an evil predator. These girls do not choose to live on the streets; rather, they are stalked, preyed upon and trafficked. Some are mentally challenged like Sarah, others are emotionally damaged, and still others simply come from broken or dysfunctional homes. A few come from good families and even go to church.

I found myself confronting my own misconceptions about slavery in the world today. I began to do the research, and I discovered that one girl alone can bring in more than $150,000 a year in cash. So, if a pimp has five girls on the street, he could be raking in well over $750,000 a year—*tax-free*. Like Sarah, the girls don't understand that their new "boyfriend"—who is saying "I love you," spending time with them, playing with the affections of their hearts—is really just trying to win their trust so he can turn them into slaves. These girls don't make the choice to sell their bodies for sex. They are coerced. This type of slavery is as evil and sinister as any type of slavery in the past.

As I dug deeper, I discovered that between 100,000 and 300,000 people—girls and boys of all ages—are sold for sex in America each year.[3] Sadly, I learned that only a few services, organizations and churches reach out to help. For too many kids, there is no place to go.

I decided that I needed to become part of the solution. In 2011, I founded Unlikely Heroes to create much-needed restoration homes for the victims of sexual slavery in the United States and around the world. Together with a team of radical modern-day abolitionists, we are doing everything we can to educate people about the realities of modern-day slavery and to create restoration homes that provide victims with the education, job skills and trauma therapy they need to have a second chance at life.

In November 2012, I traveled to the Philippines with a team of committed justice-minded people from a few nonprofit anti-trafficking organizations. In one remote region, we rescued ten girls out of brothels and opened a restoration home. One of the rescued girls named Ana (name changed) was sixteen years old and had been living in a five-foot by eight-foot room in the back of a brothel for more than a year. She told the team that she had gone to work in a bar because her family did not have enough money to feed her or her siblings. Only after she started the job did the bar owner tell her that she was to have sex with men for money. Ana is now safe.

Unlikely Heroes is also working to open an outreach center in the San Francisco Bay area to help children such as Sarah who are sold for sex.

I asked Erica to tell her story because it shows how one woman has responded and is now living out the specific destiny God has for her. Erica and Unlikely Heroes have boldly joined the growing ranks of people who are willing to say yes to God's call. Perhaps you need to be aware of (and pray about) trafficking and other justice issues, or perhaps God is calling you to something equally bold but altogether different. Either way, you can learn more about combating human trafficking from Unlikely Heroes or any of the other organizations listed below. These are just a few of the many great ministries rising to fight for justice today. God is calling us all to a destiny.

Resources on Human Trafficking

Exodus Cry (ask about the film *Nefarious*), exoduscry.com

Freeset (India) (Kerry and Annie Hilton), freesetglobal.com

Hope Foundation (Australia) (Bronwen Healy), hopefoundation.org.au

International Justice Mission, ijm.org

Justice Speaks (Sharon Ngai), justicespeaks.org

Love 146 (Rob Morris), love146.org

Moral Revolution, moralrevolution.org

NightLight (Annie Dieselberg), nightlightinternational.com

Not For Sale Campaign (David Batstone), notforsalecampaign.org

The Salvation Army, salvationarmyusa.org/usn/fight-human-trafficking/ or salvationarmy.org/ihq/antitrafficking

Shared Hope International (Linda Smith), sharedhope.org

Unlikely Heroes (Erica Greve), unlikelyheroes.com

Notes

Introduction

1. "What Americans Think About Women in Power," Barna Group, March 8, 2017, https://www.barna.com/research/americans-think-women-power/.

2. "Female Genital Mutilation," *World Health Organization*, 2017, http://www.who.int/reproductivehealth/topics/fgm/prevalence/en/.

3. "Women, Poverty and Economics," *UN Women*, 2008, http://www.unifem.org/gender_issues/women_poverty_economics/.

Chapter 1: The Journey

1. Aimee Semple McPherson, *The Story of My Life* (Dallas: Word, 1973), 72.

2. Ibid., 72.

3. Ibid., 75.

4. Gwen Shaw, *Unconditional Surrender* (Jasper, Ariz.: End-Time Handmaidens, Inc., 1986), 62.

5. Ibid., 64.

6. Ibid.

Chapter 2: Secret Pain

1. Note: I am grateful to Rich Wilkerson for his book *Private Pain: Healing for Hidden Hurts* (Eugene, Ore: Harvest House, 1987) for the concept I used to begin this chapter. I highly recommend his book.

2. Quin Sherrer and Ruthanne Garlock, *A Woman's Guide to Breaking Bondages* (Ann Arbor, Mich.: Vine Books-Servant, 1994), 181.

3. Ibid., 125.

4. Corrie ten Boom, *The Hiding Place* (Grand Rapids: Revell, 1996), 238.

5. Quin Sherrer with Ruthanne Garlock, *How to Forgive Your Children* (Lynnwood, Wash.: Aglow Publications, 1989), 66–67.

Chapter 3: Dear God, I Need a Friend

1. Joy Dawson, *Intimate Friendship with God* (Grand Rapids: Chosen, 1986), 51–53. Scripture quote is from the 1984 New International Version.

2. *The Woman's Study Bible* (Nashville: Thomas Nelson, 1995), 437.

3. Ibid.

4. Ibid., 440.

5. Dr. Fuchsia Pickett, *The Prophetic Romance* (Lake Mary, Fla.: Creation House, 1996), 29.

6. Ibid., 108.

7. Ibid.

Chapter 4: Women of Destiny

1. Ruth A. Tucker and Walter Liefeld, *Daughters of the Church* (Grand Rapids: Zondervan, 1987), 272–73.

2. Ibid., 273.

3. Finis Jennings Dake, *Dake's Annotated Reference Bible* (Lawrenceville, Ga.: Dake Bible Sales, 1963), 142.

4. Ibid.

5. Tucker, *Daughters*, 274.

6. Ibid., 275.

7. Darrow Miller, *Nurturing the Nations* (Downers Grove, Ill.: InterVarsity, 2012), Kindle Edition.

8. Beverly LaHaye, *The Desires of a Woman's Heart* (Wheaton, Ill.: Tyndale, 1993), 87. Scripture quotation from the NIV.

9. Ibid., 86–87.

10. Kari Torjesen Malcolm, *Women at the Crossroads* (Downers Grove, Ill.: InterVarsity, 1982), 30–31.

11. I first wrote about these five strongholds for a chapter entitled "Dethroning Strongholds" in Aglow International's book *Women of Prayer*. For a more complete study, please refer to pages 89–105 of that book.

12. Ed Silvoso, *That None Should Perish* (Ventura, Calif.: Regal, 1994), 155. I actually memorized this quote from Ed long before he wrote it in his book.

Chapter 5: Heroines of the Faith

1. IMB, "Lottie Moon," *International Mission Board*, 2018, https://www.imb.org/who-was-lottie-moon.

2. Edith Deen, *Great Women of the Christian Faith* (Uhrichsville, Oh.: Barbour and Company, Inc., 1959), 241.

3. Ibid., 243.

4. Tucker, *Daughters*, 303.

5. "Perpetua," *Christianity Today*, 2018, https://www.christianitytoday.com/history/people/martyrs/perpetua.html.

6. Deen, *Great Women*, 4.

7. Ibid., 5.

8. Tucker, *Daughters*, 101–102.

9. Deen, *Great Women*, 61.

10. *Encyclopaedia Britannica*, s.v. "Saint Joan of Arc," by Malcolm G.A. Vale and Yvonne Lanhers, accessed May 8, 2018, https://www.britannica.com/biography/Saint-Joan-of-Arc.

11. Ibid.
12. Deen, *Great Women*, 65.

Chapter 6: Moms and Other Great Women of Faith

1. "Saint John Chrysostom," *Coptic Orthodox Church Network*, 2014, http://www.copticchurch.net/topics/synexarion/john.html.
2. Ibid.
3. *Encyclopaedia Britannica*, s.v. "St. John Chrysostom," by Donald Attwater, accessed May 8, 2018, https://www.britannica.com/biography/Saint-John-Chrysostom.
4. Deen, *Great Women*, 23.
5. Edward Bouverie Pusey, trans., *The Confessions of Saint Augustine*, Book II, 1914, http://www.sacred-texts.com/chr/augconf/aug02.htm.
6. Ibid., Book VIII.
7. Sandy Dengler, *Susanna Wesley* (Chicago: Moody, 1987), 201.
8. *Wikipedia*, s.v. "Amy Carmichael," last modified April 11, 2018, https://en.wikipedia.org/wiki/Amy_Carmichael.
9. Tucker, *Daughters*, 305–06.
10. Wilma J. Johnson and Priscilla Pope-Levison, "Amanda Berry Smith," *BlackPast*, 2017, http://www.blackpast.org/aah/smith-amanda-berry-1837-1915.
11. Tucker, *Daughters*, 270.
12. Ibid., 271.
13. The terminology *wounded burden bearer* is from John and Paula Sandford and the teachings of Elijah House.
14. Freda Lindsay, *My Diary Secrets* (Dallas: Christ for the Nations Publishing, 1984), 14.
15. Ibid., 250.

Chapter 7: Gender to Gender

1. Gary Smalley and John Trent, *Why Can't My Spouse Understand What I Say?* (Colorado Springs: Focus on the Family, November 1988), 3.
2. H. Norman Wright, *What Men Want* (Ventura, Calif.: Regal, 1996), 14–15.
3. Jane Hansen Hoyt with Marie Powers, *Fashioned for Intimacy* (Ventura, Calif.: Regal, 1997), 36.
4. Alfred H. Ells and Gary Kinnaman, *Leaders That Last* (Grand Rapids: Baker, 2003).
5. Gary Smalley, "Advice You Can Bank On," *Focus on the Family Magazine*, February 1997, 3–4.
6. James Strong, *The New Strong's Exhaustive Concordance of the Bible* (Nashville: Thomas Nelson, 1984), #7194.
7. John Dawson, *Healing America's Wounds* (Ventura, Calif.: Regal, 1994), 246.
8. Ibid., 247.

Chapter 8: The Woman Question

1. Vonette Bright, *Women of Vision 2000*, newsletter of the AD2000 and Beyond Movement Women's Track, first quarter (1997), 4.

2. Dr. J. Robert Clinton, *Gender and Leadership: My Personal Pilgrimage* (Altadena, Calif.: Barnabas Publishers, 1995), 18–19.

3. The KJV, NKJV, NASB and earlier versions of the NIV all describe Phoebe as a "servant." See, however, Walter Bauer, William F. Arndt, F. Wilbur Gingrich and Frederic Danker, eds., *A Greek-English Lexicon of the New Testament and Other Early Christian Literature* (Chicago: University of Chicago Press, 1957; revised edition, 1979), 184, 2b, citing early second-century Latin texts that translate the Greek *diakonos* with the Latin word *minister*.

4. Dr. A. J. Gordon, "The Ministry of Women," in *Missionary Review of the World* (New York: Funk & Wagnalls, 1894), 7:916–17.

5. Charles Trombley, *Who Said Women Can't Teach* (South Plainsfield, N.J.: Bridge Logos, 1985), 194–95.

6. According to Gerhard Kittel and Gerhard Friedrich, eds., *Theological Dictionary of the New Testament* (Grand Rapids: Eerdmans, 1964), 2:93, an order of deaconnesses arose quickly in the early Church. Also, we have seen that Paul called Phoebe a *deacon*, a lofty term in the New Testament. It is significant that Philip also was a deacon (in Acts 6:2, "to serve" is the same verb used for serving as a deacon in 1 Timothy 3:10, 13). Notice that as a deacon, Philip preached, healed, taught, baptized and planted churches in cross-cultural missiological settings (see Acts 8:4–25), always in accountability to the Jerusalem elders (see Acts 8:14ff.). It is, therefore, clear that deacons could and did exercise tremendous leadership and authority.

7. Quoted in Trombley, *Who Said*, 195–96.

8. Ibid., 197.

9. Dr. Catherine Kroeger, "The Neglected History of Women in the Early Church," *Christian History Magazine*, no. 17 (1988): 6.

10. Trombley, *Who Said*, 191.

11. David Cannistraci, *The Gift of Apostle* (Ventura, Calif.: Regal, 1996), 86.

12. Such as John Piper and Wayne Grudem, *Recovering Biblical Manhood and Womanhood* (Wheaton: Crossway, 2012), 80, who argue that the name should be translated in the masculine form. The majority of Bible translations follow the feminine form.

13. Trombley, *Who Said*, 190–91.

14. Mary J. Evans, *Woman in the Bible* (Downers Grove, Ill.: InterVarsity, 1984), 160.

15. Cannistraci, *The Gift*, 90–91.

16. L. E. Maxwell, "The Ministry of Women of Salvation Army Principles" (unpublished manuscript, November 26, 1977), 1.

17. Billy Graham, *Just As I Am: The Autobiography of Billy Graham* (New York: HarperCollins, 1997), 137.

18. Ibid., 213.

19. Dr. Richard C. Halverson, quoted in *Dream Big: The Henrietta Mears Story* (Ventura, Calif.: Regal, 1990), endorsement.

20. Ben Witherington III, *Women and the Genesis of Christianity* (Cambridge: The Press Syndicate of the University of Cambridge, 1995), 220.

21. Katharine C. Bushnell, *God's Word to Women* (self-published, 1921), paragraph 195.

22. Bill Metzger, *A Textual Commentary on the Greek New Testament* (Stuttgart: United Bible Society, 1971), 466–67, referring to Acts 18:26. Most textual critics think

the manuscripts of the Western tradition of the Greek New Testament later reversed the order of the names because of a bias against women.

23. I highly recommend Dr. Bushnell's book *God's Word to Women*, self-published in 1921. She was a remarkable woman who traveled as an evangelist and social crusader with the Women's Christian Temperance Union. In addition, she was a medical doctor, was a missionary to China and was famous in the Christian community for her work against white slavery and prostitution. The book is a compilation of her Bible lessons.

24. No one is called *pastor* or *shepherd* by name in the New Testament except Jesus (see John 10:11, 14; Hebrews 13:20; 1 Peter 5:2, 4).

25. See Acts 19:22; 1 Timothy 1:3. Also see G. F. Hawthorne, "Timothy," *International Standard Bible Encyclopedia* (Grand Rapids: Eerdmans, 1988), 4:857–58.

26. Dr. C. Peter Wagner, *Blazing the Way* (Ventura, Calif.: Regal, 1995), 196.

27. Evans, *Woman*, 110.

28. Dr. Gary Greig, personal correspondence. Additionally, the following is taken from personal correspondence with Dr. Greig and Bayard Taylor: Paul and Peter tell elders to "pastor/shepherd" the flock of God (see Acts 20:28; 1 Peter 5:1–2). Elders were responsible for pastoring those under their care, but clearly both men and women were involved in the function of pastoring. . . . A pastor was not necessarily a paid Christian professional leading a local congregation; more likely a pastor would be the leader of a house church (see Ephesians 4:11). . . . Priscilla and the Marys who followed Jesus were not called pastors, but there can be no doubt that they pastored. Deacons were not at all limited simply to serving physical needs as many deacons are today. . . . Elders were not the decision-making committee for a local congregation. The biblical term *elder* seems to mean a man who has oversight over a church or group of churches in a city or in a geographical location (see Acts 14:23; 20:17, 28; 1 Timothy 5:17–19; Titus 1:5–9; 1 Peter 5:1–2).

29. Although the text of the New Testament does not explicitly call Priscilla and Lydia "deacons," they functioned as such.

30. The elders of Ephesus called together by Paul in Acts 20:17 were told to "shepherd" the Church of God (see Acts 20:28). These elders would have represented at least some of the "elders" mentioned in Ephesians 4:11. In 1 Peter 5:1–2, Peter also says that elders are to "pastor" God's flock. At least some elders, therefore, were pastors.

31. See John 13:33; 21:5; 1 John 2:1, 12–13, 18, 28; 3:7–18; 5:21; 2 John 1, 4, 13; 3 John 4.

32. C. Peter Wagner, *Your Spiritual Gifts Can Help Your Church Grow* (Ventura, Calif.: Regal, 1995), 137.

33. John Jarick, "Seven Prophetesses of the Old Testament," *Lutheran Theological Journal* 28:3 (1994): 116–21.

34. Dr. Bill Hamon, *Apostles and Prophets* (Shippensburg, Pa.: Destiny Image, 1997), 115–16.

Chapter 9: Domestic Authority (Headship and Submission)

1. I am aware that these are broad definitions and are not by any means inclusive of the theological stances of those who are in either of these categories.

2. The word *tsela* has been translated "rib" in some versions; however, to do so tends to marginalize her creation from man as being from an insignificant part. *Tsela* is used 41 times in the Old Testament and is used as rib here only in Genesis 2:21–23.

3. Taken from personal communication with Dr. Gary Greig and Bayard Taylor regarding the word *ezer*.

4. Although the work is amazing, I called in some modern-day theologians to study some of her concepts, such as her definition of the word *teshuqah*, because of my inability to read the Bible in its original languages. The personal communication I am referring to is responses to my questions from her book. Dr. Gary S. Greig (Ph.D., University of Chicago) at the time of correspondence was associate professor of Old Testament at Regent University School of Divinity, Virginia Beach, Virginia. Bayard B. Taylor (M.Div., Trinity Evangelical Divinity School) at the time was senior editor of Biblical and Theological Issues at Gospel Light Publications, Ventura, California.

5. Bushnell, *God's Word*, paragraphs 103–33.

6. Personal correspondence with Dr. Gary Greig.

7. As we can see, *mashal* in the earliest pages of the Bible and when it refers to God's rule, means "servant leadership." This meaning eventually became influenced negatively by its association with the "rule" of human kings and princes who were not servant leaders, but despotic, arbitrary, domineering, authoritarian, greedy, cruel and vain (for examples see Genesis 37:8; Exodus 21:8; Judges 8:23; 14:4; 15:11; Proverbs 28:15; 29:12; Isaiah 14:5; 52:5; Joel 2:17).

8. Priscilla, for example, was not under Apollos's authority when she and her husband, Aquila, instructed Apollos "more accurately" about Jesus in Acts 18:26. And the "elect lady" of 2 John 1 was not under the authority of itinerant male teachers; she had to discern false teaching and remove false teachers (see 2 John 10–11).

9. Strong, *Exhaustive Concordance* #5293; see also Bauer, *Greek-English Lexicon*, 847–48.

10. The evidence: (1) Greek lexicons do not agree whether *kephale* as a metaphor means "source, origin" or "authority." (2) Of 180 occurrences where the Hebrew Bible uses *ro'sh* in a figurative way to denote "ruler, leader," the Greek translation of the Hebrew Bible (the Septuagint) avoids using *kephale* at least 90 percent of the time. In only five passages does the Septuagint use *kephale* to translate *ro'sh* as "ruler, leader" (see Judges 11:11; 2 Samuel 22:44, which is the same as Psalm 18:43; Isaiah 7:8–9 [four times]; and Lamentations 1:5), and in each of these cases the translation *kephale* depends on Hebraisms or Massoretic marginal notes incorporated into the Greek text. (3) The contexts of the New Testament passages that allegedly use *kephale* as a metaphor for "ruler, leader, authority" (see 1 Corinthians 11:3–16; Ephesians 1:10; 22–23; 5:23; Colossians 1:18; 2:10; 2:19) can all be shown to point toward "source, origin" as the meaning. See Bilezikian's appendix in *Beyond Sex Roles: What the Bible Says About a Woman's Place in Church and Family* (Grand Rapids: Baker, 1991).

11. Katherine M. Haubert, *Women as Leaders* (Monrovia, Calif.: MARC, a division of World Vision International, 1993), 40.

12. Bilezikian, *Beyond Sex Roles*, 137.

13. Piper, *Recovering*, 53.

Chapter 10: Oh, Those Difficult Passages!

1. Rebecca Merrill Groothuis, *Good News for Women* (Grand Rapids: Baker, 1997), 203.
2. Bauer, *Greek-English Lexicon*, #749d; see also Strong, *Exhaustive Concordance*, #4601.
3. Ibid., 168b; see also Strong, *Exhaustive Concordance*, #1135.
4. Ibid., 25b; see also Strong, *Exhaustive Concordance*, #149.
5. Bushnell, *God's Word*, paragraph 203.
6. Ibid.
7. For possible examples, see 1 Corinthians 7:2; 8:1; 10:23; 12:1; 14:34–35; 15:12; 16:1,12.
8. Bushnell, *God's Word*, paragraph 203.
9. Dr. Jim Davis and Dr. Donna Johnson, *Redefining the Role of Women in the Church* (Santa Rosa Beach, Fla.: Christian International Ministries Network, 1997), 35.
10. Richard Clark Kroeger and Catherine Clark Kroeger, *I Suffer Not a Woman* (Grand Rapids: Baker, 1992), 47.
11. Ibid., 54.
12. Ibid., 59–60.
13. Don Rousu, "The Truth About Women in Public Ministry," *Spread the Fire*, October 1997, 5.
14. David Joel Hamilton, "I Commend to You Our Sister" (Master's thesis, Kona, Hawaii: University of the Nations, 1996), 271.
15. Piper, *Recovering*, 59.
16. Groothuis, *Good News*, 211.
17. Ibid., 99.
18. Ibid., 121.
19. Rousu, "The Truth," 6. Rousu goes on to say that this statement directly contradicts the notion that Eve was the "illuminator" and carrier of new revelation.
20. Spiros Zodhiates, Th.D., editor of the *Hebrew Greek Key Lexicon Bible*, says: "But I suffer not a woman (*gunaiki*, which should be translated as a wife or a woman in her relationship as a wife) to teach (*didaskein*, the pres. inf. of *didasko*, to teach, indicating continuity of teaching), which may be interpreted as lording it over her husband." If this were a prohibition of a woman teaching men, it would have said *authenteo*, "to usurp authority over" *andron*, the pl. gen., instead of the sing. gen., men. Instead of *andros* in the singular meaning "over man," referring to her own husband. "Paul is anxious to make very clear here that no woman through her teaching should give the impression that she is the boss and lording it over her husband. If any such impression is given at any time, then she should keep quiet. The relationship expressed in 1 Timothy 2:13 is not that of Adam and Eve as man and woman, but rather as husband and wife."
21. Bushnell, *God's Word,* paragraph 195.
22. Ibid., paragraph 314.
23. Ibid., paragraph 322.

Chapter 11: Anointed to Serve (Spiritual Authority)

1. Anne Graham Lotz, "Ministering Women," *Christianity Today*, April 8, 1996, 17.
2. "Ministering Women: A Forum with Jill Briscoe, Mary Kassian, Jean Thompson,

and Miriam Adeney," moderated by Wendy Murray Zoba and Helen Lee, *Christianity Today*, April 8, 1996, 14.

3. "Number of Female Senior Pastors in Protestant Churches Doubles in Past Decade," Barna Group, September 14, 2009, http://www.barna.com/research/number-of-female-senior-pastors-in-protestant-churches-doubles-in-past-decade/.

4. Ibid.

5. "Clergy Women: An Uphill Calling," Hartford Institute for Religion Research, 2006, http://hirr.hartsem.edu/bookshelf/clergywomen_abstract.html#women/men.

6. Vinson Synan, "Women in Ministry," *Ministries Today Magazine*, January/February 1993, 50.

7. John W. Kennedy, "More Women Heed Calling," The General Council of the Assemblies of God, February 14, 2018, https://news.ag.org/news/more-women-heed-calling.

8. Sarah Pulliam Bailey, "Women Pastors Remain Scarce," *Christianity Today*, August 7, 2009, https://www.christianitytoday.com/women/2009/august/women-pastors-remain-scarce.html.

9. The Foursquare Church, "Foursquare by the Numbers," *Foursquare News*, April 14, 2009, https://www.foursquare.org/news/article/by_the_numbers_april_2009.

10. Bill Shepson, "More Female Senior Pastors Than Ever Before, Study Finds," *Foursquare News*, September 29, 2009, https://www.foursquare.org/news/article/more_female_senior_pastors_than_ever_before_study_finds.

11. Ibid.

12. Bailey, "Women Pastors." Data were obtained from the National Congregation Study (www.soc.duke.edu/natcong/).

13. Adrienne S. Gaines, "Church of God Debates Role of Women," *Charisma*, August 6, 2010, https://www.charismamag.com/site-archives/570-news/featured-news/11656-church-of-god-debates-role-of-women.

Chapter 12: The Cultural Reformation

1. Meaning "supplement," this is a form of *baraitot* passages. This liturgical morning prayer was recited every day by all devout Jewish males during Paul's time.

2. Quoted in Hamilton, "I Commend," 43.

3. Ibid., 81.

4. Ibid., 35.

5. Witherington, *Women*, 15.

6. Ibid., 4.

7. Bushnell, *God's Word*, paragraph 8.

8. Witherington, *Women*, 5.

9. Bushnell, *God's Word*, paragraph 106.

10. Witherington, *Women*, 6.

11. Ibid., 53.

12. Witherington, *Women*, 100.

13. Ibid., 102.

14. Hamilton, "I Commend," 132.

15. Ibid., 134.

16. Bushnell, *God's Word*, paragraph 88.

17. Ibid.
18. Ibid., paragraph 619.
19. Ibid.; see diagram after paragraph 128.
20. Ibid., paragraph 142.
21. Ibid., paragraph 20.
22. Janette Hassey, *No Time for Silence* (Grand Rapids: Academie Books, 1986), 16.
23. Ibid., 3.
24. Ibid., 31.
25. Ibid., 53.
26. Ibid., 61–62.
27. Ibid., 137.
28. Charles H. Barfoot and Gerald T. Sheppard, "Review of Religious Research Prophetic Versus Priestly Religion: The Changing Role of Women Clergy in Classical Pentecostal Churches," *Review of Religious Research*, 22, no. 1 (September 1980): 9.
29. Ibid.
30. Ibid., 15.

Appendix C: Women and Justice Issues

1. Jill Dougherty, "State Department Report Ranks Countries on Human Trafficking," CNN, June 27, 2011, http://www.cnn.com/2011/POLITICS/06/27/human.trafficking/index.html.
2. Luis C. deBaca, "Release of the Ninth Annual Trafficking in Persons Report," U.S. Department of State, June 16, 2009, https://www.state.gov/j/tip/rls/tiprpt/2009/.
3. "Part 1: Victims or Perpetrators: Who Goes Free in the 'Land of the Free'," Shared Hope International, October 23, 2011, https://sharedhope.org/2011/10/part-1-victims-or-perpetrators-who-goes-free-in-the-land-of-the-free/.

Recommended Reading

Aglow. *Women of Prayer*. Lynwood, Wash.: Aglow Publications, 1993.

Barna, George. *Today's Pastors*. Grand Rapids: Baker, 1993.

Bushnell, Katharine. *God's Word to Women*. Self-published, 1921. Bible studies taught in the early 1920s by Bushnell, a medical doctor and missionary.

Cannistraci, David. *The Gift of Apostle*. Grand Rapids: Baker, 1996.

Dake, Finis Jennings. *Dake's Annotated Reference Bible*. Lawrenceville, Ga.: Dake Bible Sales, 1963.

Davis, Jim and Donna Johnson. *Redefining the Role of Women in the Church*. Quoted from manuscript self-published in 1997 by Christian International, 177 McKenny Road, Santa Rosa Beach, FL 32459.

Dawson, John. *Healing America's Wounds*. Grand Rapids: Baker, 1994.

Dawson, Joy. *Intimate Friendship with God*. Minneapolis: Chosen, 1986.

Dengler, Sandy. *Susanna Wesley*. Chicago: Moody, 1987.

Evans, Mary J. *Woman in the Bible*. Downers Grove, Ill.: InterVarsity, 1983.

Graham, Billy. *Just As I Am*. San Francisco: Harper, 1997.

Groothuis, Rebecca Merrill. *Good News for Modern Women*. Grand Rapids: Baker, 1997.

Hamilton, David Joel. "I Commend to You Our Sister." Master's thesis, Kona, Hawaii: University of the Nations, 1996.

Hamon, Bill. *Apostles and Prophets*. Shippensburg, Pa.: Destiny Image, 1997.

Hansen, Jane with Marie Powers. *Fashioned for Intimacy*. Grand Rapids: Baker, 1997.

Hassey, Janet. *No Time for Silence*. Grand Rapids: Academie Books, 1986.

Haubert, Katherine M. *Women as Leaders*. Monrovia, Calif.: Marc, a division of World Vision International, 1993.

Kroeger, Richard and Catherine Clark. *I Suffer Not a Woman*. Grand Rapids: Baker, 1992.

LaHaye, Beverly. *The Desires of a Woman's Heart*. Wheaton, Ill.: Tyndale, 1993.

Littauer, Florence. *Wake Up, Women!* Dallas: Word, 1994.

Lindsay, Freda. *My Diary Secrets*. Dallas: Christ for the Nations Publishing, 1984.

Lutz, Lorry. *Women as Risk-Takers for God*. Carlisle, Cumbria, U.K.: World Evangelical Publications, 1997.

Malcolm, Kari Torjesen. *Women at the Crossroads*. Downers Grove, Ill.: Inter-Varsity, 1982.

Maxwell, L. E. with Ruth C. Dearing. *Women in Ministry*. Camp Hill, Pa.: Christian Publishers, 1987.

Mears, Henrietta. *Dream Big*. Grand Rapids: Baker, 1990.

Pickett, Fuchsia. *The Prophetic Romance*. Orlando, Fla.: Creation House, 1996.

Piper, John and Wayne Grudem. *Recovering Biblical Manhood and Womanhood*. Wheaton, Ill.: Crossway, 1991.

Sherrer, Quin and Ruthanne Garlock. *A Woman's Guide to Breaking Bondages*. Ann Arbor, Mich.: Vine Books-Servant, 1994.

———. *A Woman's Guide to Spiritual Warfare*. Ann Arbor, Mich.: Vine Books-Servant, 1991.

———. *How To Forgive Your Children*. Lynwood, Wash.: Aglow Publications, 1989.

Silvoso, Ed. *That None Should Perish*. Minneapolis: Chosen, 1994.

ten Boom, Corrie. *The Hiding Place*. Minneapolis: Chosen, 1971.

The Women's Study Bible. Nashville: Thomas Nelson, 1995.

Trombley, Charles. *Who Said Women Can't Teach?* South Plainsfield, N.J.: Bridge Logos, 1985.

Tucker, Ruth. *Guardians of the Great Commission*. Grand Rapids: Zondervan, 1988.

Tucker, Ruth and Walter Liefeld. *Daughters of the Church*. Grand Rapids: Zondervan, 1987.

Varner, Kelley. *The Three Prejudices*. Shippensburg, Pa.: Destiny Image, 1997.

Wagner, C. Peter. *Blazing the Way*. Grand Rapids: Baker, 1995.

———. *Discover Your Spiritual Gifts*. Minneapolis: Chosen, 1979.

Witherington, Ben III. *Women and the Genesis of Christianity*. Cambridge, Mass.: Press Syndicate of the University of Cambridge, 1990.

Wright, H. Norman. *What Men Want*. Grand Rapids: Baker, 1996.

Scripture Index

General Index

Cindy Jacobs is a prophet, speaker, teacher and author with a heart for discipling nations in the areas of prayer and the prophetic. She and her husband, Mike, are the founders of Generals International, working to achieve social transformation through intercession and prophetic ministry. Cindy has written several bestselling books, including *Possessing the Gates of the Enemy*, *The Voice of God* and *The Power of Persistent Prayer*. Her television program, *God Knows*, is seen in the U.S. on God.tv in English and on other stations in multiple languages, as well as around the world. She travels and speaks internationally to groups of hundreds of thousands each year in churches and conference centers. Cindy and Mike have two grown children and six grandchildren and reside near Dallas, Texas.

More Kingdom Resources for the Spirit-Filled Believer by Cindy Jacobs

Practical, personal, biblical and motivational, this bestselling book has sold over 250,000 copies and been a definitive go-to guide to intercessory prayer for years. Fully revised and updated, with an in-depth study guide, the fourth edition of this classic text offers new and vital insights and practical tips on spiritual warfare and praying effectively.

Possessing the Gates of the Enemy

In the revised and updated edition of this classic text, you can learn how to hear the voice of God and speak it with wisdom and maturity. Through a practical, biblical examination of the gift of prophecy, this foundational, vital work helps you discover basic protocols—as well as how to avoid the pitfalls—of the life-giving movement of prophetic ministry.

The Voice of God

Chosen

Stay up to date on your favorite books and authors with our free e-newsletters. Sign up today at chosenbooks.com.

Find us on Facebook. facebook.com/chosenbooks

Follow us on Twitter. @Chosen_Books